MW00439181

INTEGRAL URBANISM

INTEGRAL URBANISM

NAN ELLIN

Routledge
Taylor & Francis Group
New York   London

Routledge is an imprint of the
Taylor & Francis Group, an informa business

Book Design by Barbara Ambach. Cover art "Eas-X" by José Parlà.

Routledge
Taylor & Francis Group
270 Madison Avenue
New York, NY 10016

Routledge
Taylor & Francis Group
2 Park Square
Milton Park, Abingdon
Oxon OX14 4RN

© 2006 by Nan Ellin
Routledge is an imprint of Taylor & Francis Group, an Informa business

Printed in the United States of America on acid-free paper
10 9 8 7 6 5 4 3 2 1

International Standard Book Number-10: 0-415-95228-X (Softcover) 0-415-95227-1 (Hardcover)
International Standard Book Number-13: 978-0-415-95228-6 (Softcover) 978-0-415-95227-9 (Hardcover)

No part of this book may be reprinted, reproduced, transmitted, or utilized in any form by any electronic, mechanical, or other means, now known or hereafter invented, including photocopying, microfilming, and recording, or in any information storage or retrieval system, without written permission from the publishers.

Trademark Notice: Product or corporate names may be trademarks or registered trademarks, and are used only for identification and explanation without intent to infringe.

Visit the Taylor & Francis Web site at
http://www.taylorandfrancis.com

and the Routledge Web site at
http://www.routledge-ny.com

Dedication

To Dan

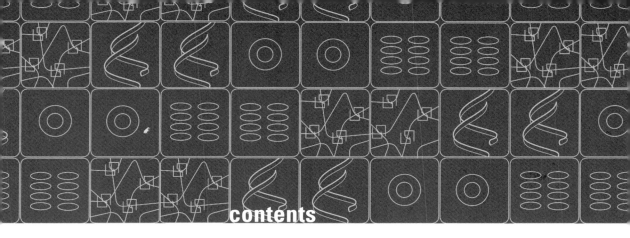

contents

ConvergencePatternsIntegration

PermeabilityFluxCatalystsArma

NetworksNodesLinksHubsPaths

TentaclesRhizomesWorldWideW

EcologyEngagementPeopleChilc

HybridityConnectivityPorosityAuth

ConnectivityPorosityAuthenticityVu

PorosityAuthenticityVulnerabilityH

AuthenticityVulnerabilityHybridityC

VulnerabilityHybridityConnectivityP

PublicSpaceProactiveSustainabi

nterdependenceDynamicProces

HarmonyAdventureFascinationE

LocalCharacterGlobalForcesRela

CommunicateCommonsCongregat

ReflectRehabilitateRevitalizeRes

DiversityRespectWell-BeingPro

ConvergencePatternsIntegration

Mobility Resilience Flourish Thrive
sFrameworks Punctuation Marks
logy Thresholds Ecotones Nature
nternet Border Edge In-Between
Community Conserve Caretaking
city **Integral Urbanism** Vulnerability
bility Hybridity Connectivity Porosity
dity Connectivity Précis Authenticity
ctivity Porosity Authenticity Hybridity
ty Authenticity Hybridity Connectivity
ymbiotic Organism Inspiring Vital
dback Complementarity Synergy
y Excitement Urbanism Landscape
ships Transparency Translucency
nverse Consider Conspire Courage
Realign Realize Reveal Rejuvenate
rity Innovation Vision Inclusivity
Mobility Resilience Flourish Thrive

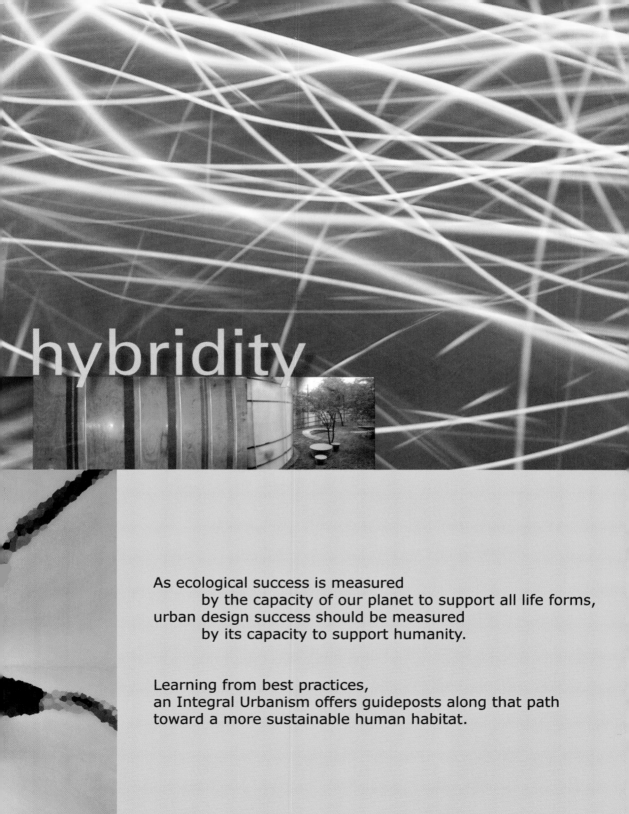

hybridity

As ecological success is measured
        by the capacity of our planet to support all life forms,
urban design success should be measured
        by its capacity to support humanity.

Learning from best practices,
an Integral Urbanism offers guideposts along that path
toward a more sustainable human habitat.

In contrast to escapist, cynical, or purely mercenary tendencies,
Integral Urbanism aims to heal wounds
inflicted upon the landscape
by the modern and postmodern eras
as manifest in:

Visually unappealing places

Impoverishment of public space and heightened perception of fear

Diminished sense of place and sense of community &

Environmental degradation.

connectivity

To accomplish this, Integral Urbanism demonstrates five qualities:

Hybridity
Connectivity
Porosity
Authenticity
Vulnerability

Hybridity and **Connectivity** bring activities and people together, rather than isolate objects and separate functions. These qualities also treat people and nature as symbiotic—as well as buildings and landscape—rather than oppositional.

Porosity preserves the integrity of that which is brought together while allowing mutual access through permeable membranes, rather than the modernist attempt to dismantle boundaries or postmodernist fortification.

Authenticity involves actively engaging and drawing inspiration from actual social and physical conditions with an ethic of care, respect, and honesty. Like all healthy organisms, the authenti-City is always growing and evolving according to new needs that arise thanks to a self-adjusting feedback loop that measures and monitors success and failure.

And **Vulnerability** calls upon us to relinquish control, listen deeply, value process as well as product, and re-integrate space with time.

In contrast to the master-planned functionally-zoned city which separates, isolates, alienates, and retreats, Integral Urbanism emphasizes **connection**, **communication**, and **celebration**.

As we are a part of nature,
so are our habitats including our cities.
Over the last century, however,
urban development has treated the city as a machine
for efficiently sheltering and protecting
and for moving people, money, and goods.

flow

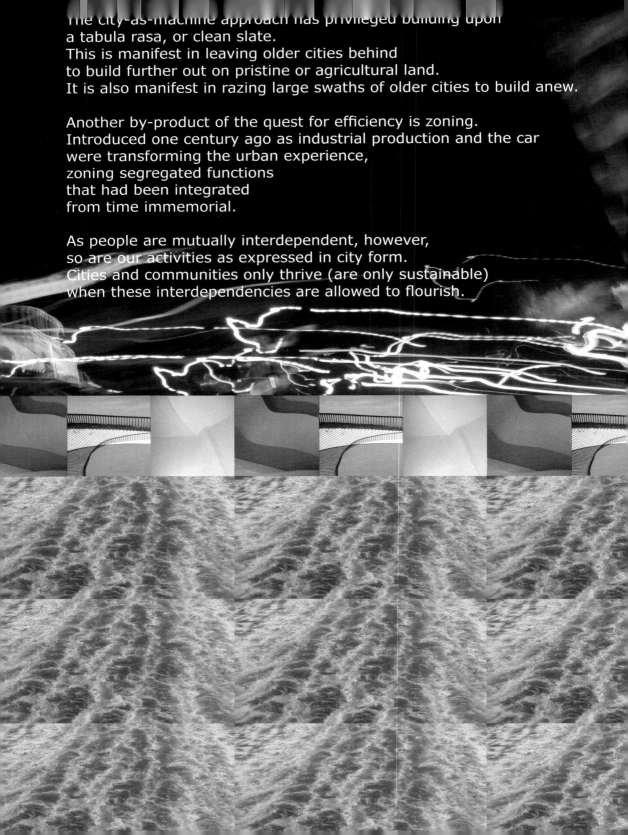

The city-as-machine approach has privileged building upon
a tabula rasa, or clean slate.
This is manifest in leaving older cities behind
to build further out on pristine or agricultural land.
It is also manifest in razing large swaths of older cities to build anew.

Another by-product of the quest for efficiency is zoning.
Introduced one century ago as industrial production and the car
were transforming the urban experience,
zoning segregated functions
that had been integrated
from time immemorial.

As people are mutually interdependent, however,
so are our activities as expressed in city form.
Cities and communities only thrive (are only sustainable)
when these interdependencies are allowed to flourish.

patterns

We are now belatedly recognizing the problems
wrought by the clean-slate tendency and land-use zoning.
However well-intended, these efforts to "renew" our cities
and render them more efficient have gone too far,
ultimately draining the life from them and contributing
to threaten our sense of community, security,
and physical and emotional health.

Rather than neglect, abandon, or erase our urban heritage, Integral Urbanism
preserves buildings, neighborhoods, and natural landscapes that we value;
rehabilitates, reclaims, restores, or renovates what is underperforming;
and **adds** what we do not have yet but would like,
as informed by effective community involvement.

Whether applied to existing urban fabrics or new development,
Integral Urbanism activates places
by creating thresholds—places of intensity—
where a range of people and activities may converge.
Providing places to congregate along with synergies and efficiencies,
Integral Urbanism offers settings—while also liberating time and energy—
for collaboratively envisioning and implementing desired change.

The result is:
more conservation & *less* waste,
more quality public space & *less* distrust and fear,
more quality time & *less* "screen time" and commuting time,
more proaction & *less* reaction.

Whereas the modern paradigm discouraged convergences
through its emphasis on separation and control,
this new paradigm encourages them.
Convergences in space and time
of people, activities, businesses, and so forth
generate new hybrids.
These hybrids allow new convergences and the process continues.
This is, in fact, the definition of development.

convergence

egral Urbanism veers away from master planning which,
ts focus on controlling everything,
nically tends to generate fragmented cities without soul or character.
tead, Integral Urbanism proposes more punctual interventions
t have a tentacular or domino effect,
alyzing other interventions in an ongoing dynamic process.

naster planning were a form of surgery on an anaesthetized city,
egral Urbanism might be a form of acupuncture on a fully alert and engaged city.
opening up blockages along "urban meridians,"
t as acupuncture and other forms of bioenergetic healing
en blockages along the energy meridians of our bodies,
approach can liberate the life force of a city and its vibrant communities.

porosity

m the machine as model (modernism),
cities of the past as model (postmodernism),
egral Urbanism finds models simultaneously in
logy and new information technologies such as
esholds, ecotones, tentacles, rhizomes, webs, networks,
World Wide *Web*, and the Inter*net*.
lso reveals a fascination with the border, edge, and in-between,
concepts as well as actual places.

contrast to earlier models, these suggest
importance of connectedness and dynamism
well as the principle of complementarity.
the ecological threshold where two ecosystems meet, for instance,
re is competition and conflict along with synergy and harmony.
ere is fear along with adventure and excitement.
not about good or bad, safety or danger, pleasure or pain, winners or losers.
of these occur on the threshold if it is thriving.

While integrating the functions that the modern city separated, Integral Urbanism also seeks to integrate:

- conventional notions of urban, suburban, and rural to produce a new model for the contemporary city
- design with nature
- local character with global forces
- the design professions and
- people of different ethnicities, incomes, ages, and abilities.

Integral Urbanism is about:
    Networks **not** boundaries
        Relationships and connections **not** isolated objects
            Interdependence **not** independence or dependence
    Natural and social communities **not** just individuals
      Transparency or translucency **not** opacity
          Permeability **not** walls
           Flux or flow **not** stasis
  Connections with nature and relinquishing control,
    not controlling nature
        Catalysts, armatures, frameworks, punctuation marks,
        not final products, master plans, or utopias

authenticity

The urban and environmental challenges of the last century
have prompted a reconsideration of values, goals, and means of achieving the
particularly over the last decade.

In contrast to the fast-paced more-is-more mentality,
the appeals of **s**implicity, **s**lowness, **s**pirituality, **s**incerity, and **s**ustainability
are clearly on the rise.

Side by side with the still prevalent reactive tendencies of
form to follow **f**iction, **f**inesse, **f**inance, and **f**ear,
myriad proactive initiatives from a wide range of contributors
to shaping the environment are shifting the paradigm toward integration.

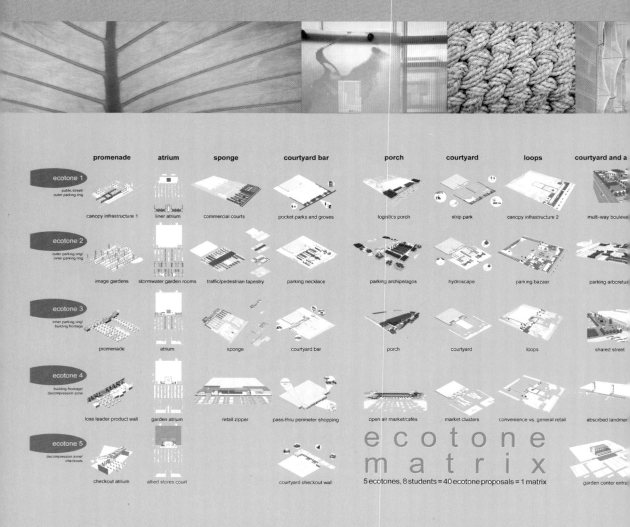

	promenade	atrium	sponge	courtyard bar	porch	courtyard	loops	courtyard and a
ecotone 1 public street/ outer parking ring								
	canopy infrastructure 1	liner atrium	commercial courts	pocket parks and groves	logistics porch	strip park	canopy infrastructure 2	multi-way boulevard
ecotone 2 outer parking ring/ inner parking ring								
	image gardens	stormwater garden rooms	traffic/pedestrian tapestry	parking necklace	parking archipelagos	hydroscape	parking bazaar	parking arboretum
ecotone 3 inner parking ring/ building frontage								
	promenade	atrium	sponge	courtyard bar	porch	courtyard	loops	shared street
ecotone 4 building frontage/ decompression zone								
	loss leader product wall	garden atrium	retail zipper	pass-thru perimeter shopping	open air market/cafés	market clusters	convenience vs. general retail	absorbed landmark
ecotone 5 decompression zone/ checkouts								
	checkout atrium	allied stores court		courtyard checkout wall				garden center entrance

ecotone
matrix
5 ecotones, 8 students = 40 ecotone proposals = 1 matrix

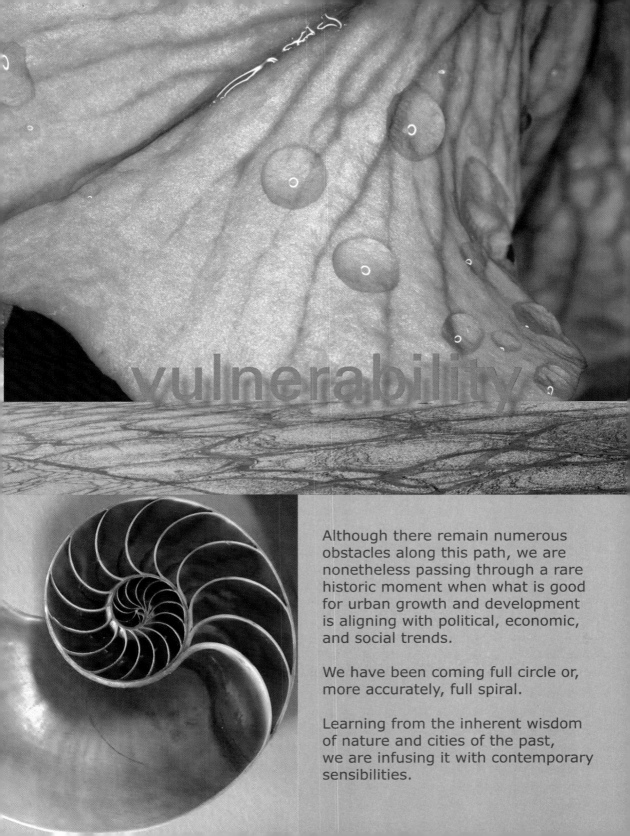

vulnerability

Although there remain numerous obstacles along this path, we are nonetheless passing through a rare historic moment when what is good for urban growth and development is aligning with political, economic, and social trends.

We have been coming full circle or, more accurately, full spiral.

Learning from the inherent wisdom of nature and cities of the past, we are infusing it with contemporary sensibilities.

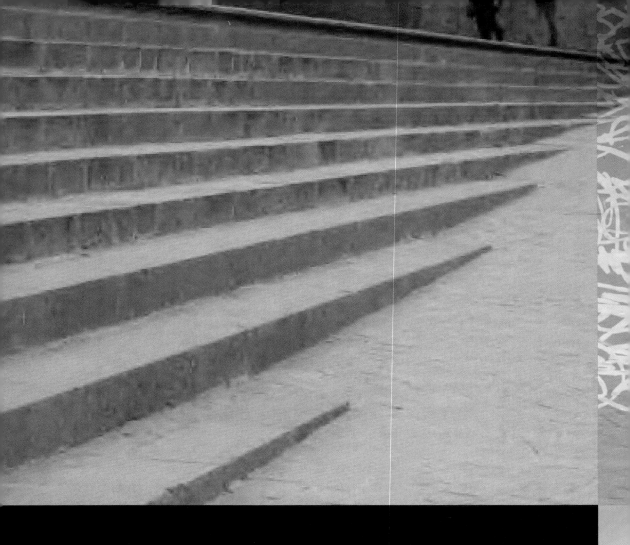

Rather than choosing to continue or abandon the modern project,
our hyper-rational reliance upon information technologies along with
a simultaneous revalorization of process, relationships, and complementarity
is conspiring to eradicate the either/or proposition.
We are doing both simultaneously,
each providing feedback for and adjusting the other accordingly,
holding potential for achieving integration at another level.

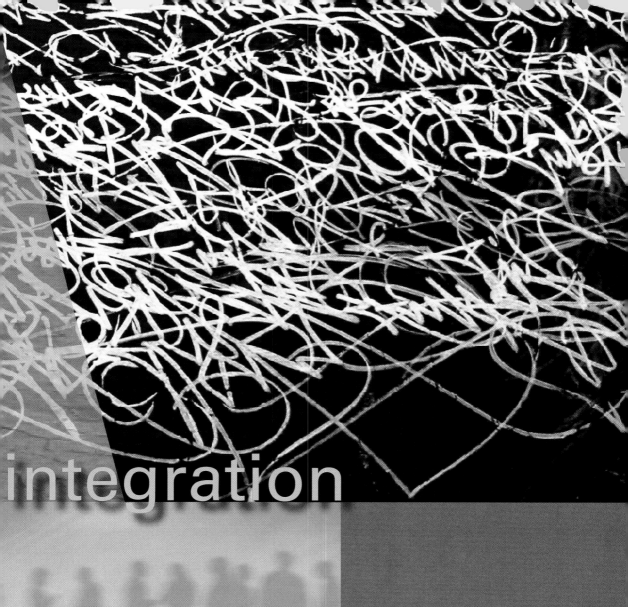

integration

The modern era divided the world and our thinking about it into fragments and our landscape followed. We are suffering the results.

Integrating disciplines and professions,
Integral Urbanism seeks to mend seams and darn holes in the urban and social fabrics.

Resolutely refusing to idealize the past or escape the present,
Integral Urbanism envisions and realizes
a new integration for an enriched future.

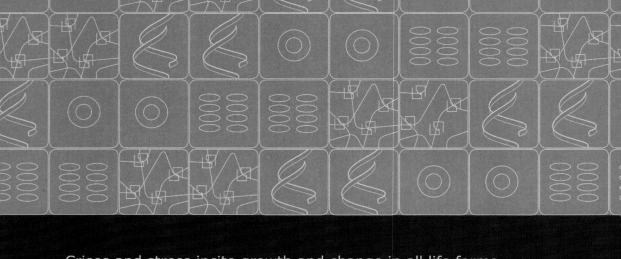

Crises and stress incite growth and change in all life forms.
The kind of change that occurs may support or detract from
the health and well-being of the system depending
upon its level of resilience and intelligence.

Applying **the five qualities of Integral Urbanism**
can offer the soul food necessary
for our cities and communities
to blossom and truly thrive.
Not merely survive.

Acknowledgments

I am deeply indebted to the late Jane Jacobs who paved the path I have had the privilege to wander and, hopefully, extend. This book shares her premise in *The Death and Life of Great American Cities* (1961) that urban vitality and public safety are complementary – not contradictory – features of a city, achieved through adjacencies of uses and people along with other "generators of diversity." I also share Jacobs' method of learning what is best for places by observing and participating in them. Most importantly, I share her view of cities as organisms that are sustained optimally through organic interventions, rather than master planning and social engineering. Much has changed since that seminal book appeared forty-five years ago, changes I consider here, still aiming first and foremost to enhance the health and well-being of our cities and our communities.

Phoenix, Arizona, my city and community of the last eight years, has been both fodder and palette for many of the ideas expressed here. The fifth largest city in the United States, Phoenix is struggling to manage its exponential growth without foregoing its spirit of independence and generosity or harming its majestic desert landscape. Through my involvement with downtown revitalization, I have had the privilege of sharing ideas and working with Don Keuth and Jo Marie McDonald of the Phoenix Community Alliance; Brian Kearney of the Downtown Phoenix Partnership; Mayor Phil Gordon, Myra Millinger, and Cyd West of the Maricopa Partnership for Arts and Culture; Deborah Whitehurst of the Arizona Community Foundation; Richard Hayslip of the Salt River Project; Arizona Attorney General and former Phoenix Mayor Terry Goddard; Grady Gammage of Gammage & Burnham; Judy Mohraz of the Piper Trust; Jon Talton of the *Arizona Republic;* Councilman Greg Stanton; Pat Grady of the Downtown Development Office; Phil Jones of the Phoenix Office of Arts and Culture; Dean Brennan and Jane Bixler of the planning department; Matt Baker of Metro Arts; and John McIntosh of Arizona State University's Joint Urban Design Program. For their life-affirming spirit, tenacity, and soul gift to Phoenix, I am also thankful to the arts community, especially Kimber Lanning, Greg Esser, Cindy Dach, Gregory Sale, Beatrice Moore, Susan Copeland, Mies Grybaitis, Wayne Rainey, David White, Carrie Bloomston, Susan Krane, Marilu Knode, Lara Taubman, and Shelley Cohn. For creating places of value in this desert metropolis, I gratefully acknowledge talented architects and friends Will Bruder, Eddie Jones, Wendell Burnette, Marwan Al-Sayed, Chris Alt, Christiana Moss, and Christy Ten Eyck.

My students over the years at New York University, University of Southern California, Southern California Institute of Architecture, University of Cincinnati, and Arizona State University have listened to and provided valuable feedback on many ideas in this book. I especially wish to thank the participants in my Slash City seminar for their contributions to "For Phoenix to Flourish," a special issue of *Shade Magazine*: Sophia Meger, Jesus Lara, Jens Kolb, Jay Valenzuela, Shawn Goetzinger, Rob Merrill, Regina Belsanti, Jonathan Wright, Julia Fuller, Tyler Kimball, Mitu Singh, Sweta Bonsal, and Joshua Mulhall. For designing this issue, I thank Shannelle Cook, Molly Schoenhoff, Brian Prout, Mike Sullivan, and Toni Gentilli. I extend a heartfelt note of appreciation to Josh Rose, whose vision, talent, and collaborative spirit animated *Shade Magazine* for a magical few years.

Arizona State University has provided an oasis to step out of and reflect upon the rapidly changing urban scene. I extend my utmost gratitude to Ron McCoy and John Meunier for the atmosphere of creative inquiry and collegiality they fostered for many years and to Darren Petrucci, Catherine Spellman, and Duke Reiter for their ongoing contributions to our school and college. I would also like to thank my Ph.D. students who inspire me through their dedication and desire to effect positive change as well as Cindi Fernandez for flawlessly holding it all together. For a Catalyst Grant benefiting this book, I thank Janet Holston and the Herberger Center for Design Research.

David McBride of Routledge has graciously stewarded this book along each step of the way. Architect and graphic designer Barbara Ambach skillfully integrates these fields to produce "diagraphics," here beautifully animating the concepts of integral urbanism. The work of Brooklyn-based artist José Parlá resonates with the urban qualities advocated in this book – particularly layering, connecting, authenticity, flow, dynamism, and marking our places. I thank him for providing the stunning "Eas-X," which graces the cover.

I am ever grateful to my parents Carole and Morty Ellin, whose Baltimore community models many aspects of integration, for their unfailing support and encouragement. My twelve-year-old daughter Theodora shares my affection and hopes for Phoenix as we have participated in its revitalization efforts over the years. I am deeply thankful for her perspectives, manifold talents, companionship, good will, and good grace. To Dan Hoffman, collaborator in life and twin flame, I dedicate this book.

Phoenix, 2005

Preface

Specialists without spirit, sensualists without heart; this nullity imagines that
it has attained a level of civilization never before achieved.
    MAX WEBER (1905)[1]

Il faut réculer pour mieux sauter.
(You have to take a step back in order to jump further.)
    FRENCH PROVERB

There has been a stalemate in the urban design professions, manifested in historicism, on the one hand, and razzmatazz image-ready architecture, on the other. Both of these trends have their merits and proper place. The nostalgia of the former, however, suggests a denial of contemporary issues and an exhaustion of creative energies. The devil-may-care attitude of the latter reveals a deep and highly infectious cynicism.

These urban design trends ultimately suppress critical thinking, problem solving, and concern for the larger community. They offer little in the way of creative or personal sustenance to emerging urban designers. They are largely unequipped to heal what ails our neighborhoods, towns, and cities.

Over the last decade and a half, a range of proactive practices spanning the Western world has been bucking these reactive trends. These practices emerged *on the borders* between traditional schools of thinking and on geographical borders between nations and between city, suburb, and countryside. They emerged *from the border* to include voices that were suppressed or had chosen silence. Moreover, they have been *pushing the border*. Sprouting initially from the crevices of mainstream architectural and planning practices, they have more recently been moving from the urban design wings into the spotlight.

Despite the growing popularity of these approaches, examples of urban design excellence remain scattered, particularly in the United States. As a result, much of the landscape is lacking in vitality, unfriendly to the pedestrian, and a contributor to contaminating our air and water. We also lack a convenient way to describe these proactive practices and, thereby, transmit, evaluate, and refine them. *Integral Urbanism* offers steps in these directions.

This book was fueled by equal parts indignation and inspiration: indignation about the resistance to improving our landscapes emanating from many quarters, and inspiration from the exemplary practices that have been gathering force. The resistance, I believe, draws in large part from an inability to apply a wide-angle lens to the many issues that bear upon the shape of our environment. A fragmented understanding of contemporary problems only generates fragmented solutions. Whereas, the division of labor occasioned by industrial production approximately one century ago allowed for tremendous progress in terms of productivity and rational efficiency, it also enabled the decline of central cities, social isolation, and environmental degradation. Failure to address urban problems holistically has indeed taken its toll.

It is precisely the work of synthesis that I have undertaken in *Integral Urbanism*. Ambitious, yes. Foolhardy, perhaps. City building and community building have grown so divided and subdivided that myopic specialists can sometimes only see the fragment that pertains to them, rather than the whole. Invariably, they also tend to dismiss synthetic overviews as shallow, incomplete, reductive, and derivative (lacking depth, breadth, and originality). Clinging to habitual ways of thinking and acting is often the default response to rapid change, rather than venturing into new territories, taking risks, and aspiring to improve the human condition.

By assembling and distilling these divergent, proactive, urban design practices to reveal a wider perspective, I hope to make this journey safer and well traveled. Taking a step back to view the big picture is imperative if we are to move forward, leaving aside for a moment the many important daily tasks of design professionals and the general public that add up to our cities: responding to requests for proposals, meeting with client representatives, design development, checking punch lists, attending city meetings, participating in neighborhood, community, and merchant associations, and so much more.

Just as ecological success is measured by the capacity of our planet to support all life forms, so urban design success and excellence should be measured by its capacity to support humanity. Integral Urbanism aims to steer that course. To inform, inspire, and incite a better human habitat.

INTRODUCTION

Integral – Essential to completeness, lacking nothing essential, formed as a unit with another part.

Integrate – To form, coordinate, or blend into a functioning or unified whole; to unite with something else; to end the segregation of and bring into equal membership in society or an organization; desegregate.

Integrity – Adherence to artistic or moral values; incorruptibility; soundness; the quality or state of being complete and undivided; completeness.

In architecture and urban planning, a revolution has been taking place aiming to heal the wounds inflicted upon the landscape by the Modern and Postmodern eras. These wounds are manifested as sprawl, the growing perception of fear, a declining sense of community, and environmental degradation. This design revolution is relatively quiet because its practitioners are not unified under a single banner and because their sensitivity to people and the environment translates into design that may not call attention to itself. Nonetheless, numerous stones have been thrown around the globe, and their still small but growing ripples are beginning to reshape dramatically our physical environment while enhancing our quality of life.

In Western society, generally, we are witnessing a gradual reorientation toward valuing slowness, simplicity, sincerity, spirituality, and sustainability in an attempt to restore connections that have been severed over the last century between body and soul, people and nature, and among people. For architects and planners, this has been apparent in the shift from the machine as model (Modernism), to cities of the past as model (Postmodernism), to seeking models simultaneously in ecology and new information technologies (e.g., thresholds, ecotones, tentacles, rhizomes, webs, networks, the World Wide Web, the

Internet). Along with these new metaphors, there has been a fascination with the border, edge, and in-between, as concepts as well as actual places.

In contrast to the earlier models that bespoke aspirations for control and perfection, these current models suggest the importance of connectedness and dynamism as well as the principle of complementarity. On the ecological threshold, where two ecosystems meet, for instance, there is competition and conflict but also synergy and harmony. There is fear but also adventure and excitement. It is not about good or bad, safety or danger, pleasure or pain, winners or losers. All of these occur on the threshold if it is thriving.

Widespread frustration with the escapist tendencies of recent urban design along with the sorry state of market-driven urban growth and development has inspired more proactive approaches. These share an emphasis on reintegration (functional, social, disciplinary, and professional), on permeable membranes (rather than the Modernist attempt to dismantle boundaries or Postmodernist fortification), and on design with movement in mind, both movement through space (circulation) and through time (dynamism, flexibility).

From "less is more" to "more is more," the byword has become "more from less."[1] Louis Sullivan's dictum that form follows function (1896) was supplanted by the deeply cynical late twentieth-century tendency for form to follow fiction, finesse, finance, and foremost fear (see Ellin 1997, 1999). At the turn of this third millennium, form is once again following function, but function is redefined. Rather than primarily mechanistic and instrumental, function is understood more holistically to include emotional, symbolic, and spiritual "functions," in fact, Sullivan's initial (but widely misinterpreted) intent.[2] At the same time, the attitude among designers toward rapid change has been shifting. From attempting to deny or control change, an attitude characterizing most of the twentieth century, we are now witnessing an acceptance, sometimes even an embrace, of change.

This reorientation carries deep implications for urban design. The result is a departure in theory and practice – in concept and implementation – ranging from small-scale interventions to regional plans. The selective synthesis of exemplary trends presented here offers an overview of recent urban design that supports the complex and wondrous range of human needs, allowing us not only to survive but also to thrive. Integral Urbanism is the rubric under which I gather these creative solutions.

Applying Abraham Maslow's "hierarchy of needs" advanced in 1943, we could say that these landscapes satisfy our physiological and security needs as

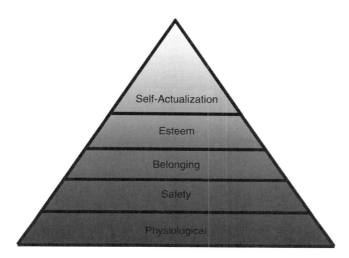

Figure 1

well as our higher needs for belonging, self-esteem, and self-actualization (see Figure 1). We might define such urban design as the "art and science dedicated to enhancing the quality of the physical environment in cities, to providing civilizing and enriching places for the people who live in them."[3] Integral urbanism may also be regarded as the urban design analogue to, or container for, what philosopher Ken Wilbur describes as integral psychology (illustrated by "nested spheres"[4]) and the "Spiral Dynamics" of Don E. Beck.[5]

Crises and stress are what incite growth and adaptation in all life forms. The kind of change that occurs, however, may support or detract from the health and well-being of the system depending upon its level of resilience and inherent wisdom. The health and well-being of the human habitat is currently perched upon a tipping point. While proactive practices continue to proliferate, so do obstructionist and reactionary tendencies. By not contributing to the solutions, these latter only contribute to the problems. Ultimately, they are unsustainable.

By distilling here the principal qualities of the more sustainable practices, I hope to tip the scales toward proactivity. That is the challenge for urban design today.

WHAT IS INTEGRAL URBANISM?

Essentially, Integral Urbanism seeks to integrate:

- Functions or uses — living, working, circulating, playing, and creating [*program, typology*]
- Conventional notions of urban, suburban, and rural as well as the private and public realms [*morphology*]
- Center and periphery (local character and global forces) [*scale*]
- Horizontal and vertical [*plan and section*]
- The built and unbuilt — architecture and landscape architecture, structural and environmental systems, figure and ground, indoor and outdoor [*people with nature*]
- People of different ethnicities, incomes, ages, abilities (universal design), locals and tourists, etc. [*people of all kinds*]
- Design professionals (architecture; planning; landscape architecture; engineering; interior, industrial, graphic designers) as well as designers with construction and real estate professionals (design, build, develop), clients with users, and theory with practice [*the design disciplines and professions, designers and nondesigners, concept and implementation*]
- Process and product [*time and space, verb and noun*]
- System and serendipity, the planned and spontaneous, principle and passion [*approach, attitude*]

FLOW

Everything flows.
Heraclitus

In the end the urban truth is in the flow.
Spiro Kostof[1]

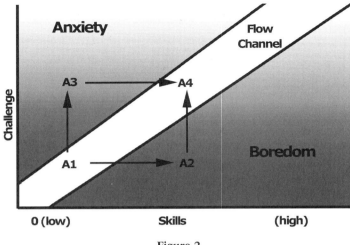

Figure 2

The goal of Integral Urbanism is to achieve *flow*. As defined by psychologist Mihaly Csikszentmihaly, flow is the intense experience situated between boredom and overstimulation (see Figure 2). It is characterized by immersion, awareness, and a sense of harmony, meaning, and purpose.[2] While generally intended for enhancing individual performance, such as playing sports, it is also useful to consider how places might be "in flow."

We know intuitively when a place is in flow. It strikes a balance between boredom and overstimulation through, for instance, combining monuments with background buildings, defamiliarizing features with familiar ones, and a wide range of people and activities. It is not the unrelenting grid, but nor is it deconstructivism on the urban scale. Places in flow also allow ease of movement of people, goods, and information. Too much ease of movement would produce boredom and stasis, eliminating mystery and wonder, ultimately the Achilles heel of the modern city. Places that are truly in flow thus have interesting and unexpected detours and zigzags. We might call these ebbs or the rocks around which the flowing stream navigates.[3] Because people require varying amounts of stimulation to be in flow, places that are in flow offer choice and may be experienced in different ways.

When speaking of places in flow, their formal attributes and people's experiences of them are inseparable and reliant upon one another. Given the heightened significance of movement, it makes sense that fluency – or flow – becomes even more important. The concept of flow and ebb also represents the form of this movement, three-dimensional webs or networks, in contrast to the traditional model of central places and hinterlands.

Even though architecture and planning espoused a machine model throughout much of the twentieth century, popular consciousness never relinquished the earlier organic understanding of places. Encountering a place that is not in flow, the French typically remark that it lacks soul (*Il n'a pas d'âme*). Americans tend to say that it lacks character. Places that are in flow are characterized by the French as *animé* (animated, spirited, or soulful) and by Americans as lively. Such characterizations presume that places ideally should have these human attributes.[4]

The well-intentioned, and in many respects laudable, modern efforts to cleanse the city of illness and to render it more efficient have gone too far, "draining the life" from them, as we say, or "cutting off their lifeblood." Simultaneously, globalization and attendant standardization have been endangering the soul and character of our landscapes and ourselves. We crave unique and authentic experience along with more opportunities for freedom of expression. Just as people are mutually interdependent, so are our activities as expressed in city forms. Cities only thrive (are only sustainable) when these interdependencies are allowed to flourish.

Integral Urbanism simply validates our intuitive understanding of how places should be – dirt, disorder, and unpredictability included – rather than propose some ultimately undesirable as well as unattainable utopia. Places of urban integrity exemplify certain qualities. Places in search of the vitality that these qualities endow might learn from them.

FIVE QUALITIES OF AN INTEGRAL URBANISM

> Dull, inert cities, it's true, do contain the seeds of their own destruction and little else. But vital cities have marvelous innate abilities for understanding, communicating, contriving, and inventing what is required to combat their difficulties ... Lively, diverse, intense cities contain the seeds of their own regeneration, with energy enough to carry over for problems and needs outside themselves.
>
> JANE JACOBS[1]

Important qualities for places to be in flow include *hybridity, connectivity, porosity, authenticity,* and *vulnerability.* Together, these qualities describe a shift from emphasizing isolated objects and separating functions to considering larger contexts and multifunctional places. These qualities suggest a departure from the presumed opposition between people and nature and between buildings and landscape to more symbiotic relationships. These qualities also place a premium on borders, the site of these relationships. In addition, they regard process as paramount, rather than a finished product. The values expressed by these qualities veer away from master planning which, in its focus on mastery, control, and efficiency, tends to generate fragmented cities without soul or character.

Instead, Integral Urbanism proposes more punctual interventions that contribute to activating places (enhancing flow) by making connections and caring for neglected or abandoned "in-between" spaces or "no-man's lands." In the best-case scenarios, these interventions have a tentacular or domino effect, catalyzing other interventions in an ongoing and never-ending process.

If master planning were a form of surgery on an anaesthetized city, Integral Urbanism might be regarded as a form of acupuncture on a fully alert and engaged city. By opening up blockages along "urban meridians," just as acupuncture and other forms of bioenergetic healing open blockages along the energy meridians of our bodies, this approach can liberate *chi*, or the life force of a city and its dynamic communities. Opening urban meridians may be applied to existing built environments as well as new development, and it can take various forms, depending on the context. It may call for the creation of vital hubs of activity, a quality civic space or green space, easing movement and facilitating connections, or other appropriate responses.

Because Integral Urbanism does not aim to produce master plans, it is not obsessed with control and determining outcomes. Instead, it aims to allow things to happen, things that may even be unforeseen. Produced by people for people, these interventions are arrived at intuitively as well as rationally. They are inspired by the physical context as well as the social and historical contexts.

In contrast to conventional planning, these interventions are not always developed and represented primarily in plan and section. Rather, they might be conveyed through imagery suggesting the latent experiential quality that the intervention would activate. This imagery may be representational or abstract, and it may refer to or draw from other fields (see example below, p. 93). In addition, interactive methods are often applied to generate dialogue and incorporate user feedback.

As urban design theory and practice have evolved, there have been corollary and intersecting shifts in social and cultural theory. One of these shifts is from Structuralist thinking in binary oppositions (e.g., the Hegelian thesis + antithesis = synthesis, Marxian base and superstructure with mediating ideology, Freudian id and superego with mediating ego) to Poststructuralism. Poststructuralism applies a nondialectical approach that acknowledges differences without trying to unify or synthesize them.

While seeking to correct the limitations of Modern thinking, however, Poststructuralism has fallen into many of the same traps. In regarding any kind of communion and things we share (language, ritual, customs, and so forth) as "prison houses" or "repressive codes," Poststructuralism understands relationships through a competitive and instrumental paradigm rather than one of mutual caring and growing. It, therefore, places a premium on separateness, autonomy, and control, valorizing the individual who is nomadic, undomesticated, and unattached to a family, a community, or the Earth.

Philosopher Charlene Spretnak locates the origins of this attitude "in patriarchal culture's brutal and self-destructive divorce from the body – the Earthbody, the female body, the body of the mother."[2] This intense denial of our human nature, Spretnak maintains, led to "a flattened valuelessness in which nothing is left but the will to power."[3] Poststructuralism is, she contends, a philosophical justification for deeply engrained perceptions of profound separateness that yield "alienation, deep-seated rage, and reactive cravings for autonomy and control."[4] Embracing this position, she claims, is ultimately repressive for it is a "cultural construction of the deepest loneliness."[5]

Alternatively, the ecological approach is also nondialectical, but avoids falling into the traps of Poststructuralism or Modernism. Ecological social and cultural theory encourages us to see the gestalt obscured by the Modern project's attempt to control situations scientifically, which ends up valorizing certain fragments while ignoring others such as nature and native peoples.[6] In doing so, this perspective seeks to preserve "the positive advances of the liberal tradition and technological capabilities but is rooted in ecological sanity and meaningful human participation."[7] The ecological approach counters the traditional Eurocentric patriarchal values of rational objectivity, separateness, autonomy, and control with those of transactive subjectivity, community, dialogue, and flexibility.

Ecological design, as architect Barbara Crisp explains, "reconnects mind and body, fostering a sense of place and time and true well-being."[8] To accomplish this, ecological designers have been advocating "integral design," "integral systems,"[9] and "biomimicry."[10] Learning from nature and aspiring to design in a way that supports it, these approaches emphasize the importance of permeable membranes, system diversity, and the ability to be self-adjusting and always evolving. In the words of Sim Van der Ryn and Stuart Cowan, "It is time to stop designing in the image of the machine and start designing in a way that honors the complexity of life itself … we must mirror nature's deep interconnections in our own epistemology of design."[11] For instance, in place of using "hard energy," which is centralized, expensive, and very polluting, ecological design opts for "soft energy," benefiting from natural energy flows and renewable resources. Instead of relying upon human-made machines to service our environments, "living systems" or "living machines" assemble the correct cast of species so that the waste of one biological community becomes food for another.

It is just over the last decade and a half that scientists have acknowledged the importance of biodiversity to ecosystem functioning.[12] Diversity ensures that the plant community (which sustains animal life) will not be wiped out in times of stress such as a drought. Rich biodiversity ensures the health and resilience of the system.[13] In landscape ecology, the loss of biodiversity is referred to as fragmentation. It can result from human interventions or other disturbances, such as the disruption of a wildlife corridor by building a highway or suburban tract development.[14]

Architect Ken Yeang points out that unsustainable building practices simplify the ecosystem, leading to diminished resiliency. "The overall effect," he says, "is that humanity and its built systems have become not less dependent upon the functioning of the ecosystems within the biosphere, but on the contrary, have now become more dependent."[15] To improve resiliency, Yeang recommends that design become "a form of applied ecology."[16]

While designers at all scales from household products to regions are emulating nature, other fields are undergoing analogous paradigm shifts. Anthropologists and cultural theorists are increasingly regarding culture as a part of nature rather than in opposition to it.[17] Scientists, in their search for a "theory of everything," are describing our cosmos in terms of natural principles. Evolutionists now understand human evolution as a "web of life" rather than a "tree of life."[18] Physicist Lee Smolin has proposed that our universe is part of an endless chain of self-reproducing universes that make their own laws, evolving as natural species evolve, according to processes of natural selection.[19]

In urban design, the parallel shift was from the central city model to the polycentric or integrated model. Christopher Alexander's article "The City Is Not a Tree" (1965), which demonstrated the flaw of understanding the city in terms of mathematical models, marked the beginnings of the parallel theoretical shift, now significantly widespread (see pp. 35–7, 49–55, 120–4).

At the same time, we have been witnessing a widespread call for substituting traditionally feminine for traditionally masculine values or, at least, redressing the balance. Seeking to avert the deleterious effects of economic restructuring, for instance, John Logan and Todd Swanstrom propose replacing "the masculine metaphor of cutthroat competition for mobile capital" with "a more feminine image of nurturing the strength of the local context" of "economic development based on embeddedness."[20] Rachel Sara writes in her award-winning article, "The Pink Book," that "The old conception of architecture has a masculine bias; the movement for change is fundamentally feminizing … The new paradigm values qualities traditionally considered feminine such as empathy and collaboration, community and evolution, holism and versatility, negotiation and enabling, emotion, experience and responsiveness."[21] Exposing the privileging of masculine values in architecture, artist Alison Dunn and musician Jim Beach ask, "Why do we always hear about the world's tallest building? Why don't people compare the widest building?

Or the most accommodating? Or the most supportive? Most soulful? Most nurturing?"[22] Acknowledging this bias, architect James Stewart Polshek claims to be feminizing his design "so that there is more nurturing and less swaggering," vowing "I will never be defensive about taking human comfort seriously."[23]

Contemporary attitudes toward place and connectedness have age-old, as well as more recent, precedents in science, philosophy, religion, and design. These include Asian geomancy (or *feng shui*) and Vedic architecture, which emphasize the need for cities and buildings to breathe, Native American attitudes toward regarding our buildings as part of nature, the Renaissance view of the city as having a life force and a soul,[24] the early twentieth-century Chicago School of Urban Ecology's understanding of the city as organism, the Japanese Metabolists' interest in dynamic design,[25] Archigram's notion of "city synthesis" (1960s),[26] and the Gaia hypothesis,[27] which holds that the earth is a living organism that is interdependent at all levels and all scales.

There is, however, something qualitatively different this time around. The current version of the everything-is-related-and-follows-certain-universal-laws approach incorporates the notion that information technologies have irrevocably and irreversibly reconfigured space and time. Now, there is no longer a perceived battle or need to choose between the city-as-organism and city-as-machine. Instead, it is perhaps the Cyborg City, or simply the Cyburg. It may no longer be possible, or relevant, to clearly separate the organism and the machine. However troubling it may be to ponder, we too are increasingly cyborglike. We may have machine components such as pacemakers or artificial limbs; we may be dependent upon hearing aids, insulin-monitoring devices, or other devices; or we may have been created with technical assistance (bioengineering). At the very least, we are interdependent with the machines in our lives, from personal digital assistants to computers, phones, cars, and more.

Indeed, new technologies have been enabling the ecological approach. Instead of only the ideal shapes of classical (Euclidean) geometry, computers can represent the "anexact" (self-similar not self-same) shapes found in nature, also described as fractals of time and space and "fluid or topological geometries." In architecture and urban design, these technologies are allowing us to represent and design cities as dynamic rather than static entities. The Internet and mobile technologies also allow more organic and flexible patterns of settlement and forms of communication.

For instance, new technologies have incited interest in the "folding" of space and time in contrast to more conventional "framing." Folding seeks to connect places (usually through modulating ground planes) and to connect the present with the past and future, without blending these all together.[28] Neither homogenous, like the Modern city, nor heterogeneous like the Postmodern city, folding seeks to acknowledge and support complexity.

What we are witnessing is a significant step beyond the binary logic that reigned supreme in the Western world for centuries. Supplanting linear, hierarchical, and static models (the tree metaphor)[29] are holistic, multicentric, nonhierarchical, and dynamic models (the web or network metaphor). From cells to cities, culture, and cosmology, theories are converging on the same universal principles of development and codevelopment, characterized by dynamic webs of interdependencies[30] and the inextricability of people, nature, and technology.

The five qualities of Integral Urbanism recall other formulations of five. In *The Image of the City* (1960), Kevin Lynch reported that *paths, nodes, districts, landmarks,* and *edges* are the organizing principles of our mental maps of cities. These categories bear similarities to those of Integral Urbanism with nodes offering hybridity, paths providing connectivity, edges allowing porosity, and districts and landmarks endowing authenticity. Focusing on literature, not cities, Italo Calvino called for preserving five values in *Six Memos for the Next Millennium* (1988).[31] *Lightness* intersects with the qualities of vulnerability and porosity; *quickness* refers to connectivity in that it is "based on invisible connections;"[32] *exactitude* recalls authenticity as well as porosity and vulnerability; *visibility* carries traits of porosity and connectivity; and *multiplicity* parallels hybridity. Interestingly, Calvino never penned what was initially conceived as Memo 6 – that of consistency.[33] More recently, Anita Berrizbeitia and Linda Pollak identify five "operations" describing relationships between landscape and architecture: *reciprocity, materiality, threshold, insertion,* and *infrastructure.*[34] Jonathan Barnett posits five principles of good urban design: *community, livability, mobility, equity,* and *sustainability.*[35]

The following chapters array the five qualities of Integral Urbanism into a quilt of many fabrics woven by design and planning practices as well as the rough-and-tumble world of business and real estate development, the more removed studio and theory of academia, and the day-to-day concerns and activities of neighborhoods and communities. I begin by describing the new integration that features *hybridity* and *connectivity.* The subsequent chapter looks at the seams where differences meet to demonstrate *porosity*. I then turn to the central issues of *what* an Integral Urbanism aspires toward – *authenticity* – and *how* best to achieve it – *vulnerability*. Stitching together these swatches of various textures, colors, and sizes, Integral Urbanism offers a "live theory"[36] for enhancing the places we live in.

Mercury, with his winged feet, light and air-borne, astute, agile, adaptable, free and easy, established the relationships of the gods among themselves and those between the gods and men, between universal laws and individual destinies, between the forces of nature and the forms of culture, between the objects of the world and all thinking subjects.
Italo Calvino

Only connect! . . . . Only connect the prose and the passion, and both will be exalted and human love will be seen at its height. Live in fragments no longer. Only connect, and the beast and the monk, robbed of the isolation that is life to either, will die.
E.M. Forster

We live in Flow City. Systems are the roots of design, nourishing the spaces we try to make beautiful . . . . Projects in urban design, architecture, and landscape architecture that aren't made with an understanding of flows and connectivity are destined to fail.
Kristina Hill

Our concern is for the poetry of movement, for the sense of connectivity.
Alison and Peter Smithson

We are building too many walls and not enough bridges.
Scott Carson

Hybridity & Connectivity

Connections missed
Connections made
Connections illusive
Longed for and imagined.

Connections lost
Found
Severed
Invented
Disconnected
And secured.
Nan Ellin

The time has come to conceive of architecture
urbanistically and urbanism architecturally.
Aldo Van Eyck

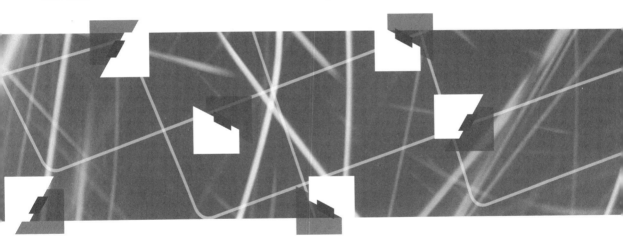

The great challenge of the 21st century
is to strengthen the forces of integration
and weaken the forces of disintegration
and destruction.
Former President Bill Clinton

Urbanism is something that creates potential, and
architecture is something that exploits potential,
exhausts potential …. Urbanism is generous, and
architecture is egotistical.
Rem Koolhaas

HYBRIDITY & CONNECTIVITY

TOWARD A NEW INTEGRATION

The creation of great civic spaces with strong connections between them was a primary goal of city design from antiquity to the nineteenth century, most famously exemplified in Ancient Greek cities, sixteenth-century Rome of Sixtus V and Domenico Fontana, and nineteenth-century Paris of Napoléon III and Baron Haussmann. The mass production and consumption of cars in the early twentieth century, however, transformed city building as it altered the logic and scale of movement.

Privileging vehicular movement over the pedestrian experience, the "city functional" plans that proliferated throughout the United States during this period were motivated primarily by getting from point A to point B as quickly as possible, rather than valuing the journey. Pedestrian and vehicular paths thus separated. So did land uses, activities, buildings, and districts resulting in cityscapes composed of freestanding high-rises and suburban tract houses linked by highways. Largely absent from this "megalopolitan development"[1] of the last century were quality public spaces, local character, multifunctional places (combining housing, work, circulation, and recreation), and an integration of the built and natural landscapes. Dispersal and fragmentation occurred hand in hand, spelling an end to the connectedness, walkability, and sense of place of the prevehicular landscape.

Integral Urbanism aims to bring these back through *hybridity* and *connectivity*. Hybridization connects people and activities at points of intensity and along thresholds. Emanating from these are other paths that connect elsewhere. While Modern Urbanism espoused the separation of functions in urban form, Integral Urbanism reaffirms their symbiotic nature by combining and linking (or "slashing," see pp. 133–4) them.[2] In doing so, it learns from ecology and from past urban forms. From ecology, it adopts the logic that the health and well-being of places derive from optimizing numerous variables rather than trying to maximize one variable.[3] From city-building wisdom, Integral Urbanism learns about juxtaposition, simultaneity, and collective decision making, adapting these to contemporary needs and tastes as well as to the landscape we have wrought over the last century.

Whatever happened to the earlier city-building wisdom? In the United States, the rise of mass culture and mass production at the beginning of the last century followed by mass suburbanization (allowed by the car) and widespread television viewing after the Second World War conspired to fray both quality public space and a vibrant self-confident popular culture. During this same period, the extended family was largely supplanted by the nuclear family (particularly in middle-class culture). This shift was assisted in part by the "New Fatherhood Movement" (of the 1920s) that encouraged fathers to be involved in child raising, effectively dismantling the webs of women and elders that had been caring for children. These coincident changes in family structure, urban development patterns, leisure activities, and popular culture contributed to a sense of disconnectedness from self and the places we live.

Focusing specifically on urbanism, Jane Jacobs prescribed diversity in *Death and Life of Great American Cities* (1961): "In our American Cities, we need all kinds of diversity, intricately mingled in mutual support ... [M]ost city diversity is the creation of incredible numbers of different people and different private organizations, with vastly differing ideas and purposes, planning and contriving outside the formal framework of public action. The main responsibility of city planning and design should be to develop – insofar as public policy and action can do so – cities that are congenial places for this great range of unofficial plans, ideas and opportunities to flourish, along with the flourishing of the public enterprises."[4] To generate such diversity, Jacobs recommended districts that serve many functions, short blocks, comingling of old and new buildings, and dense concentrations of people.[5] Although Jacobs' recommendations struck a chord among the general public, the professions of urban design and development were not yet sufficiently equipped to heed them.[6]

In more recent years, numerous architects and city planners have been attempting to readdress the ever-growing sense of disconnectedness. In contrast to the purist and essentialist tendencies of Modernism,[7] many are extolling the virtues of "hybridity." Steven Holl, for instance, champions hybrid building programs, hybrid construction techniques, and hybrid detailing of buildings.[8] Rem Koolhaas asserts that the city's primary connective principle is constituted by "exacerbated difference," or a permanent hybridity.[9] In *Delirious New York*, he celebrates the "poetic density" of Manhattan, the potential of each block to support "an infinite number of superimposed and unpredictable activities." Describing programmatic hybridity variously as complexity, density, congestion, contamination, and "thematic intensification,"[10] Koolhaas maintains, "programmatic elements react with each other to create new events – Bigness returns to a model of programmatic *alchemy*."[11] Architects Marc Angelil and Anna Klingmann similarly advocate a "hybrid morphology [that] unfolds from a system of relations between different, sometimes contradictory forces, no longer as an absolute but in reference to other structures," in a process that is "unceasingly renegotiated."[12] In addition, urbanist Roger Trancik, in *Finding Lost Space*, calls for mixing uses to ensure greater richness and vitality in cities.[13]

Intensifying program (also described as cross programming or programmatic integration) can be accomplished spatially (plan and section) as well as temporally over the course of a day, week, or year. It allows people and activities to comingle and converge in ways that the separation of functions does not. Robert Putnam, in *Bowling Alone*, describes the benefits of these casual interactions, often among strangers, saying, "Like pennies dropped in a cookie jar, each of these encounters is a tiny investment in social capital."[14] Urban sociologist William H. Whyte coined the term "triangulation" to describe this phenomenon. In his now classic documentary, "The Social Life of Small Urban Spaces," Whyte demonstrates how a piece of public art, a fountain, a street performer, or a kiosk can enrich the urban experience. As a former Whyte student and current president of the Project for Public Spaces, Fred Kent explains, triangulation occurs when "certain uses that seem unlikely partners can, if put together, create a synergy that exceeds anyone's imagination. The idea is, if you take a children's reading room in a library, and put it next to a children's playground in a park, and then you add a coffee shop, a Laundromat, and a bus stop, that would be a very vital place."[15]

Programmatic integration can be accomplished through deliberate intentions of designers, planners, and developers or more spontaneously and serendipitously by small business owners and neighborhoods. Some contemporary integrations recall preindustrial ones such as housing above the store and live/work spaces. Others are preindustrial with a twist such as housing above the big-box store, time-share condominiums, the movie theater/restaurant, bookstore/coffeehouse (both mega versions and small boutique versions), the urban plaza or parking lot by day/outdoor movie theater at night (see Figures 3 and 4), and advertising integrated with buildings through murals, billboards, and animated screens. Others still are completely of the moment. Such emergent

Figure 3

Figure 4

examples of cross programming include the office building with basketball court and daycare center, the intergenerational community building (combining day care, teenage community center, continuing education, and senior center), the public school/community center, the integrated parking structure (parking blended into office buildings, retail centers, and parks), the cybercafé (sometimes combined with computer retail as well), the laundromat/club, and the dive-in (watching movies while floating on rafts).

As many of these contemporary integrations reveal, parallel shifts have been occurring in regulatory, real estate, and business practices without regard for, but allowing, the hybridization architects and planners have been advocating. Epitomized perhaps by the Barnes & Noble–Starbucks partnership, the explosion in business partnering is not confined to books and coffee, but extends exponentially and virtually such that online services are partnering (developing alliances) to garner larger market shares and to encourage "stickiness" so people do not click away to other "sites." The buzzword *convergence* describes such technological integration.

E-commerce offers a virtual example of the new integration, permitting recycling, redistribution, greater access to goods and information, and price equity, all without a central authority or surveillance. Selling art online, for instance, provides artists with a larger audience, eliminates middle-person fees, and allows consumers far greater access to artistic production. No longer do art lovers and potential customers need to worry about appearing stupid or unhip by snotty gallery owners or even to travel to galleries or artists' studios. Through e-commerce, customers can purchase original art, as well as other items, from home and have them delivered to their door with just a few clicks, thereby gaining access to worlds previously out of reach. Although not contributing to a sense of community derived from a shared place (the preindustrial model), e-commerce allows another sense of community, entered into voluntarily and connected by common interests.

An actual example of the new integration might be a children's center (or "cc"[16]), a twenty-four-hour indoor/outdoor center equipped with a playground, indoor gymnastics equipment, library, arts and crafts, trained caretakers, and access to health care. Instead of thirty-two individual nannies or babysitters who may not be very competent or enthusiastic about this sort of work and who are isolated with children in their homes, a cc could employ four experienced childcare workers in a beautiful well-equipped facility for the same number. Children would be with other children in a safe, enriching setting away from home with well-trained caretakers. They could benefit from numerous activities unavailable at home, such as mounting their own performances or art shows, hosting guest speakers on various topics, and taking field trips to local factories, farms, seniors' centers, or the theater. The caretakers would have a far superior work environment than if they were isolated in someone else's home with one child. Parents would not only be offered the assurance that their children are in a good environment, but would also be offered flexibility. As a twenty-four-hour center that charges by the hour, the cc would accommodate a work schedule that departs from the conventional 9 to 5, a last-minute meeting, a night out, or an emergency. If the cc is located adjacent to other amenities, workplaces, and homes and if some of its amenities such as the library were shared with the larger community, opportunities for social interactions (a public realm) would be in place. It would also catalyze other developments.

Transposing programmatic hybridity onto the urban and regional scales can increase density of activity without necessarily increasing building density or increasing it only slightly in certain places to produce a low-density urbanism. The outcome is new hybrid typologies and morphologies that pool human and natural resources to the benefit of all. Resources conserved include time, effort, talent, money, water, energy (fuel, electricity, and human energy), building materials, paper (less paperwork and less junk mail), space, and more.

Although recalling the consolidation and increased efficiency applied to the factory, this new integration can occur without "Taylorization," the scientific management style introduced by Frederick Winslow Taylor in the 1910s that increased production but also led to dehumanization, demoralization, and class conflict. Rather than dehumanize, this new integration holds the potential for empowering people to fulfill their needs and desires more effectively. This is because a central authority does not impose it and because it contributes to revitalizing the public realm thanks to the time saved and new gathering spaces generated. This kind of integration can reduce commuting, enhance convenience, preserve the natural environment, increase quality public space, and greatly multiply opportunities for social encounters.[17] With more time and interaction, people discuss common concerns and generate innovative resolutions.

NEW TYPOLOGIES

Numerous architects and urban designers have been exploring new typologies – or variations on old ones – with the goal of combining the best of city and suburb while also darning holes in existing urban and suburban fabrics. For instance, at Swan's Marketplace in Oakland, California, Pyatok Architects Inc. adaptively reused the Market Hall (originally built between 1917 and 1940) to provide cohousing condominium units with a common house, affordable rental units, live/work spaces, a farmers' market hall, commercial office space, and parking, as well as space for the Museum of Children's Art (MOCHA) (see Figures 5 and 6).

Figure 5

Figure 6

Inside a large auto warehouse in Portland dating from the turn of the nineteenth century, the Sienna Architecture Company ingeniously combined three levels of parking, using the existing ramps, with condominiums so that residents may park adjacent to their units.[18] To achieve these urban (or inner suburban) densities, Sienna has engaged in creative client and financial arrangements by purchasing air rights over commercial and office spaces in Portland and Seattle to build housing.[19]

The possibilities allowed by cross programming inspire innumerable architectural proposals. Michael Gamble, for instance, suggests reprogramming midtown Atlanta to include (1) A (Con)Temporary Film Institute: A parking lot that has a double feature every night inside and outside, constructed of aluminum so it can be easily disassembled and reconstructed elsewhere if a client comes along with plans for more permanent structures (see Figures 7 and 8); and (2) Another Atlantic Steel: A figure-8 track through the brownfield site of the defunct Atlantic Steel for defensive driving classes, NASCAR and Grand Prix events, and auto conventions as well as (in the infield) affordable housing, workspace, and retail, producing overlapping multiple speeds and layers of movement (see Figure 9).

New typologies were in full force at the Venice Biennale of 2004.[20] George Yu proposed weaving together elements of conventional commercial spaces with a landscape of terraced residential buildings and public park space. In a project called "Parking Sections," the firm Lewis.Tsurumaki.Lewis (LTL) combined parking with retail, commercial, and residential components. In a "New Suburbanism," LTL overlaps suburban houses with big-box stores intersected by parking garages and athletic fields. For "Park Tower," a drive-up skyscraper features a double-helical system combining a continuous parking surface with stacked retail, office, and housing. Reiser+Umemoto suggested rethinking the highway

Figure 7

Figure 8

ANOTHER ATLANTIC STEEL

ANOTHER
ATLANTIC
STEEL

1.9 Mile Nascar Circuit

A. Grandstands
B. Housing
C. Department Store
D. Convenience Store
E. 400 Car Parking
F. Recreation Fields
G. Developable Infields
H. Office Block
I. Existing Shed/Pit Area
J. Hotel + Convention
    Center
K. Grandstand with 1400
    Car Parking
L. Underpass at Train
    Tracks
M. New 16th Street Bridge
N. Existing Institute of
    Paper Science
O. Park

Figure 9

interchange by introducing a bridge made of laminated-wood members that would incorporate housing, pedestrian circulation, and landscaping.

When designing large structures, many architects are attempting to emulate the fine grain of traditional cities. According to Kenneth Frampton, the Metabolism of the 1960s evolved into a "fragmentary urbanism at a higher symbolic level," exemplified by Maki's Makuhari Exhibition Hall (540 by 120 meters) built at Chiba in 1989 and the smaller Tokyo Municipal Gymnasium of 1990, both of which feature dematerialized shell structures and offer "a new kind of urban enclave."[21] Large structures are also emulating the programmatic textures of old cities such as the Triangle des Gares in Euralille, France, designed by Jean Nouvel (1994) to create a link between two train stations with a shopping mall, small office towers, hotel, school, theater, and housing. The Salt Lake City Library, designed by Moshe Safdie (2003),

Figure 10

includes a "Main Street" with shops along it (see Figure 10). Airport renovations around the globe incorporate the kinds of shops, restaurants, and art galleries found in the cities they serve, producing an internal "urbanism."

SUBURBAN REVITALIZATION

Much of the contemporary hybridity and connectivity is taking place in older suburbs. As Ellen Dunham-Jones recounts, "Some suburbs are renovating older malls or building new ones to create town centers and main streets where none existed. Hybrids combining libraries, post offices, shops, recreation, restaurants, and even residences, these centers are generally more innovative in their mix of programs than in their design expression or commitment to civic purposes, but they do reflect an interest in urbanizing suburbia."[22] Many abandoned or underutilized shopping malls built after the Second World War around the United States are being retrofitted into street-friendly shops and cafés with live/work spaces or condos above them.[23] Old shopping malls in Chattanooga, Tennessee; Pasadena, California; and Kendall, Florida, have been retrofitted to face outward toward the street while brand new "downtowns" are being built in cities that never had an urban core.[24]

Other efforts are focusing on the streets themselves. Designing a highway corridor for the town of Chanhassen, Minnesota, the architect William Morrish and landscape architect Catherine Brown aspired to retain the small-town character that its inhabitants valued, preserve the natural environment, and integrate the new road into the community rather than allow it to divide and conquer the community.[25] A multidisciplinary team including architects Jude Le Blanc and Michael Gamble is retrofitting sixteen square miles of sub-urban strip along Buford Highway in Atlanta. The University of Arkansas Community Design Center has generated a matrix of "recombinant infrastructures" to provide more amenities along the suburban arterial Highway 9B extending from Fayetteville (see Figures 11 and 12).

In addition to these initiatives undertaken by the public sector, private developers, and designers, many mid-twentieth-century strip malls have been transformed by the business owners themselves, often reflecting changing demographics. Museologist Elaine Gurian keenly observes this phenomenon in her neighborhood outside Washington, D.C.: "the Laundromat has pool tables, a child's play area and a barbershop. It had a money order and check-cashing booth but that moved to its own shop next door and combined with the utility bill-paying function that used to operate out of the Asian food

Figure 11

Figure 12

market. The Asian owners speak Spanish, sell both Asian and Latino food and beer and liquor. Not to be outdone, the Latino food market sells lottery tickets, phone cards, and is the French pastry outlet. The Halal food store rents videotapes and sells clothes. The hours of use are nearly around the clock."[26]

This widespread urbanization of the suburbs recalls Lewis Mumford's advice almost one-half century ago: "If we are concerned with human values, we can no longer afford either sprawling Suburbia or the congested Metropolis" (1961).[27] The low-density urbanism accomplished through programmatic densities connected by mass transit in inner suburbs can overcome the drawbacks of both sprawl and congestion. In addition, concentrating development into these cores and corridors allows greater conservation of the natural environment.

HYBRIDS

Whether in large cities, small towns, or suburban areas, people are increasingly asking how they can add to the mix in order to generate synergies and efficiencies along with higher revenues. As a result, mixing uses has been occurring widely in transit hubs, cultural institutions, retail, health clubs, community centers, the workplace, and outdoor public spaces.

A number of proposals for subway and light rail stations for the Los Angeles metropolitan area seek to retain and enhance what local communities value. Johnson Fain and Pereira Associates devised a plan for the Chatsworth Station that includes a replica of the historic Chatsworth Station, a childcare center, and other civic and commercial services, all linked to the natural landscape by pedestrian and bicycle paths.[28] For a more urban site in Hollywood, Koning Eisenberg Architects proposed a station that expresses neighborhood identity by preserving the small scale of residential blocks while providing market stalls clustered around the station with housing and a single-room occupancy hotel above.

The public library has lately been demonstrating its commitment to remain on the forefront of resource efficiency and quality public space by offering much more than books. The Central Library of Phoenix designed by architects Will Bruder and Wendell Burnette features a state-of-the-art teen center, bookstore, auditorium, gallery, indoor/outdoor children's section, and (planned) café (see Figure 13). The Red Deer Public Library in Alberta, Canada, has a café in the reading area. The Chungmuro Intermedia Playground (2001) in Seoul, Korea, designed by Cho Slade Architecture with Team BAHN includes a lounge area, video screening room, video editing room, auditorium, and exhibition space. Museums are following suit with, for instance, a café within the exhibition space at the National Museum of New Zealand (Te Papa).

Among the most prevalent hybrids is the bookstore/café for large chain retailers as well as local independent businesses such as the Red Canoe Children's Books & Coffee House in Baltimore. However, there are many other flavors of mixing. An updated and upscaled version of the now extinct lunch counter in five-and-dime stores, Barney's in Beverly Hills features a full bar on its top floor. No longer just for the ladies-who-lunch crowd, it has become a

Figure 13

destination in itself for women and men at any time of day or night and no doubt inspires numerous purchases of the men's ties and women's bikinis displayed adjacent. Ulta, a chain of 160 cosmetics/spa/salon superstores in 20 states in the United States also offers its customers a pharmacy, shoeshine, e-mail and fax, makeover counter, and delivery service. Farrelli's Cinema Supper Club, in Scottsdale, Arizona, is a cinema/restaurant/bar, and Lucky Strike Lanes, in numerous locations throughout the United States and Canada, offers an upscale blend of bowling alleys with restaurant/lounges. In California, the William L. Morris Chevrolet dealership, which was offering breakfast and lunch to clients waiting for their cars to be serviced, expanded into a full Italian restaurant within the car showroom upon the suggestion of its chef Franco.[29] From within the design world, architects Coop Himmelblau proposed a BMW showroom that doubles as an entertainment space for the 2002 Venice Biennale.

Intensely competitive for clients, health clubs have been ratcheting up their offerings (as well as their design), with daycare, massage therapy, and healthy cafés becoming standard features. The Silverleaf Club, nestled in the McDowell Mountains in Scottsdale, Arizona, is composed of locally quarried stone and salvaged building materials imported from France including 200–400-year-old handmade roof tiles, limestone for window accents, and doors reclaimed from a *château*.

Accessible only to those who reside in the neighborhood, the 51,000-square-foot rural Mediterranean expanse sits amid a sprawling golf course, two pools, a labyrinth for walking meditation, and a large indoor/outdoor courtyard for events. The club includes a fitness room, spa, *watsu* (small pool for water massage), large dining room, private dining area, bar, and well-appointed locker rooms. Inside the 12,000-square-foot women's locker room, there is a "conservatory" featuring a full-service menu, full bar, linen table cloths, and magnificent mountain and pool views from the terrace seating[30] (see Figure 14).

A precursor to this women's locker room may be found in the late nineteenth-century–early twentieth-century ladies' lounges adjacent to rest rooms of department stores. For the women who shopped there, these lounge areas were places to gather with other women and their small children and sometimes to organize for political causes. A public precursor to the entire private club is the French cafés/dance gardens, often located along rivers, for locals as well as tourists, for people of all ages at all times of day, offering meals and snacks, drinks, dancing, swimming, and boating.

Figure 14

Some cities are offering greater convenience while conserving resources by combining community centers with libraries, schools, and recreational areas (see administrative porosity, p. 75). While bringing programs together, this cross-programming is also bringing together people of different incomes, ethnicities, and ages (social integration). Urban seniors' villages are being planned to offer residents the vitality of cities and to offer cities more "eyes on the street,"[31] unofficial neighborhood "mayors," and the mutual assistance and learning benefits of age diversity. Grassroots efforts are also forging the new integration with, for instance, community workshops for woodworking, metallurgy, sculpture, and painting combined with art classrooms, studio space, galleries, and cafés.

Progressive workplaces are also adopting hybrid programs, emulating cities within, and integrating with cityscapes around them (see Microsoft, p. 77).[32] When TBWA\Chiat\Day moved to Playa del Rey, California, in 1998, it modeled its new offices in a large warehouse after the city, including a "central park" with trees and park tables, a basketball court, and a "main street" flanked by stacked "cliff-dwellings" on either side described as "neighborhoods."[33] Some workplace designers call this "community-based planning."[34] Richard Florida explains that office layouts today tend "to be traffic-oriented rather than hierarchical."[35] This new workplace places an emphasis on flexibility and mobility, with casters on just about everything. The "laptop chair" is a lounge chair with a tablet arm for laptop computers, allowing employees to shift locations and sit by windows. Small cafés are integrated throughout the workplace with laptop ports and built-in flat screens so that employees may hold meetings or work there.

Turkish designer Ayse Birsel created the 120-degree connector desk that can be assembled to create pods or constellations, emulating the patterns of honeycombs, for Herman Miller [Resolve System, 1999 (see Figure 15)]. Lacking right angles, these desks produce aisles that meander like the streets of the premodern city. Fabric panels between desks or pods can be raised or lowered to offer collaborative or separate work areas while transforming the appearance of the space. Birsel's Resolve System entered the permanent collection of the Museum of Modern Art in 2001.[36]

Observing that people working in technology sales spend a lot of time on the phone and that they like to walk while talking, the offices designed for Mainspring in New York City (2000), now IBM, feature a "track" with "telephone rooms" dispersed along it for those wishing to converse in private (see Figure 16). One of the squash courts from the New York Sports and Racquet Club, which occupied the space prior, was retained as a squash court that can be converted into a conference room using mobile furniture.[37]

Figure 15

Figure 16

Outdoor public space is also growing more hybrid. Landscape architect Walter Hood, for instance, designs "hybrid landscapes" to satisfy diverse user group needs (see p. 126) by juxtaposing qualities such as urban park/woodlands, plazas/parks, and park/parking. On Poplar Street in Macon,

Georgia, Hood created four 650-foot-wide "yards" that combine parks, parking, and public art. The art is intended to be meaningful to the local community as well as functional, such as white cubes that recall cotton bales while also serving as picnic tables.

Numerous efforts to reclaim vacant lots also demonstrate this hybrid and holistic approach. Landscape architect Achva Benzinberg Stein designed the Uhuru Garden in Watts, Los Angeles, to include gardens as well as facilities for instruction in gardening and for selling what is grown. Incorporating native California vegetation as well as indigenous irrigation techniques, this garden is used by residents of an adjacent public housing project, students at the local public school, and clients at a drug rehabilitation center.[38] Other efforts to convert vacant lots into community gardens in the United States have been undertaken by the HOPE Horticulture Corps, the Los Angeles Regional Food Bank Garden, Food from the Hood, and the Green Guerrillas. In addition to community gardens, vacant lots are also being reclaimed for temporary tree nurseries, playgrounds and parks, infill housing, and mixed-use development.

To describe a hybrid condition between architecture and landscape, Mark Lee introduced the term "topological landscape." Rather than represent "spaciousness by merely dissolving spatial confines," Lee explains, "the topological landscape actively seeks to redefine new boundaries while simultaneously transgressing established ones ... It is not a stable entity but a performative state ... "[39] An offshoot of geometry, topology originated in the nineteenth century to study those properties an object retains under deformation – specifically bending, stretching, and squeezing, but not breaking or tearing.[40] Practitioners of topological landscape include Greg Lynn, Bernard Cache, Foreign Office of Architects, Ushida Findlay, and Rem Koolhaas.

CORES AND CORRIDORS

Combining the qualities of hybridity and connectivity, large-scale design interventions are focusing on the creation of cores with adjoining corridors. Planner Marion Roberts and cohorts advocate reorienting "urban design away from its traditional focus on sites and centres towards an inclusion of networks, transport interchanges and suburban sub-centres" with a particular emphasis on connectivity "between centres and sub-centres and between public and private."[41] They recommend that the most significant paths and nodes constitute an "armature" forming "a core of movement, activity and meaning" including "key routes and places"[42] in the public and semipublic realm of the "most significant stretches of the key channels of movement."[43] Each element of this armature, they explain, should be mutually reinforcing. Transportation networks should be integrated with each other and with pedestrian networks forming "natural nodes for the development of a new style of urban sub-centres."[44] All of this, they emphasize, should be accomplished "without recourse to an overly detailed master plan,"[45] allowing for natural growth and change.[46]

Rather than large arterials leading to pods of housing on the cul-de-sacs of conventional suburban development, the New Urbanism applies a dispersed traffic pattern to create a network of streets, town centers, and districts. In the new town of Verrado outside of Phoenix, for instance, a major town center is connected to smaller town centers by boulevards and a series of parks are connected by pathways (see Figure 17).

The New Urbanism, which began as Neo-Traditional Urbanism in the 1970s, revisits and updates the themes of Jacobs and of the English townscape movement.[47] Form-based coding (see pp. 38–41), as opposed to use-based zoning, prescribes building locations and size, largely allowing the market

Figure 17

to determine uses (with some restrictions). Transect-zoning acknowledges the transition in quality from urban to rural but insists upon a certain mix in each. While initially focused on greenfield sites, the New Urbanism has been evolving to engage in urban infill and to incorporate ecological design principles.

In retrofitting existing cities and suburbs, Peter Calthorpe proposed the "Urban Network," composed of boulevards, avenues, and streets that mix cars, transit, bicycles, and pedestrians.[48] He describes this network as a "cross between our historic grid, streetcar avenues, and the suburban arterial."[49] The Urban Network retains the freeway and grid of major arterials and adds connector streets for traffic dispersal. The arterials are redesigned to become "transit boulevards" that allow mixed-use, pedestrians, bikes, and transit. Village centers, town centers, and urban centers are located where boulevards intersect.

With William Fulton and Robert Fishman, Calthorpe applies this logic at the regional scale to produce networks of communities, open space, and economic systems.[50] European social democracies, most notably France, Sweden, and the Netherlands, have been applying network theory to large-scale urban planning over the last several decades, channeling large-scale growth into concentrated areas connected by transit lines.[51]

Smart growth initiatives around the United States are supporting integration at the regional scale. Wisconsin's "smart growth" legislation, for instance, assists cities in linking transportation, land-use, and quality of life issues.[52] National organizations and policies are also assisting such integrations. Reconnecting America works to link transportation networks – planes, trains, autos, and buses, as well as walking and bicycling. Robert Yaro, President of the New York Regional Plan Association and Armando Carbonell, of the Lincoln Institute of Land Policy recommend that the United States become a true intermodal network of air, road, rail, and water linkages to alleviate congestion and the risks associated with attacks and natural disasters.[53]

Real estate developers have been hopping happily upon the density and mixed-use bandwagon, because more square feet combining residential with office space and retail translates into greater revenues. Amenities such as pathways and parks have also proven to add value. As a result, the industry is actively involved in building mixed-use projects, transit-oriented development, pedestrian-oriented development, and something called "manufactured density," which is the square footage and uses that will support mass transit.

Regulatory practices that support these trends include mixed-use zoning, also called "integrated land use," as well as the less common "performance" zoning. Performance zoning regulates land use through the application of standards based on public objectives and community visions. In contrast to conventional zoning, it does not restrict land uses, but specifies the intensity of land use that is acceptable, allowing for hybridity. Common objectives include ensuring that development does not burden existing infrastructure or that it does not eliminate access to parklands. The marketing principle of "adjacent attraction" also generates the hybridity and intensity that urban designers have been seeking.

The most recent refinement in regulatory practices that support hybridity and connectivity is form-based coding. In contrast to conventional land use zoning, which largely segregates functions, form-based coding presumes that what happens within a building is less important than the form of the building and its relationship to other buildings and to the street. The goal is to produce high-quality public space that will support healthy civic interaction while allowing uses to change according to owner's wishes and market demand from, say, a warehouse to artists' studios to a restaurant/club with condos. Form-based codes (FBCs) regulate certain uses but accomplish this differently than land-use zoning.[54]

The FBC is developed through a community visioning process and is conveyed through clear illustrations and diagrams along with explanatory text. The code designates building types, assembling plan and section diagrams for each type on one 8½-by-11-inch page or combined on a matrix formatted as a poster. These standards typically establish maximum and minimum building heights, placement in relation to adjacent buildings and street, and location and configuration of entrances, windows, porches, parking, yards, and courtyards. General uses are labeled (retail, housing, and so forth) on the section diagrams, allowing for different uses on each floor, instead of the often confusing land-use method of indicating uses in the plan with colors, stripes, and cross-hatching. Section diagrams indicate dimensions for cars, parking, medians, sidewalks, planting strips, and property lines. FBCs often include landscape standards as well, identifying appropriate locations and species.

Form-based coding was introduced in 1982 for Seaside, a new town located on the Florida panhandle, designed by the firm Duany Plater-Zyberk (DPZ) for developer Robert Davis beginning in the late 1970s (see Figures 18 and 19). Thanks to the success of Seaside, as measured by consumer demand,

Figure 18

Figure 19

DPZ has developed over two hundred more FBCs since. Other developers along with the public sector have also been adopting FBCs for the creation of new towns, the revitalization of old ones, suburban revitalization, and infill. These ordinances are a spur to development because they offer a level of confidence and predictability to private investors. Because of the public involvement in elaborating the ordinances, they also increase community spirit and trust, sometimes allowing for development that had previously stalled.[55]

Instead of beginning from scratch each time, DPZ has developed the SmartCode, a template based on the "transect" that organizes metropolitan regions into zones from most urban to most natural. Elaborating upon this template, places may create their own customized FBCs. After the city of Petaluma, California, successfully applied the SmartCode, following years of futile efforts to adopt a more conventional scheme, California officially endorsed form-based coding in its general plan guidelines in 2004.[56]

There are numerous advantages to form-based coding. Because these codes are prescriptive (stating what communities want), rather than proscriptive (what they do not want), FBCs can achieve a more predictable physical result. Because they allow people to visualize what will take place, FBCs encourage public participation and with that, a greater comfort level and ability to accept things they would not have without the process, such as density, mixed uses, and mass transit.

Because FBCs can regulate development at the scale of an individual building or lot and because they are easily accessible (not requiring specialist knowledge), they encourage independent development by multiple property owners, eliminating the need for large land assemblies along with the mega projects often built on these. Thanks to the public process, stylistic diversity compatible with the overall code usually results. Taking the place of land-use zoning and its sometimes compensatory design guidelines, form-based coding simplifies the standard legal and design process of city building, thereby conserving time, energy, money, and aggravation, while also reducing financial risk. Because the goal is healthy cities as determined by their citizens, the codes are not enforced on the basis of aesthetics but on the basis of the public good.

As the FBC suggests, urban designers are expanding their purview beyond transforming the physical environment to effecting changes in public policy and in public opinion regarding the potential value of urban design. Along with DPZ and Calthorpe, urban designer William Morrish also engages in larger issues. His public art plan for Phoenix "used art as a bridge between the public and those who make public policy" (1991). Projects in Minneapolis include efforts to generate jobs while providing a series of small neighborhood parks at the Hennepin County Works and to integrate public housing with private-sector housing.[57] Also branching out from design to policy, architect Michael Gamble proposes applying special public interest (SPI) and community improvement district (CID) funding to the infrastructural development essential to his proposals for retrofitting Atlanta (see pp. 25–6).

ADMINISTRATIVE HYBRIDS

Interventions at the urban or regional scales require integration (or hybrids) at another level, that of political and administrative units such as school districts, parks and recreation departments, transit authorities, zoning boards, neighborhood and homeowners' associations, and real estate concerns (see administrative porosity and "sharing opportunities," pp. 75–6). As Project for Public Spaces reports:

> Fortunately, there is a new wave of interdisciplinary collaboration that adopts a more cooperative approach to knit neighborhoods together, and it brings real economic and social benefits to cities. Parks departments are partnering with transportation officials to create greenways and other transportation networks for pedestrians and bicyclists. Transportation agencies are teaming up with economic development organizations to bring housing, businesses, and a sense of vitality back to downtown streets. And community development groups are investing in parks, plazas, and other public spaces with the goal of reviving urban neighborhoods.[58]

One example is found in the redevelopment of the 2.2-kilometer inner-city beachfront, the Strand, in Townsville, Australia, after devastation by Cyclone Sid in 1998. The Parks Services and Environmental Management Services worked with the police department and community groups to create an inclusive, safe, well-maintained "boulevard by the sea." The Strand offers four beaches along with a showcase for public art, state-of-the-art youth recreation facilities and children's playgrounds, fresh water swimming pool, fitness trail, fishing jetty, basketball court, amphitheatre, restaurants, kiosks, gardens, and parks where they have planted 16,000 trees. Preparing for any future storms, they have incorporated storm water control, cleaning without chemicals, and associated damage prevention educational programs. To be responsive to community needs, the Townsville City Council conducts regular surveys to obtain feedback. The Strand's success has catalyzed revitalization in the adjacent suburb of North Ward.[59]

In the United States, partnerships among several agencies allowed a community-based health center in Wisconsin, the Sixteenth Street Community Health Center (SSCHC), to go well beyond traditional health care provider models. The SSCHC led a Sustainable Development Design Charrette in 1999 and subsequently hosted a 2002 design competition with sponsorship from the National Endowment for the Arts subtitled Natural Landscapes for Living Communities. The winning submission by Wenk Associates of Denver called for restoring the ecological systems of the area, including the Menomonee River Valley adjacent to downtown, by building a storm water park to prevent water pollution along with recreational open space. It also proposed building an industrial park to provide jobs and increase the city's tax base. The charrette and competition demonstrated sustainable redevelopment practices and served as catalysts for cleaning up contaminated sites, redeveloping the area, and contributing to economic revitalization.[60]

MAKING CONNECTIONS

Along with intensifying activity and opportunities through hybridity, tremendous attention has been paid in recent years to facilitating movement within and between urban nodes. This is often accomplished by reclaiming abandoned infrastructures or constructing new ones.

Conveniently and effectively, contemporary transit/recreational corridors often reuse abandoned infrastructures. The Rails-to-Trails Conservancy was founded in 1988 to assist in converting abandoned railroad corridors around the United States into public "linear parks," also called rail-trails or rails-with-trails. Over one thousand miles of trails have been constructed and many more are in progress. Studies of rail-trails in Baltimore, Seattle, and the East Bay of San Francisco report significant increase in property values adjacent to the trails along with revenues generated by the trails for the communities through which they pass.

Landscape architect and urban designer Diana Balmori proposed building a light rail system and greenway on the site of an abandoned canal and rail line that passes through New Haven to unite segregated communities and to enhance a pedestrian orientation.[61] William Fain of Johnson Fain and Pereira Associates developed the Greenway Plan for metropolitan Los Angeles to revitalize four hundred miles of abandoned rail and infrastructure rights-of-way as well as river and flood control channels to create a grid of public space, recreational trails, and a coherence and structure to the city, as well as an important source of employment.

Abandoned infrastructures may also serve as cores, sometimes combined with corridors. Eric Owen Moss proposed A.R.City (Air Rights City) in 1995 with developer Frederick Smith above an abandoned rail corridor in Culver City, California, to unite separated neighborhoods and revitalize the area. A.R. City would create a half-mile long linear park along the rail line with buildings above it at points, raised on steel columns twenty-one feet off the ground. The Samitaur Building designed by Moss for Smith and located a few blocks from the rail spur could be a prototype. Named after Smith's development company and intended to house creative enterprises, the Samitaur connects two existing industrial buildings creating a bridge or *porte cochère* above a driveway.

The nonprofit citizens' group Friends of the High Line in New York City has worked to protect this elevated rail structure on the west side of Manhattan from demolition. Built in 1930 for freight trains, and abandoned in 1980, this line passes through two buildings and measures thirty to sixty feet wide, is one-and-a-half miles long, and encompasses seven acres. Selected in 2004, the design team of Field Operations (James Corner) and Diller Scofidio + Renfro envisions the High Line, "as a string of discrete urban moments, ranging from contemplative gardens to an outdoor theater and distant views of the river. The idea is to savor the nuances of everyday urban life, to heighten the contrast between vast scale and intimate spaces that give the city texture."[62] The designers have proposed a system of "agri-tecture," "a flexible and responsive system of material organization where diverse social and natural habitats may grow." This system is intended to blur the boundary between plantings (softscape) and pathways (hardscape) with an innovative planking system that integrates hard and soft surfaces.[63]

A two-mile stretch of waterfront along the East River Esplanade of Lower Manhattan offers another example of creating an amenity from an abandoned infrastructure. SHoP Architects,[64] Richard Rogers Partnership, and Ken Smith have proposed a scheme that weaves together the fine-grained fabric of the surrounding neighborhoods with the monumental scale of the freeway. The designers propose cladding the underbelly of the freeway in metal and concrete panels as well as bands of fluorescent light strips. They also insert glass pavilions under the freeway to house flower shops, restaurants, and other uses. They apply landscaping to scattered areas along the waterfront including gardens along the piers and they propose tiny parks and reflecting pools where the esplanade meets with neighborhoods. Architecture critic Nicolai Ousoroff maintains, "The plan shows how a series of small interven-

Figure 20

tions, when thoughtfully conceived, can have a more meaningful impact on daily life than an unwieldy urban development scheme"[65] (see Figure 20).

Reclaiming waterfronts and riverfronts for public use, after serving industrial or highway uses, is widespread. Examples include La Nova Icaria in Barcelona; Riverwalk in San Antonio; Cincinnati Banks; WaterFire in Providence, Rhode Island (see pp. 77–8); Embarcadero in San Francisco; Making Waves in Toronto; and the Waterfront Plan for Chattanooga. All of these emphasize connecting the city and community with the waterfront as well as connecting communities along the waterfront with one another.

The importance of circulation has rendered connectivity an important theme, and sometimes a principal generator, of urban design interventions. Architect Alex Wall notes that designers have been interested in providing "flexible, multifunctional surfaces," creating connective tissue between city fragments and programs to support the diversity of uses and users over time.[66] In order to discover existing networks, architects Ben van Berkel and Caroline Bos advocate "movement studies" that analyze "the directions of the various trajectories, their prominence in relation to the forms of transportation on the site, their duration, their links to different programs, and their interconnections."[67] Applying this method to the Arnheim (Netherlands) train station (1996–99), van Berkel and Bos skillfully accommodate existing vehicular and social networks that also inspired their design.

Although we tend to think of movement horizontally by foot or vehicle, it can also be vertical, allowing hybridity and connectivity in section as well as plan. For his 1997 proposal for the Museum of Modern Art, Rem Koolhaas made circulation his organizing idea by applying Otis Elevator's "Odyssey: The Integrated Building Transit System," which moves horizontally as well as vertically in glass-enclosed modules. Zaha Hadid also used circulation as a point of departure for the Cincinnati Museum of Contemporary Art (2003), identifying "energy lines" reflecting the movement of bodies and vision through space as well as the larger urban context.[68]

FORGING PATHS

Another way of connecting people and places is through the creation of extensive systems of pathways. Many of the recent large-scale public space projects trace a direct lineage to the nineteenth-century parks and boulevards designed by Frederick Law Olmsted. Exemplary descendants of the Olmsted parks include the sophisticated public space networks composed of bike and pedestrian paths, mass transit, parks, plazas, and neighborhoods found in Denver, Colorado, and Bogotá, Columbia.

Greater Phoenix has considered and embarked upon numerous initiatives over the years to knit together its sprawling metropolis that extends over 9,300 square miles. The public art plan produced by William Morrish and Catherine Brown (1991) aspired to connect places. Landscape architect Frederick Steiner proposed a "Turquoise Necklace," in reference to Olmsted's Emerald Necklace for the city of Boston (1870s), combining existing waterways in the Phoenix area with newly created ones. Architect Vernon Swaback advocates preserving large networks of open space throughout the Phoenix metropolitan area around which dense pockets of urbanism develop, rather than the formless sprawling suburbs (1996).

Figure 21

Figure 22

Currently, ambitious regional multimodal trail systems for the entire Phoenix metropolitan area are linking existing paths with canals, parks, and flood-control land, and creating miles of new trails.[69] The Rio Salado Habitat Restoration project along with the Rio Oeste extension is reclaiming natural systems while providing park and recreational space as well as an important connector through the center of the city (see Figures 21 and 22).[70]

Figure 23

North of the Rio Salado, along the Papago Salado Trail, Studio Ma[71] is implementing "Portals and Loops," the winning entry in a National Endowment for the Arts Public Works competition. This project includes a series of entrances (portals) connecting the trail with existing patterns of movement (streets, trails, and canals) to provide opportunities for alternative circulation while creating vibrant urban/desert hubs. Acknowledging and expanding upon existing uses, this intervention provides amenities – such as seating areas, water fountains, lighting, and cooling devices – to weave a rich tapestry of desert, suburbia, industry, history, and archaeology (see Figure 23).

CAR-CHITECTURE

A significant aspect of the new integration and its emphasis on flows is an interest in integrating car spaces into the larger connective web of the city, or "car-chitecture."[72] Instead of being considered merely functional or leftover space, the approximately 25 percent (more in some cities) of our landscape composed of highways, roads, parking, driveways, gas stations, and garages is increasingly valorized and reconsidered. Rather than eviscerate the city, these interstitial car spaces are linking previously isolated parts of the city. Spaces for cars can connect with other kinds of public spaces, such as parks, and with other people-moving networks, such as transit stations and airports.

In Northern Europe, places combining parking with trees, planters, public benches, artwork, and children's play areas were introduced in the 1960s.[73] Described as home zones (in the United Kingdom), *woonerfs* ("living yards" in Dutch), or *Wohnstrasses* ("living streets" in German), these usually involve the community in design and management. In addition to offering quality public spaces, the lack of distinction between street and sidewalk and the sharing of space by motorists, cyclists, pedestrians, and children have a traffic-calming effect.[74] The University of Arkansas Community Design Center has been designing shared streets for several U.S. projects (see Figure 24).

There are numerous other recent examples of integrating car spaces into the city. In Barcelona, Andreu Arriola's Plaça de les Glories Catalanes (1992) converts a traffic interchange into a place for moving cars, parking, and a park.[75] In many instances, parking serves simultaneously as a park using landscaping, perforated concrete paving filled with grass (e.g., "Grass-crete") in place of asphalt, and street/park furniture including shade structures. In other instances, parking is fully integrated into buildings as in SHoP's V-Mall in the Queens borough of New York City. For this small site, SHoP proposed a vertical interior car passageway that simultaneously transports shoppers to the

Figure 24

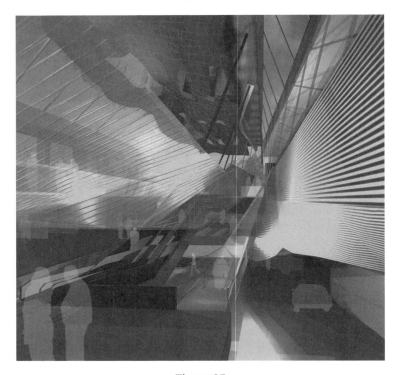

Figure 25

retail portion of the mall while also connecting the commercial boulevard to the adjacent residential area (see Figure 25).

The result is that the distinction between car spaces and people spaces breaks down, acknowledging that cars *are* people spaces (because people drive them) and that we need not relegate them to leftover, neglected, separate places that ultimately tear the urban fabric to shreds. The car – initially inspiring separation when separation of functions was the goal (during the Modern period) and ignored when separation was no longer the goal (during the Postmodern period) – is now being brought into the mix, generating new urban forms along with new urban experiences.

NETWORKS AND NATURE AS MODELS

As recent best practices demonstrate, networks offer an appropriate model for urbanism.[76] The same rules apply to networks in nature (e.g., molecules in a cell, species in an ecosystem), networks of people, and the Internet. All of these networks contain many nodes with very few links and a tiny number of nodes with a great many links or "hubs."[77] If the small nodes fall off, the larger network is not interrupted, but if the hub is eliminated, the whole system can break down. As a result, these systems are stable and resilient but prone to occasional catastrophic collapse. Thanks to the hubs, everything in a network is usually connected by no more than six links, the "small-world phenomenon" popularized by the play *Six Degrees of Separation*.[78] Another feature that all these networks share is the "rich get richer" effect.[79] As new nodes are added to a network, they tend to form links with others that are already well connected. So the new kid at school tends to become friends with those who already have lots of friends. New scientific papers are more likely to cite those already cited many times.[80] New shops tend to appear in places where there are already other shops.

All of these networks share other features as well. Nodes shift naturally, moving tentacularly along connectors. Nodes may grow larger or become smaller. New nodes are formed. Others disappear. Cutting-edge collaborations are the product of "hot groups," people joining together out of mutual interest until that interest fades and they disperse, eventually forming new nodes. Physically, nodes are places of intensity or density. Connectors are "channels," like channels of water (or canals), allowing or impelling movement through them. Connectors may channel information and ideas as television channels provide conduits for programming or as spiritual channels serve as a conduits between the living and deceased. Connectors may also serve as channels for people, natural resources, products, and money. Networks are never static but always changing in search of a dynamic equilibrium.[81]

Although profoundly interconnected into a network at a higher register, we may discern six types of networks (or flows) for urban designers to consider. These include natural networks (wildlife corridors, weather patterns, waterways, mountain ranges, etc.), networks for people moving (roads, paths and trails, railroads, airways, elevators, escalators, and stairs), exchange and economic networks, communication and virtual networks, social networks, and networks of history and memory. A *connected* urbanism investigates these existing networks as a focal point and source of inspiration in contrast to Modern planning, which ignored them or regarded them as irritants to be eliminated or disguised. Integral Urbanism enhances these flows and allows them to flourish, taking cues from ecological thresholds. While bringing things together, such urban thresholds and their larger networks also preserve the integrity of each other – specificity of time, place, culture – and diversity.[82]

Obstructing the natural flows of these networks can have an adverse effect. One example is the urban growth boundary. Although an attempt to preserve undeveloped land and encourage urban revitalization, the imposition of an urban growth boundary can act as a noose, strangling the natural growth and development of a city. Instead of negative reinforcement through the imposition of boundaries, we might instead implement strategies of positive reinforcement by enhancing existing networks through incentives or "attractors." These enhanced hubs, nodes, and connectors might include a range of quality housing, educational and recreational opportunities, workspaces, retail, and restaurants. Rather than negatively saying, "don't go," as the urban growth boundary does, these say "please participate in creating our community." Such positive urban reinforcement allows for a naturally growing and changing polycentric city rather than an artificially imposed and bounded monocentric city. Not incidentally, similar methods have proven effective in child development. Rather than teach children through punishment (create barriers), we teach through "redirecting behavior" and "positive reinforcement."

A lesson may be learned from efforts to prevent shoreline erosion. Experience demonstrates that building huge and very costly walls is ineffective because these walls eventually collapse. As the Army Corps of Engineers discovered, *undercurrent stabilization* – an intervention in the ocean itself that allows the waves to roll in more gently – effectively prevents shoreline ero-sion.[83] In similar fashion, we need to invest in our central cities so that resources and people do not pour out of them. As we learn from shoreline erosion, erecting walls to avert natural processes is ultimately counterproduc-tive. Instead, we need to redirect growth and offer positive reinforcement, ren-dering such walls unnecessary and supporting sustainable urban and community building.

Nature offers an overarching model, including networks, for urbanism today. Urban design can emulate, for instance, the similar branching patterns of trees, rivers, and capillaries in the body, all of which derive their form and function from water movement. Janine Benyus identifies three levels of emu-lating nature, or biomimicry: form, process, and living systems (large-scale and long-term). She recommends designers apply biomimicry when designing at all scales from household products to cities.[84] Others have been advocating the application of permaculture (permanent agriculture) principles to environ-mental design,[85] as in the new towns of Civano, Arizona, and Prairie Crossing outside of Milwaukee.

With the rise of nature as a model for urban design, the organic metaphor, popular until the early decades of the twentieth century,[86] has been making a comeback. Now, however, it is more than a metaphor. As Jane Jacobs posits in *The Nature of Economies* (2000), economies and cities are part of nature.

Ironically, it is new technologies that are supporting this full circle (or spiral) return to emulating the processes and forms found in nature.[87] By allowing us to design and represent buildings and cities as dynamic and exact entities rather than static self-same ones, computer-based technologies are allowing for a convergence of human-made with natural processes and products.[88]

These contemporary urban design approaches, which take cues from existing traces of form and activity, recall novelist Italo Calvino's description of landscapes as "spider webs of intricate relationships in search of form."[89] An Integral Urbanism is keenly aware of and inspired by these webs com-posed of flows including contour lines, property lines, utility lines, wildlife corridors, roads and transit lines, flight paths, pedestrian paths, waterways, and lines of sight.

THE NEW DENSITY

While new transportation and communication technologies are, in theory, making physical proximity less necessary, the reality is that cities are growing in popularity, and correspondingly in land values, around the world. Saskia Sassen has identified a "logic of agglomeration," a tendency among major firms and advanced telecommunications facilities to centralize economic functions in large cities with top-level management capacity and highly specialized services necessary for "global control capability."[90] Proximity helps specialized firms by making joint production of certain services possible. The city is also a marketplace where buyers and sellers can converge. In brief, density is good for business.

Cities are also growing in popularity because, as Alvin Toffler forecast in *Future Shock* in 1970, the more high technology we embrace, the more "high touch" we become. We need compensatory human connection such as face-to-face interaction and handwritten notes sent by snail mail. Cities are growing in popularity because the new generation of knowledge workers prefers to live in vibrant cities. According to a study by the Urban Design Associates, those entering the workforce today "tend to reject the suburbs in favor of funky city neighborhoods. They're into authenticity. They like old buildings or new buildings that look like old buildings. They wouldn't be caught dead in a suburban campus." In *The Rise of the Creative Class,* Richard Florida emphasizes the importance of offering what this "creative class" values: diversity, tolerance, authenticity, walkability, active forms of recreation, and a range of cultural or arts venues.

In addition to becoming desirable for many residents and businesses, concentrated human settlements also contribute to protecting the natural environment and conserving natural resources. The exponential increase in smart growth measures since 1998 in the United States has been slowing down the powerful centrifugal force of urban development. Moreover, as journalist and designer Laurie Kerr points out, "The dense old cities are becoming the new exemplars of environmental sustainability, since they accommodate people in a way that saves space, resources, and energy ... A recent study found that New York State is the nation's most energy efficient state on a per-capita basis. In 1999, each New Yorker used less than two thirds the energy consumed by the average American." While cities have long been regarded as the nemesis of ecological living and the countryside its embodiment, it is now apparent that cities can be the most sustainable of human habitats.

Contrary to initial assumptions that the digital economy would render cities less important, cities have grown even more important as social, political, economic, and technological hubs. Add to these justifications for urban concentration, the developers' bias toward density, the urban-philic tradition within the architecture and planning professions, and the movement toward preserving the natural landscape, and we have a recipe for continued intensification of existing cities in the near future.

REPRESENTING, TEACHING, AND PRACTICING THE NEW INTEGRATION

To *demonstrate* and *describe* such urban and architectural hybridity and connectivity, designers have been adapting their forms of representation and expression accordingly. Numerous designers such as Paul Lewis, Marc Tsurumaki, and David Lewis as well as Hani Rashid and Lise Ann Couture of Studio Asymptote have introduced hybrid forms of representation combining hand drawings, computers, and other technologies. The book *Hybrid Space* by Peter Zellner profiles the real/virtual hybrids of designers including Greg Lynn, UN Studio, dECOi, and NOX.

Beaux Arts and Bauhaus pedagogy, though divergent in many ways, shared a predilection for the ideal and universal, pure geometries, proportional relationships, formal composition, and internal programmatic hierarchy. In both of these traditions, architect Wendy Redfield points out, "Only after the *parti* has achieved a degree of self-sufficiency and completion is it introduced to the site. At this point, the relationship between *parti* and landscape can only be one of accommodation – not of mutual generation. And this accommodation is generally quite one-sided, with the building's geometry and internal logic calling the shots. The result is a view of architecture as primary – as active – as only figure – and a treatment of the ground as secondary, reactive, even residual." Correcting this bias, Redfield teaches interpretive site analysis, using diagramming, collage, and *bas-relief* models to "render landscape, urban, and architectural systems as integral, reciprocal, and equivalent."

To "find lost space" in cities, Roger Trancik advocates an "integrated approach to urban design," combining figure-ground, linkage, and place theories. Figure-ground theory pays attention to the relationship between built and unbuilt as well as public and private space, linkage theory to the connectivity of a place, and place theory to cultural aspects. This integrated approach calls for organizing geometries of axis and perspective to provide a sense of orientation, "integrated bridging" where buildings provide an uninterrupted mesh of activity along passageways, and the fusion of indoor and outdoor to ensure year-round usage and energy efficiencies.[91]

Architect and theorist Stan Allen suggests adopting the score, the map, the diagram, and the script to describe or intervene in "this new field ... where visible and invisible streams of information, capital and subjects, interact in complex formations [forming] a dispersed field, a network of flows." Allen explains: "The score allows for the simultaneous presentation and interplay of information in diverse scales, on shifting coordinates and even of differing linguistic codes. The script allows the designer to engage program, event and time on specifically architectural terms."[92] Allen advocates the use of diagrams and maps that demonstrate formal as well as programmatic elements, describing "potential relationships among elements."[93] These methods, Allen suggests, would also allow interaction with other fields such as film, music, and performance.

Whereas Allen's use of the score imagines the architect as the composer and conductor of the city, architect Jusuck Koh applies the score analogy to suggest a creative collaboration with users, asking, "What would happen if architects conceptualized their design as musical scores and as choreography open to creative interpretation by performances of users and builders?"[94]

Rem Koolhaas has introduced hybrid terms, or "MERGE©," that connect separated phenomena. For example, golf course and urban fabric equals "SMOOTH© green crust of THIN© urbanism."[95] "SCAPE©" encompasses townscape and landscape[96] in an effort to erase distinctions between figure and ground, inside and outside, center and periphery. SCAPE© conveniently allows for the convergence of architecture, landscape, and infrastructure.

The New York City firm SCAPE epitomizes the new integration. Founded by landscape designer Kate Orff, after working in the offices of Hargreaves Associates and Rem Koolhaas, SCAPE describes its goal as connecting "people to their immediate environment." Inspired by the structure and function of nature and incorporating sustainable design principles, SCAPE aspires to "understand and enhance connections between ecological systems and public infrastructures to create dynamic, textured outdoor spaces, in concert with long-term, phased strategies for their implementation."[97]

Another exemplar of Integral Urbanism is the University of Arkansas Community Design Center (UACDC). A collaborative enterprise under the direction of Stephen Luoni, UACDC aspires to enhance the physical environment and quality of life in the community by simultaneously addressing social, environmental, economic, political, and design issues. As UACDC explains: "Integrative design solutions add long-term value and offer collateral benefits related to sustained economic capacity, enhanced ecologies, and improved public health – the foundations of creative development."[98] The design center acknowledges that the contemporary landscape calls for new approaches to designing civic spaces and has undertaken this challenge in numerous contexts.

In a proposal for retrofitting Wal-Mart, a group of fourth-year architecture students working with Luoni sought to enhance the civic responsiveness of these big-box stores while respecting the organization of the discount retail industry. They proposed appropriately adapting urban traditions such as the porch, courtyard, atrium, promenade, arcade, bar, and conservatory to this context. They also introduced updated interpretations of these such as the "sponge" between building and parking lot and the "hydroscape," which allows natural water flows to animate a site. In addition, they adapted ecological principles by, for instance, establishing five "ecotones" where these "ecosystems" meet: public street, outer parking ring, inner parking ring, building frontage, store compression zone, checkouts. The result is an environment that enables new combinations of work, leisure activities, and commerce, ultimately supporting the community as well as private enterprise (see Figures 26 and 27).

Not only are the various components of urbanism reintegrated, so are design practices and pedagogies. For many, this transition is welcome and intensely liberating. For those who cling to older paradigms, it can be a struggle and source of frustration.

Figure 26

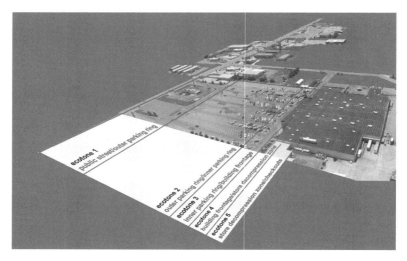

Figure 27

PRECEDENTS

"Context" comes from the Latin *contextere*, meaning to weave together or make connections. Seeking inspiration from site and situation (from context) in building our habitats has deep precedents. For indigenous cultures, this has always been a matter of course. In the western tradition, first-century B.C. Roman writer, architect, and engineer Vitruvius asserted that the first act in making a building is access to site. Sensitivity to local places informed building and urban design until, ironically, Neo-Classicism sought inspiration from another place and time. Then, twentieth-century Modernism became largely nonreferential with place supplanted by generic space, a *tabula rasa* upon which to impose personal utopian visions or displays of architectural virtuosity.

Numerous architects, urbanists, and social theorists resisted the Modernist tendencies to design without regard for context and to segregate functions. Victor Gruen, for instance, proposed shopping centers with parking lots on the roof and pedestrian malls (1950s and 1960s). The Japanese Metabolists produced multifunctional megastructures (1960s) such as Fumihiko Maki's "city-in-miniature." Planner David Crane advanced the capital web theory of city planning (1961–65) and sociologist Henri Lefebvre advocated "multifunctional" and "transfunctional" buildings and spaces that would generate new kinds of sociability (1967). Other examples include Archigram's Plug-In City and Instant City (1960s);

many of Team 10's proposals, such as the "mat" or "carpet" buildings[99] (1950s–60s); the Situationists' unitary urbanism (*urbanisme unitaire*), which critiqued the Modern city and called for an integrated urban environment (1957); Mies van der Rohe's plazas on plinths (1960s);[100] Paolo Soleri's Arcosanti (1960s–present); and Josep Lluis Sert's urban design for Roosevelt Island (1970s).[101]

Lewis Mumford advocated "biotechnics," an approach to urban design that supports a balanced and self-regulating relationship between the built and natural environments (1938).[102] Hans Scharoun spoke of "urban-landscape" composed of natural forms, built forms, and communities of people in the 1950s.[103] His vision of the "city as a gently modeled landscape incorporating the existing topology into the movement of built structures" was a postwar response to the natural landscape now visible beneath the debris. Scharoun's vision was also a reaction to the ordered and hierarchical city, but fell into disrepute as economic development accelerated.[104] Victor Gruen called upon architects to design a landscape as well as a "cityscape" (1955).[105] Constantinos Doxiadis developed a theory of architecture encompassing landscape and site in the 1960s.[106]

Nor is considering circulation as a principal generator of design new.[107] The advent of the automobile contributed greatly to a fascination with movement and its relationship to the built environment, especially after the Second World War. Erich Mendelsohn was interested in movement and designed a pathway on a hill to the Weizman Mansion of Rehobeth (1936–37). The Greek architect Dimitri Pikionis expressed this interest in designing the "Paths" ascending to the Acropolis (1950–57).[108] Architects Mary Otis Stevens and Thomas McNulty designed the Lincoln House, which was featured in *Life Magazine* in 1965 as "a passageway" and "channel for flow and movement."[109] Other precedents include Le Corbusier's *promenade architecturale* as realized in the original plan for the Carpenter Center at Harvard University (1960); the Radburn plan developed by Clarence Stein and Henry Wright (1928); Polish architect Matthew Nowicki's plan for Chandigarh later elaborated by Le Corbusier (1951–54); Louis Kahn's plan for Philadelphia (1953), which examined its "hierarchy of flow"; Kenzo Tange's plan for Tokyo (1960); elements of Team 10's work; and the French new town of Toulouse-Le-Mirail (1961) designed by George Candilis, Alexis Josic, and Shadrach Woods.[110]

Woods, a New Yorker who spent much of his career in Paris (working in Le Corbusier's Paris office before starting his own), expressed interest in "space measured not by inches but by the speed of a moving pedestrian."[111] He applied the concept of the "stem" to urban design (1960s). As described by Alexander Tzonis and Liane Lefaivre, "Stem goes beyond the *plan masse* and the plastic architectural composition, prescribing a topological order, a way of linking locations that accommodates human activity and interaction. The Stem is a support system, very similar to the network of paths in a traditional town." The Stem was "an approach based not on space alone, but on human mobility in space." This evolved into the Web, which "was not just a circulation system; it was an environmental system, 'a way to establish a large-scale order' which *by* its existence made possible 'an individual expression at the smaller scale.' More than a technical device, the Web was 'a true poetic discovery of architecture.'"[112]

These mid-twentieth-century sympathies toward hybridity and connectivity were largely overshadowed, however, by the Modernist orthodoxy of functional separation. While recalling many of these precedents, the voices advocating integration today fall upon more receptive ears, eager to learn lessons that might contribute to remedy the fragmentation of our cities.

As recent trends suggest, while motives may diverge, the goals of businesspersons (large and small) and of urban designers are converging fortuitously. The attempt by urban designers to identify and intensify latent opportunities in the city is paralleled (and manifest) by the entrepreneur's attempt to identify and supply latent markets. In addition to supporting density and mixed use, designers and developers are also converging on best practices regarding residential development as both are valuing density, infill housing, urban residential typologies, natural and transportation networks, and connected public spaces. Happily, good design has become good business, and sometimes, vice versa.

Although hybridity and connectivity in architecture and urban design are not new, there are differences in the current crop. The efforts of the last two decades clearly depart from the preautomobile era because of the dramatic transformations in landscape and lifestyle wrought by the car. They also depart from the bulk of the last century's attempts in recognizing polycentrality rather than the more traditional center surrounded by a suburban ring that is surrounded by countryside. These more recent efforts also turn their gaze to previously neglected or abandoned corners of our landscapes, places left in the wake of the industrial revolution — what we now refer to as brownfield sites – or of postwar suburban mall building, what we are calling greyfield sites. Metaphors for these initiatives include creating ligaments (connective tissues), mending seams, darning holes, and healing wounds inflicted upon the landscape. The following chapter describes what happens when and where such juxtapositions or connections take place.

Identity is only a consistent entity in mathematics. The self is formed on relationships . . . How can the city cling to its walls? Doesn't the opportunity of the city lie in the complexity of integrated worlds that become so likely they want to be realized? This form of urbanity needs transcendence and permeability.
Sabine Kraft

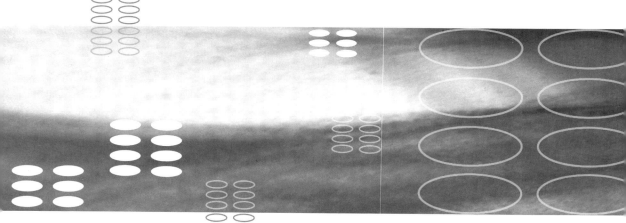

The sun never knew how wonderful it was until it fell on the wall of a building.
Louis Kahn

Walls do not contain, they bestow.
Stacy Alaimo

Porosity

*But for the boundary, the mind is still
Trapped within a frame
The mind exerts its highest creativity.*
Akira Yamamoto

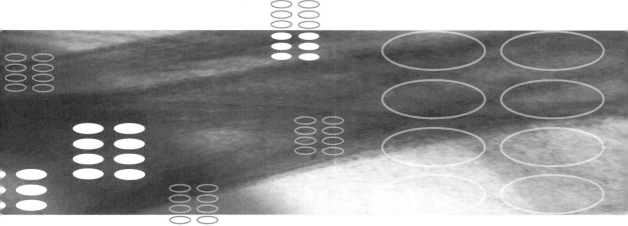

*Everything happens in the space between
the skin/body and the clothes.*
Issey Miyake

POROSITY

A TRANSLUCENT URBANISM

If something or someone is "transparent," we can "see through" to what lies beneath or beyond the surface. Translucency, in contrast, reveals only some of what is underneath, behind, or inside and conceals the rest. By simultaneously revealing and concealing, translucency lends interest to what lies beneath or beyond, such as the cloaking or wrapping of environmental artists Christo and Jeanne-Claude, or Roland Barth's "writerly" text,[1] or the geisha's kimono. From the Latin root meaning "to shine through," translucency might even be understood as revealing *through* concealing.

A translucent urbanism similarly enhances our experience of the city. It accomplishes this through *porosity*, an urban condition that allows some seepage but not free flow. In fact, the French word for flow is *couler* from the Latin *colare*, meaning to filter. Walls – both real and symbolic – preclude a translucent urbanism. Such a lack of porosity occurs around shopping malls, walled or gated communities, and schools that do not share facilities with the surrounding neighborhoods. At the other end of the continuum, too much porosity also precludes translucency. This is apparent inside big-box retail stores where a variety of uses blend together indiscriminately or in the sprawling suburbs where, as Gertrude Stein famously remarked about Oakland, California, there is "no there there."

Both instances – no porosity or too much porosity – diminish the quality of life. How then might we achieve a happy medium of porosity and, thereby, a translucent urbanism? Learning from successful instances, we glean many different kinds of porosity depending on what is permitted to seep through and what is not.

Visual porosity allows us to see through but not move through a space. This is most commonly accomplished through the use of glass, such as the large shop window that allows those on the street to peer in and those inside to gaze out onto the street. Shop windows may entice passersby to enter, while also lending vitality to the street through their rotating displays and inside activity.

Visual porosity is being applied in less conventional ways as well. Health clubs are increasingly offering pedestrians and motorists a view of the aerobics, dance, karate, basketball, and other activities inside, whether located in a bustling urban area or more sedate suburban settings. These views provide free advertising for the clubs and brief live performances for the pedestrian or motorist. A glass partition in a synagogue outside of Baltimore separates its childcare center from the main auditorium allowing the children to share in the religious service without disrupting it. The recent vogue of filming television programs in studios separated from the street by a glass wall, such as NBC's *Today Show* and MTV in New York City, offer home viewers a dynamic streetscape and a sense of place, while offering pedestrians a chance to watch the filming process and to appear in the backdrop. In similar fashion, the new Paseo in Phoenix, a long thin indoor suture between the U.S. Airways Center (the former America West Arena) and the surrounding city, features a bar and television studio, and live performance stage that extends from the arena allowing live broadcasts with the arena directly in the background. New airports of all sizes around the world are increasingly bringing the ongoing spectacle of flight into full view. These include the Barcelona airport designed by Ricardo Bofill and the Taller de Arquitectura (1988); the T. F. Green Rhode Island airport (1996); the airport of Victoria, British Columbia, designed by Campbell-Moore; the Ronald Reagan National Airport of Washington, D.C., designed by Cesar Pelli (1997); and Terminal 2 at San Diego Airport, designed by The Gensler Group (1998).

Visual porosity may also allow us to see only partially, due to a screening device, scrim, landscaping, or other means. One example, prevalent during the 1950s and 60s, was the use of concrete pattern blocks to create walls that allow us to see through – but not move through – them (see Figures 28 and 29). More recently, this is being accomplished through metallic wire mesh screens, slatted wood (or wood–plastic composites), sandblasted glass, polycarbonate, and other means.

Figure 28

Figure 29

Swiss architects Jacques Herzog and Pierre de Meuron often use metal-lic screens that filter light and views as in a small residential building in Basle (1991) where the façade is fully covered with cast-iron slats. Referring to their use of these metallic screens along with ample translucent glass, the

New York Times architecture critic, Herbert Muschamp, remarked, "the architects treat walls as porous membranes between public and private spaces." Rem Koolhaas applied wire mesh for a floor/ceiling in the Kunsthal in Rotterdam, allowing museum visitors to glimpse into other galleries and to capture unusual perspectives of other people (see Figures 30 and 31). French architect Dominique Perrault has also used wire mesh extensively, as in the Cambridge, Maryland building for mesh manufacturer GKD. Helmut Jahn used stainless steel wire mesh to cloak Europe's largest parking structure at the Cologne–Bonn airport, and Junquera Perez Pita has used the mesh for parking structures at the Barcelona airport. This steel mesh is self-cleaning and recyclable as well as elegant, reflecting the changing light and movement around it. It can also be used for projections of advertising or film. Though appearing delicate, it maintains the ability to absorb explosions without exerting pressure on the structure.

Figure 30

Figure 31

Peter Zumthor's Archeological Museum for Roman Artifacts in Chur, Switzerland, features wood slatted walls through which visitors may peer and press a button to illuminate the interior of rooms. At night, these permeable walls glow, keeping the town center alive. For the addition to the Diocesan Museum in Cologne, Zumthor created a perforated screen wall of elongated bricks. Steven Holl's "hinged space" allows a visual but not necessarily experiential connection, as realized for instance at the Storefront for Art and Architecture in New York City. Alongside a promenade separating the Experience Music Project in Seattle from a surface parking lot, a public art installation allows people to see and move through it, while also providing a screening device so that the lot is not in full view, thereby enhancing the quality of the promenade[2] (see Figure 32).

Another example of visual porosity is the abandonment of dropped ceilings in favor of exposed systems allowing for greater height, ease of maintenance, and more attractive and interesting rooms. Drawing too much attention to ceiling ducts, however, can detract from the elegance of a place. The Stone House Pavilion at the Phoenix Zoo designed by Swaback Partners resolves this dilemma through skillful visual porosity. The ceiling and ductwork are painted black and white tensile fabric panels are placed strategically to deflect attention from the pipes, while also deflecting the exposed lighting (see Figure 33). By simultaneously revealing and concealing, the Pavilion feels grand as well as intimate, inspiring both majesty and mystery.

Figure 32

Figure 33

Related to visual porosity is *solar porosity*, simply allowing, or inversely prohibiting, natural light and heat into a space. We see this at the Chapel de las Capuchinas Sacramentarias (outside of Mexico City 1952–55), where architect Luis Barragán applied yellow paint to windows to screen the view, while allowing light and sound to penetrate. More recently, solar porosity is commonly achieved through the use of translucent materials to bring daylight into subterranean spaces. Examples include the New York City intermodal transit stations and Jones Studio's Lattie Coor Building at Arizona State University.

To screen light out, the variety of sunscreens and shade structures is wildly proliferating with the production of new textiles and increased awareness of risks posed by sun exposure. Along with precursors such as Le Corbusier's *brise-soleil*, a concrete sunscreen device for tropical regions, and Frank Lloyd Wright's patterned light screens, more recent examples include the flat metal filigree version in Richard Meier's residential towers at 173 and 176 Perry Street in New York City (2003) and the range of lightweight tensile shade structures of all shapes and sizes located around the world. For his first building commission in the United States, Santiago Calatrava designed a *brise-soleil* for the Milwaukee Art Museum, an operable winglike sunscreen that raises and lowers to regulate light and heat (2001). At the Salt Lake City

Figure 34

Library, designed by Moshe Safdie, the children's section is equipped with horizontal fabric blinds that can be drawn during the brightest hours to protect books and people from the sun, while not separating them from the outdoors entirely, creating a pleasant dappling effect as the sun filters through (see Figure 34). The slatted walls described above offer solar as well as visual porosity. A Phoenix office building designed by Jones Studio features a structural glazed wall with a slatted lattice wall suspended several feet beyond that diminishes exposure to direct sun as well as direct vision.

Translucent concrete could allow for visual and solar porosity, creating visually arresting places, while also offering greater security. After speaking with Rem Koolhaas about the possibilities of translucent concrete, architect Bill Price began developing it in 1999, while he was the director of research and development at Office for Metropolitan Architecture (OMA), by adding glass

Figure 35

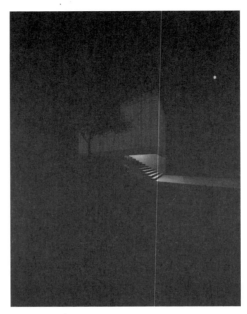

Figure 36

fibers to crushed stone, cement, and water[3] (see Figures 35 and 36). Hungarian
architect Aron Losonczi began working on developing translucent concrete
while studying at the Royal University College of Fine Arts in Stockholm in
2001 and formed the company LiTraCon (light-transmitting concrete) based in
Germany in 2004 to commercialize it.[4] A sidewalk in Stockholm demonstrates
the properties of the translucent concrete, appearing to be an ordinary sidewalk
during the day, but illuminated at night thanks to lighting beneath. An exhibition at the National Building Museum in Washington, D.C., entitled "Liquid
Stone: New Architecture in Concrete" (2004–6), presents this work.

Functional porosity allows access to a place or modulates our relationship
with it. The inverse of visual porosity – that which allows us to see through but
not move through – functional porosity is found at the entrances to airport
bathrooms where jogging walls permit free entry while ensuring privacy through
visual opacity. At the urban scale, functional porosity can subtly, yet effectively,
transform the quality of places. This can be achieved through "permeable building
edges" that combine with porticos, arcades, windows, and outdoor seating.[5]
Functional porosity may also inflect the public or private nature of a space. For
instance, Lake/Flato Architects converted a 1930s motor court in Austin, Texas,
into the boutique Hotel San José by artfully inserting a range of semiprivate
spaces defined by lath walls or trellises (1997) (see Figures 37 and 38).

Figure 37

Figure 38

Provisional porosity allows access on a temporary basis. House tours and art walks offer examples of provisional porosity, with homes and studios becoming public spaces for a designated time period before resuming their private status. Similarly, garage and yard sales provisionally blur the usual boundary between the street or sidewalk and a private residence.

Temporal porosity occurs when a place transforms over the course of a day, a week, or year. Examples include parking lots, plazas, and parks transformed into farmer's markets; street frontage overtaken by outdoor restaurants; and places that are cafés or retail by day and performance space or clubs at night. The Prada store in SoHo, New York City, designed by Rem Koolhaas, demonstrates temporal as well as visual porosity, featuring a Wave that provides an arena for flexible presentations. During the day, one slope of the wave displays shoes and handbags and at night, it becomes stadium seating. The opposite slope contains a small platform that folds down to become a stage. Cast-iron columns form a (visually and functionally) porous wall along one side of the display area/theatre.[6]

Historic porosity preserves remnants of the past while building new. An exemplary instance is the addition to the Rhys Carpenter Library at Bryn Mawr College. Designed by architect Henry Myerberg (2000), the addition's old/new porosity is enhanced by indoor/outdoor porosity. Historic porosity is also seen at the new City Hall of Phoenix designed by HOK and Langdon Wilson Architects (1993) to incorporate an exterior wall of the adjacent historic Orpheum Theatre as one of its interior walls. Generally, most buildings and neighborhoods that aim to preserve their historic character, while updating to accommodate changing needs and tastes, also demonstrate historic porosity.

Ecological porosity integrates nature and natural processes into the built environment. Building in a way that does not alter existing nature and perhaps incorporates it is one means. Homes built around large existing boulders in Scottsdale, Arizona, and an outdoor bar built around an existing tree at a restaurant in Tempe, Arizona, offer examples. The Desert Broom Library

Figure 39

Figure 40

designed by Richärd + Bauer Architecture in Cave Creek, Arizona, offers an indoor/outdoor reading space with a roof that extends sixty feet into the natural desert and a series of coiled metal screens, inspired by the form of the adjacent arroyo (see Figures 39 and 40). Ecological porosity might also be achieved by actively bringing nature into a place through interior "home-scaping" and exterior landscaping. Foliage allows both light and air to penetrate, changing appropriately with the seasons. Sometimes this involves bringing nature back into a place or "reclamation." Many have been reclaiming the biodiversity of places that have been "desertified,"[7] including landscape architects Frederick Steiner, Carol Franklin, and Leslie Sauer and artists Laurie Lundquist (see Figures 41 and 42) and Newton and Helen Harrison.

Figure 41

Figure 42

Ecological porosity is also apparent in design that accommodates existing flows of water, air, and wildlife. Unpaved streets without curbs and simple infiltration swales, for instance, allow surface runoff to filter back into the soil and absorb rain and snow more easily. They are also much less expensive than paved streets with curbs and storm drains.[8] Pervious paving surfaces, as found at the Dia Beacon museum grounds designed by artist Robert Irwin, allow the infiltration of nature while producing a pleasing effect for visitors (see Figure 43). In cities, pervious surfaces can mend seams in the urban fabric and provide a quality public space while also providing long-term ecological dividends, decreasing the heat island effect, and reducing storm water runoff.[9]

Figure 43

Effectively integrating nature into design can also reduce air conditioning as well as heating loads and pollutants by cleaning the air of ozone and sulfur dioxide. It encourages walking and social interaction, produces shade, provides food supplies as well as recreational opportunities for all ages, and significantly raises property values.[10]

Designing with nature is not, of course, new, but became secondary during much of the twentieth century. Even then, many mid-century architects emphasized linking indoors with outdoors such as Aldo Van Eyck (1959), Frank Lloyd Wright, and Nikolaus Pevsner. Buckminster Fuller proposed intelligent membranes for buildings that can adapt in response to changes in the environment. Landscape architect Ian McHarg influentially advocated "design with nature" in 1969.[11] The need for ecological porosity in our landscape has only grown over time, while the tools for implementing it have multiplied.

Circulatory porosity is found where the street, sidewalk, and parking are not clearly defined and are used variously depending upon need. It is found in places where the car and people happily coexist like the "shared streets" (see pp. 47–8). It is also found in building types that integrate car spaces and people spaces, or "car-chitecture" (see pp. 47–9), rather than relegate the car to decidedly inferior dedicated car spaces. Characteristics of this building type include easy entry and exit by car and, most essentially, cars becoming part of the architecture. Taking this logic further, new typologies are emerging that consider large-scale vehicular movement through the site and parking requirements as design generators rather than annoying programmatic requirements.

Experiential porosity allows us to discover a place. Access is gained by invitation, choice, or chance. Everyone has their own favorites. Children have a knack for discovering these nooks and crannies in their neighborhoods, unprogrammed leftover spaces where they are free to create their very own meanings and experiences.

Administrative porosity occurs when administrative units communicate and collaborate with each other to consolidate and conserve resources. In search of greater efficiencies and synergies, these collaborations are growing, especially with "joint-use schools" sharing visual and performing arts spaces with the public and libraries blending with community and recreational centers. Steven Bingler designed a high school in Tishimongo County, Mississippi, that consolidates three previous high schools and provides a gymnasium that also serves as health club to the community outside of school hours, a library that is also the public library, and an auditorium and other rooms available to the community for gathering spaces. This new high school has not only brought previously isolated groups of people together, but is also credited with increasing student performance. The Tenderloin Community School in San Francisco, an elementary school with 1,000 students, many of whom are recent immigrants from Southeast Asia, offers services to their entire families including medical and dental facilities, counseling, adult education, a child development and parent resource center, a community garden, and a community kitchen.[12] In a ripple effect, joint-use schools have incited joint-use planning for the areas surrounding them.[13]

Such "sharing opportunities" are occurring throughout the Phoenix metropolitan area, in large part due to an increasingly strapped public sector. The Maryvale neighborhood has pooled its resources to build a community center with a library and recreational area, designed by Gould Evans Associates and Wendell Burnette Architects (2006). In Peoria, a middle school that opened in 2004 doubles as a community center with an outdoor amphitheatre and dining area. Designed by Brett Hobza of the DLR Group, classrooms for children become classrooms for adults as well as other city-sponsored programs by night. Peoria also shares a public library with one of its high schools and partners with the school districts to build municipal swimming pools and coordinate scheduling for sports activities. Nearby, the city of Glendale shares a public library with Mountain Ridge High School and Goodyear is building one in its Agua Fria High School. On the southeast side of town, Chandler High School shares a large theater and gallery with the community.

The hallowed and historically remote "ivory tower" of higher education is also becoming more permeable with emphases on service learning, "social embeddedness," "responsive Ph.D.s," "situated cognition" (learning while doing rather than learning and then doing), internships and apprenticeships, and more. Philosopher and cultural critic Mark Taylor advocates "piercing" the walls of universities to render them screens that will allow what is outside to come in and vice versa. He remarked, "These changes are coming, as sure as the tide, and trying to avoid these changes is like telling the tide to turn back."[14]

Spatial porosity, or programmatic porosity, occurs when activities seep into each another as in the many hybrid examples described in the previous chapter. Neither isolated from one another nor blended together, each program retains its integrity thanks to effective means of functional and visual porosity. Although the concept of "folding" is typically applied to building form (see p. 14), spatial porosity might be considered its programmatic analogue.

Urban porosity is spatial porosity at the scale of the city, achieved when permeable membranes separate and unite buildings from and with the surrounding physical and cultural landscape. This occurs, for instance, when cafés of bookstores or libraries spill out onto the streets, providing a linkage with the city while also drawing in potential customers or patrons.

An exemplary instance of urban porosity occurs in Providence, Rhode Island, where, in the 1980s, architect William Warner was instrumental in the reclamation of three rivers passing through the middle of the city by removing a highway. Artist Barnaby Evans designed the installation Water-Fire for this site placing one hundred bonfires just above the surface of the reclaimed rivers and using twelve of the remaining highway pillars as bases. The one hundred braziers are filled with firewood twenty-eight evenings a year to create a stunning spectacle. Evans also wired the entire site to emit hours of carefully choreographed classical and world music. Since the first WaterFire event in 1994, over one million have strolled along the two-third-mile stretch of public parks watching the fires and the black-clad volunteers in boats who tend them, smelling the scent of the fragrant cedar and pine, and listening to the mesmerizing sounds. What had been a wall between the town (downtown core) and gown (location of Rhode Island School of Design and Brown University) has become a permeable membrane that serves as a social magnet and allows easy passage from one side to the other (see Figures 44 and 45).

Urban porosity is also apparent in the workplace. After decades of suburbanizing, many companies are relocating to urban hubs in search of a more stimulating environment for employees, translating into higher morale and productivity. Leaving behind an isolated corporate campus, for instance, Microsoft hired Peter Calthorpe to integrate offices, restaurants, and a health club into the new town center of Issaquah Highlands outside of Seattle (2000).

Figure 44

Figure 45

Architectural strategies that lend toward urban porosity include the interpenetration of indoors with outdoors and buildings with cityscapes, as successfully plied by architect Zaha Hadid at the Cincinnati Center for the Arts. Koolhaas's Prada on Rodeo Drive in Beverly Hills (2004) takes urban porosity to its logical extreme with a completely retractable façade. When opened, all that separates the inside from the outside is the second-story aluminum-covered box that cantilevers over it, an air-curtain system to modulate air quality, and security sensors hidden in the floor to prevent shoplifting. Koolhaas explains, "We wanted to use this absence of facade to let the public enter absolutely freely, to create a hybrid condition between public and commercial space."[15]

Integration is also occurring at a deeper level, as arts and cultural institutions spin webs of relationships with local communities and seek diverse audiences by offering a range of programming and by physically sharing spaces. The Centre Georges Pompidou in Paris, designed by Rogers and Piano in the 1970s, was a vanguard in this respect. Not only does it combine galleries with libraries, bookstores, a gift shop, auditoria, and cafés inside the building, it also maintains strong linkages with its western neighbors via a lively plaza and large fountain, drawing street performers and crowds on a regular basis.

More recently, when the Detroit Symphony Orchestra decided to move back into a hall it had previously occupied, its board began buying land around the hall and proceeded to develop an office building that generated significant rental income. The board then donated land to the city for a School of Fine, Performing, and Communication Arts for 1,200 students who will interact with symphony musicians. This bubbling creative hub has been successful in generating additional private sector revitalization around the hall as well.

For the recent renovation of Lincoln Center in New York City, architects Diller Scofidio + Renfro with FX Fowle Architects sensitively remodeled Pietro Belluschi's Brutalist building (1968) by introducing a series of permeable membranes. Once-opaque walls at the ground level of Juilliard have been replaced by transparent facades and light-emitting diode (LED) screens with animated signs. A glass box holding a dance studio descends at one street corner allowing passersby to observe the dancers and dancers to catch glimpses of the street spectacle. A new, broad double staircase/bleachers where people can sit provides a threshold between the street and the plaza above.

Santiago Calatrava's addition to the Milwaukee Art Museum reestablishes a pedestrian connection to the city after a highway had obscured it. A transparent atrium offers a visual connection between urban streets and Lake Michigan.

The current vogue of building "gateways" into cities or districts illustrates the appeal of porosity. These gateways invite us to penetrate into places while simultaneously calling our attention to their boundaries and to linkages with adjacent areas.

Symbolic porosity occurs when a permeable membrane is perceived although there may be no separation at all or, conversely, a wall.[16] Even where there are no walls or fences around single-family houses and their lawns, for instance, we perceive a boundary and typically do not trespass onto the private property. Penetrating actual walls has grown increasingly easier, especially thanks to new communication technologies. An architectural gesture may suggest a connection that is purely symbolic. By emulating mesas, for instance, the ASU Fine Art Museum designed by Antoine Predock suggests a link between the building and the landscape as well as between the land and sky.

Business porosity involves accommodating business and commercial practices to the new economy or consumer demands. Urban big-box retail adapts the big-box store to urban settings by putting it in older buildings (e.g., Home Depot in Manhattan) or providing new buildings that fit in with urban context [e.g., Target in Chicago and Minneapolis (see Figures 46 and 47)].

Figure 46   Figure 47

Other kinds of porosity include *virtual porosity*, which allows virtual access through online communication, and *emergency porosity*, which allows for escape (e.g., fire escapes, helicopter lifts, alerting systems).

EXEMPLARS

The architecture of Fumihiko Maki exemplifies porosity. Most of his work features indoor and outdoor spaces that interact at least visually, such as the Tepia Science Pavilion (1989) with expansive views from the exhibition spaces and café to a large courtyard garden. At the Hillside Terrace Apartments in Tokyo (1966–91), Maki applied a strategy of transparent layering to create threshold spaces between intimate courtyards linked by winding passageways, a densely wooded interior, and the busy street.

Perhaps the reigning practitioners of porosity are Liz Diller and Ricardo Scofidio along with partner Charles Renfro (since 2004). In addition to the renovation of Lincoln Center and the High Line mentioned above, some of their more experimental projects have been taking porosity to new levels. At the Brasserie in New York's Seagram Building, video cameras boost visual porosity by capturing images of entering patrons and projecting them onto screens above the bar. The Institute for New Media project (winner of Eyebeam competition 2002) is a twelve-story building with floors divided by a continuous ribbon of cast fiberglass and concrete containing all the cables, fiber optics, and ducts for high-tech delivery. A horizontal truss system makes it column-free allowing public and private spaces to intermingle and "Liquid-crystal glass walls turn from translucent to transparent at a switch, letting visitors and residents visually eavesdrop on each other."[17]

At Diller + Scofidio's Blur Building on Switzerland's Lake Neuchatel for the National Exposition 2002, a three-hundred-foot-wide web frame with misters spraying continuously appeared to be a cloud floating seventy-five feet above the lake's surface. The architects describe it as "immaterial architecture,"

Figure 48

Figure 49

a building whose substance appears to be dissolving, blurring the boundary between material and immaterial, inside and outside, object and context. At night, the blur was intended to become a screen for projected images. Allowing engagement with the space, people were to wear plastic raincoats called Brain Coats programmed according to a questionnaire taken by each person. If you encounter someone who is a "match," the coats would turn red or pink. If not, green. The Blur Building also included a Water Bar (cocktail lounge) (see Figures 48 and 49).

With Koolhaas/OMA, Diller Scofidio + Renfro developed the master plan for the BAM Cultural District. This plan interweaves a range of programs, including an "urban beach" to draw in passersby, a streetscape conceived as connective tissue with the surrounding area, and a "vertical garden." It emphasizes bringing the inside performance activity outside, "enculturation" into the neighborhood, and phasing.

In all of these examples of porosity, the combination of concealment and revelation renders the city accessible, interesting, and lively. Philosopher and literary scholar Walter Benjamin attributed the "organic" quality of Naples, Italy (in 1924), to its porosity of old and new, enduring and fleeting, public and private, sacred and profane, interior and exterior, hidden and apparent. Celebrating such porosities today, Integral Urbanism refuses to stay within the lines.

ENGAGING THE BOUNDARY

Whereas Modernism aspired to transparency as manifested in structural honesty, the free plan, and the ideal of an open society, Postmodernism reacted with opacity, often described as a fortress urbanism. The Modernist approach resulted in overexposure, homogeneity, and lack of legibility. The Postmodern approach was accompanied by extreme cynicism, a growing sense of fear and anxiety, and a declining sense of community.

In a translucent urbanism, the attitude toward the border, boundary, or edge contrasts with the Modern attempt to eliminate these as well as with the Postmodern tendency to fortify them. A translucent urbanism does not eliminate or fortify borders, boundaries, and edges. Rather, it engages and enhances them to reintegrate (or integrate anew) places without obliterating difference. It retains, in fact, enhances distinctions by bringing differences (of people and activities) together through the range of porous membranes described above.

Natural systems must be open to receive solar energy and to thrive, but they also need boundaries in order to increase movement or flows within them.[18] It is along the edge of species' ranges where plants and wildlife are the hardiest and most "tolerant" of diversity and change. Consequently, those at the edge are more adaptive and will survive even when those at the center of a range do not. This principle of landscape ecology recalls Jacques Derrida's remark that "something is not the most itself at its center, but near its edge, near what it is not – the essence is found at its boundary."[19] The edge is where adaptation and change occur.

Like larger ecological systems, a translucent urbanism achieves porosity by allowing some things in but not others. On the scale of the city, the layering that produces these permeable membranes creates urban thresholds, resembling ecological thresholds where ecosystems meet such as an arroyo (or "wash") in the desert or an estuary where the sea meets the shore. Ninety percent of all living things coalesce along ecological thresholds because that is where most sustenance is found. People are similarly drawn to urban thresholds because they are lively, unpredictable, and ultimately, sustainable.

Thresholds – both ecological and urban – are naturally diverse, dynamic, and self-adjusting. The challenge for urban design and development is to make connections without losing the integrity of individual parts, providing something greater than their sum. The question is what to allow in and what not. What to reveal and what to conceal. The answer lies in translucency.

FROM OBJECTS TO CONTEXT (ON RELATIONSHIPS)

Nothing exists in isolation, only in relation (or context), whether it is a building, a city, or a person. It is only in mathematics that things may exist in isolation.[20] The twentieth century is characterized, however, by numerous struggles to achieve this ideal.[21] The western notion of the self as autonomous and free-willed, reflected and reinforced by the notion of "ego boundaries" in psychology, has contributed to numbing our empathy with others and with the rest of nature.[22] Countering the alienation aroused by this understanding of self, more recent notions about identity recognize permeable boundaries between self, others, and the rest of nature.

Cultural anthropology has undergone similar transformations over the last several decades from its earlier interpretation of cultures as monolithic and functioning like machines to current views regarding cultures an inextricably intertwined and organic. These current views have precipitated studies of "multiple subjectivities," "cultural hybridity," "hybrid cultures," "border cultures," "border matters," "border cities," "the third space," "the third place," and "multi-sited ethnography."[23] In anthropology and cultural studies, the border has become a place (both geographic and conceptual) where people can negotiate their identities endlessly, a condition that permits new opportunities but can also be destabilizing. Anna Lowenhaupt Tsing reports that the shaman with whom she studied in the Meratus Mountains of Indonesia taught her that survival is "creative living on the edge."[24] Michel Serres describes the "educated third" (*le tiers-instruit*) as the nomad who is always *becoming*, moving across established categories without blurring boundaries.[25] Renato Rosaldo speaks of "border crossings" as "sites of creative cultural production," where interconnections may take place.[26] bell hooks, in her essay "Choosing the Margin," declares:

> This is an intervention. A message from that space in the margin that is a site of creativity and power, that inclusive space where we recover ourselves, where we move in solidarity to erase the category colonized/colonizer. Marginality as site of resistance. Enter that space. Let us meet there. Enter that space. We greet you as liberators.[27]

Such understandings of culture and society[28] closely parallel developments in urban design. Kenneth Frampton describes "borderline manifestations" that "flourish sporadically within the cultural fissures," offering "interstices of freedom."[29] Frampton importunes: "With what power is left to us, it is our ethical responsibility to use our ingenuity to engender an urban fabric aggregated out of topographic fragments within the metabolic interstices of the megalopolis."[30] Acknowledging that most biological activity occurs in nature where different zones meet, sociologist Richard Sennett suggests that "urban design has similarly to focus on the edge as a scene of life."[31] This shift in focus from the center to the edge can be attributed to the decline of the public realm, rise of privatism, and diminished faith in progress. Concurrent with this shift were developments in astronomy and physics that suggest new ways of conceiving centrality, order, and chaos.[32]

In certain respects, the work of Gilles Deleuze and Feliz Guattari could be the social theory analogue to Integral Urbanism. Whereas, the Structuralists maintained that we think in binary oppositions, and the Narrativists that we think in stories, Deleuze and Guattari posit a nondialectical (non-Hegelian) approach that acknowledges difference without unifying or synthesizing it. They describe a world made of flow. Everything flows from water and air to electricity, people, ideas, culture, conversation, products, natural resources, and so forth. What distinguishes these flows from one another is the places they meet, or thresholds. Free flow, without constraints, is the "body without organs." Deleuze and Guattari see desire as the force of all history and they propose schizoanalysis as the study of the circulation (flows) of desire (and creativity).[33]

According to this formulation, modern society tries to control or tame desire by territorializing and coding it.[34] People, therefore, need to decode or destroy the striated or closed boundaries characterized by rigid identities, hierarchies, and stratifications (molar lines that are dendritic) and to facilitate the smooth (open-ended and self-organizing) deterritorialization (molecular lines that are rhizomatic). The breaking of binaries constitutes intensities, a new mysticism, a "resistance," a "radical politics," "a politics of desire" that breaks with repressive identities by liberating difference and, thereby, combating totalizing modes of thought, social regulation, and state control. Rhizomatics is the method for analyzing social flows and finding leaks (lines of escape) for transformation, the search for molecular lines of flight from molar lines, such as ways in which criminals escape the legal system or women escape patriarchy. It is a "nomadic" way of thinking. (In French, the word *nomades* is often used to refer to gypsies who move from place to place and resist attempts to settle them.) Socially and politically, the result is a nonhierarchical network that connects microstruggles without homogenizing them, or "transversality."

Parallel shifts have been occurring in the sciences, governance, and general worldviews over the last several decades. As Charlene Spretnak explains:

Just as modern scientists discounted and ignored perturbations observed outside of the accepted model, so modern economists ignored the effects of unqualified economic growth on the "fragment" of the whole that is nature. Modern statesmanship proceeded by ignoring the sovereignty of native people, a "fragment" that was clearly outside the accepted model, and modern rationalists denied any spiritual perceptions as anomalous quirks not to be mentioned. [Now], however, scientists engaged in chaos research ... try to absorb into their conclusions everything they observe through their measurements; ecological economists consider the total costs of production, including the depletion of our primary "capital," the biosphere; advocates of a postmodern world order defend the precious diversity of cultures that comprise the planetary whole; and people no longer boxed in by the tight constraints of highly selective modern rationalism now allow themselves subtle perceptions of the grand unity, the ground of the sacred.[35]

With regard to creativity and innovation, psychologist Howard Gardner maintains:

The critical thing in terms of creative impulse seems to be that when something aberrant or unusual happens – either in your life or in your work – that you don't ignore it. The easiest thing is to ignore when something strange happens. If I'm a scientist and my experiment doesn't work out, the easiest thing is to assume that I made a mistake rather than to become interested in the anomaly. But the roots of innovation lie in taking seriously and developing something which nobody else has paid attention to and which you and the rest of the universe might be inclined to ignore. You need to have a lot of fortitude to do this because most other people aren't going to be giving you a lot of positive signals.[36]

Expressing this shift from an emphasis on separation to holism, Arthur Erickson observed that "By ceaselessly bombarding particles of matter to get at the core of things, science has found that, as Einstein inferred, *relationship is the only reality.*"[37] Indeed, Einstein once remarked that the notion that we are separate entities is an "optical delusion of our consciousness."[38]

Manuel DeLanda describes a shift from understanding time or history as linear to regarding it as cyclical and from understanding the world as a hierarchy to regarding it as a meshwork or network. The nineteenth-century Darwinian notion that evolution leads to fittest design (linear causality) and that thermodynamics leads to thermal equilibrium was revolutionized by Ilya

Prigogen who demonstrated in the 1960s that as long as there is an intense flow of energy coursing through a system and mutual interaction among components, it will experience transitions between stable states (bifurcations) and will be nonlinear (because of feedback). Therefore, there is no "fittest design" and no equilibrium. Instead, systems are always changing with multiple coexisting forms (static, periodic, and strange attractors).[39]

Instead of a hierarchy, we have meshworks that are self-organizing and diverse. Meshworks may include hierarchies and there may be hierarchies of meshworks. The phenomenon of "emergence"[40] describes the process, whereby systems build higher intelligence from simple components. They self-organize through self-adjusting feedback mechanisms. Without a central authority, embryo and brain cells form, ants build colonies, people create neighborhoods, and simple pattern computer-recognition hardware can anticipate our needs based on past choices.

Interestingly, this idea of self-organizing change through feedback is not new, but has only recently gained widespread acceptance, thanks to computer technologies that are capable of graphically rendering this process along with the emergent sensibility described above. With the assistance of computers, we can now represent fractals (geometry of the irregular), waves, folds, undulations, twists, warps, and more, providing a hyperrational means of representing a "higher level order" that has long been integral to the divergent worldviews of Buddhism, Taoism, and the Romantics, as well as cosmologies proposed by Albert Einstein [quantum mechanics (1905)], Arthur Koestler (the holonic), Alfred North Whitehead, and others.

The conundrum that scientists have been trying to unravel corresponds to the crisis in urban design in the concerted efforts to reconcile constant change and diversification, on the one hand, with some sense of order and predictability, on the other. In architecture and urban planning, this debate has been articulated as critical regionalism, alternative or appropriate modernities, and ecological and sustainable design.[41] Intimations of this shift are widespread and variously articulated.[42]

As described above, the concurrent shift in architecture and urban planning has been from the earlier emphasis on objects and the separation of functions to context and programmatic hybridity. In brief, the essentialism and purism characterizing earlier twentieth-century pursuits is being supplanted by an acknowledgment of diversity, complexity, embeddedness, and an element of unpredictability.

As globalization proceeds apace, many of our habitual ways of categoriz-ing the world no longer suffice. One of these is the distinction between center and periphery. Rather than being the locus of activity and innovation, the traditional center has imploded or dissolved, and we have a condition of mul-ticentrality or lack of centers, a characteristic feature of the contemporary landscape. Activity and innovation have shifted to the borders between the city, suburb, and countryside; between neighborhoods divided by ethnicity, social class, or physical barriers; between functional uses of the landscape; and to the more metaphorical borders between disciplines and professions and between designers and their constituents.

In the environmental design fields, this recent shift in attitude must contend with the longstanding privileging of objects and the largely arbitrary division of labor that characterizes our professional practices, our academic curricula, and our landscape. Just as the modern city separated functions in its quest for machinelike efficiency, so modern practice divided and subdivided over the last century into architecture, planning, landscape architecture, inte-rior design, industrial design, and graphic design, each with their circum-scribed responsibilities and their respective professional organizations, journals, and academic departments. Productive collaborations among them have been all too rare and the precious talent and energy wasted over turf skirmishes is a tragedy and embarrassment, going a long way toward explain-ing the sorry state of our built environment as well as the crises suffered by the design professions.[43]

Our current task is mending the seams in our disciplines, professions, and urban fabrics that have been torn asunder. Rather than presume an opposition between people and nature, buildings and landscape, and architecture and landscape architecture, Integral Urbanism regards these as complementary or contiguous. Rather than generate perfect objects or separate programs and functions, Integral Urbanism aims to build relationships. The emphasis thus shifts from centers to the border, boundary, edge, periphery, margin, inter-stices, and in between. It also shifts from objects to relationships.

In a recent letter to the *New York Times*, the Project for Public Spaces described this as a shift from projects to places:

> It's a step away from the 20th Century vision of the architect's work as an iso-lated triumph of aesthetic devotion (even fetishism) to a more inclusive 21st Century idea of the designer as part of a vibrant, messy, exhilarating process of creating a living, breathing community ... Making this leap from project to

place has profound implications for the profession ... Ideas, decisions, and even inspiration will come from a wider assortment of sources, including people who live there, work there, or visit there. And a number of disciplines must be drawn upon to create places that meet the various needs of people using them. Architects, landscape designers, traffic engineers, community development advocates, and economic development authorities, among others, will be in the mix, jostling and debating about how to best make a place where people will want to be. This is different. This is unprecedented. And it's scary to some.[44]

In contrast to the Modern attempt to eliminate boundaries and the Postmodern tendency to ignore or alternatively fortify them, Integral Urbanism seeks to generate porous membranes or thresholds. By allowing for diversity (of people, programs, and more) to thrive, this approach seeks to reintegrate (or integrate anew) without obliterating differences, in fact, preserving and celebrating them. This approach and the landscape it generates reflect the complementary human urges to merge (connect) and to separate (distinction, individuation), with the resultant ongoing tension and dynamism. It recalls Martin Heidegger's contention that "A boundary is not that at which something stops but, as the Greeks recognized, the boundary is that from which something *begins its essential unfolding*. That is why the concept is that of *horismos*, that is, the horizon, the boundary."[45]

This reaction to Modernism began a half century ago with the British Townscape Movement, which criticized the Modernist tendency to regard the city "as a kind of sculpture garden"[46] and emphasized the "art of relationship"[47] among all elements in the landscape. The reaction was also manifest in the "postwar humanist rebellion"[48] of Team 10 among others. Dutch architect Jacob Bakema maintained that "the modern architect must be able to communicate with people ... beauty has to express openness in human relationships."[49] Shadrach Woods emphasized the importance of "human associations." Alison and Peter Smithson advocated creating "the forms of habitat which can stimulate the development of human relations" and offered a list of relationships between different kinds of spaces.[50]

While a sustained critique of Modernism has ensued, it is largely formulated from within the modern paradigm and, therefore, lacking the insight and force to offer effective alternatives.[51] Rather than simply allow relationships to occur, for instance, it tended toward environmental determinism and social engineering. Over the last decade, however, the paradigm has been shifting to enable this critique to pave a more solid, or in this case perhaps, a more pervious path.[52]

As conduits of information, connectors and boundaries might be understood as information networks or as porous membranes. This understanding of the boundary conceives *identity as relational* whether it is individual identity or that of a neighborhood or district or ecological zone. As Angelil and Klingman maintain, this "hybrid morphology ... unfolds from a system of relations between different, sometimes contradictory forces, no longer as an absolute but in reference to other structures," in a process that is "unceasingly renegotiated."[53]

Architect and landscape architect Linda Pollak understands the boundary "as a space of communication rather than a line of sharp division," as demonstrated by her project with Sandro Marpillero for Petrosino Park in New York City (1996). In an effort to simultaneously engage and be separate from its urban surroundings, Marpillero and Pollak proposed "a new kind of public space" that negotiates multiple scales (local, metropolitan, regional, ecosystem, virtual) and "activates its boundaries as thresholds." To accomplish this, the project bridges layers of "infrastructural relationships" – natural layers, transportation infrastructures, and virtual layers – allowing the built environment to operate "at a theoretically unlimited number of scales"[54] (see Figure 50).

Along with Anita Berrizbeitia, Pollak updates the use of the term "infrastructure." Rather than simply a technical program (roads, pipelines, electrical systems), infrastructure becomes a process (or strategy). This activated infrastructure should make connections between places and activities. It should be

Figure 50

catalytic, providing opportunities for new connections to occur. These connections usually take place through grafting. When grafted, the seams remain evident but each piece acquires characteristics of the host structure, producing a hybrid. Hybrids may be programmatic such as a park and highway or they may combine functional and formal elements as well as natural processes with artificially imposed ones. Architecturally and urbanistically, these connections often take the form of multiple ground planes and undulating or modulating ground planes. Expressive of the grafting, joints and details are carefully treated.[55]

According to Stan Allen, "Infrastructure works not so much to propose specific buildings on given sites, but to construct the site itself. Infrastructure prepares the ground for future building, and creates the conditions for future events."[56] Allen contends:

> Infrastructural work recognizes the collective nature of the city, and allows for the participation of multiple authors. Infrastructures give direction to future work in the city not by the establishment of rules or codes (top-down), but by fixing points of service, access and structure (bottom-up). Infrastructure creates a directional field, where different architects and designers can contribute, but it sets technical and instrumental limits to their work. Infrastructure itself works strategically, but it encourages tactical improvisation … Infrastructures are flexible and anticipatory. They work with time and are open to change … They do not progress toward a predetermined state (as with master planning strategies), but are always evolving within a loose envelope of constraints.[57]

Landscape ecology has inspired a basis for this approach, often described as "landscape urbanism."[58] The tradition of landscape ecology[59] incorporates people and all we create into natural systems. Landscape ecologist Richard T. T. Forman[60] defines ecologies as dynamic complex assemblages of resources, species, and climates operating in multiple feedback loops. Landscape Urbanism, as James Corner explains, is "an attitude of looking at cities as if they are landscapes and landscapes as if they are cities."[61]

The notion that all is connected and that everything has wide-ranging consequences appears throughout time and around the world. A central tenet of Japanese Buddhism is *esho funi*, the oneness of life and its environment. Artist Georges Braques expressed this sensibility saying, "Echo replies to echo – everything reverberates." In his "Letter from a Birmingham Jail" in 1963, Martin Luther King wrote, "We are caught in an inescapable network of mutuality, tied in a single garment of destiny. All life is interrelated." Derrida has maintained, "The world is a texture of traces which exist autonomously as 'things' only as they refer to or relate to each other ... No entity has a unique being ... apart from the web of relations and forces in which it is situated."[62] Thinking in terms of relationships, connectedness, and context is also described as systems thinking.[63]

Nothing exists in isolation, only in relation. As Jorge Luis Borges eloquently reminds us, "The taste of the apple ... lies in the contact of the fruit with the palate, not in the fruit itself; in a similar way (I would say) poetry lies in the meeting of the poem and the reader, not in the lines of symbols printed on the pages of a book."[64] Indeed, poetry itself is about bringing together ideas in new ways, about making connections. Social change emerges from connections. It is not primarily an outcome of power and money, as Malcolm Gladwell demonstrates in *The Tipping Point*, but of influence. It is about relationships.

Just as colors will appear differently depending on the colors adjacent,[65] so a person, activity, or form is inflected by that which is in relation to it. The goal of Integral Urbanism is to allow these relationships to develop and flourish in the urban and social mix. Rather than distill and separate the functions of living, as Modern Urbanism did, this entails ensuring that the correct cast of characters is there.

Most important are the edges or borders, whether they are actual locations or the shared thoughts and behaviors that define a relationship between two or more people. Integral Urbanism tends to these relations. Although the boundaries between public and private spaces have been changing, they are not disappearing. The question now is where to place them and how. It is about making connections or building bridges without detracting from the integrity of the individual parts, but instead providing them with something greater.

Integral Urbanism regards boundaries as important validators, identity markers, and thresholds. "Freedom" from them would be annihilation. Everyone knows that children need boundaries to feel secure; adolescents need boundaries against which to rebel; and grown-ups need boundaries too. They are essential to culture, community, and creativity. Philosopher Karsten Harries claims we need boundaries to center us in the "terror of space," a condition he attributes in part to the Copernican revolution that "transformed the Earth ... into a mobile home."[66] Our fear of endless space and of not being in the center is reflected in our resistance to the Copernican revolution. We still say the sun rises and sets when the sun really does not move; it is the earth that is moving around the sun. We are egocentric and geocentric.

Trust is at the core of relationships and of communities. An "architecture of fear" filled the void generated by lack of trust resulting from the breakdown of community during the second half of the twentieth century.[67] Integral Urbanism fills this void in a way that rebuilds a sense of community and quality public space appropriate to the twenty-first century. It does this by cultivating relationships among functions of the city with their mutually supportive networks of people. The trust on which relationships and communities rely ensues.

FROM OPPOSITION TO SYNERGY (ON COMPLEMENTARITY)

Reenvisioning urban design practice as well as product suggests a paradigm shift away from binary logic and (perhaps back) toward the principle of complementarity. Complementarity presumes that, as Tadao Ando intones, "There must be darkness for light to become light." It presumes that there would be no sound or music without silence, no fullness without emptiness, no slowness without velocity, no self without other, no exaltation without lamentation, no inhaling without exhaling, no harvest without cultivation, no pleasure without pain and suffering, no hope without despair, no strength without weakness, no ease without difficulty, no health without illness, no creation without destruction, no life without death, no something without nothing.

Complementarity departs from Modernist binary logic because it does not regard the pair as oppositional nor does it seek a synthesis or resolution. Rather, it understands each as not only allowing the other, but also embracing or embodying the other. Prometheus's punishment of having his liver eaten each day by vultures and healed each night suggests the importance of darkness for becoming whole or healing, even if the harm will inevitably come again. Adam and Eve's banishment from the garden allowed for agriculture and childbearing, not to mention architecture and clothing. Although the Tower of Babel faltered, it allowed for diaspora and cultural diversity. Even though these risks may have opened the door to suffering, they were also acts of heroism that permitted creative opportunities otherwise denied.

The shift away from binary logic and toward complementarity is variously manifest in thinking about cities. Lars Lerup in *After the City* advocates "trialectical thinking" as opposed to the binary thinking, which pits architecture against the city and the city against the suburb.[68] Charles Landry in *The Creative City* emphasizes the importance of overcoming "the habit of thinking in binary opposites which is such a common barrier to imaginative problem-solving." Instead, he recommends that we "address urban problems in an integrated way." Landry observes: "Urban creativity thrives when those in charge can be open-minded and centred, can link the capacity for focus with lateral thinking, can combine practical with conceptual thinking. If these qualities do not exist in one individual they can be present in a team."[69]

The goal of intervention, then, is not to resolve conflict or to produce clearly intelligible landscapes, but to generate places of intensity with the lovely tensions they embody. The goal is not to produce cities that are entirely in flow or places that are consistently in flow over time. This is because, as the principle of complementarity maintains, flows require ebbs. From the designer's perspective, these interventions may resist analysis, recalling Isadora Duncan's remark to a reporter: "If I could tell you what it meant, I wouldn't have to dance it." Form follows function once again, but function is defined more holistically now to include emotional, symbolic, and spiritual "functions."[70] Rather than simply satisfy basic needs, places may be designed to be joyful, interesting, surprising, illuminating, even sublime.

This approach brings our subjective, transactive, qualitative, and intuitive ways of knowing back to complement the objective, autonomous, quantitative, and rational ways of knowing valued by the modern project. Produced by people for people, these interventions are inspired by the physical context (site) as well as social, historical, and virtual contexts. Accordingly, they may not be developed or represented conventionally. For instance, Dan Hoffman's abstract imagery for Cool Connectors in Phoenix suggests the latent experiential quality these interventions could activate (see Figure 51). And the hybrid hand-drawn/

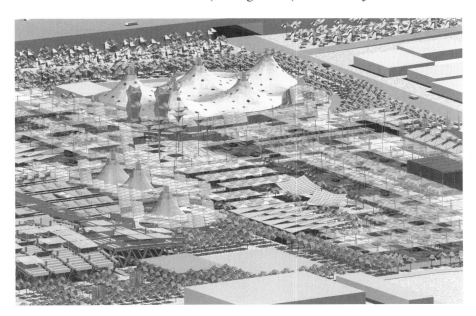

Figure 51

computer-rendered forms of Lewis Tsurumaki Lewis "produce multiple and simultaneous readings not available in typical drawing formats."[71]

The shift from the machine and utopia as models to ecological models (see pp. 11–12) is indicative of this paradigm shift. In contrast to the earlier models that bespoke aspirations for control and perfection, these current models suggest connectedness and dynamism as well as the principle of complementarity.

In psychology, the "integrated personality" was applied by Carl Jung to describe the blending of both light and dark (the shadow) components of a personality. The integrated personality acknowledges and accepts the shadow that might emerge deviously in other guises such as projection and self-sabotage if suppressed. The same could apply to the city. In contrast to the modern search for perfection, Integral Urbanism revels in the exception and imperfect. In contrast to the Modern and Postmodern fear of change, and consequent controlling and escapist tendencies, an Integral Urbanism celebrates it. Rather than neglect or abandon "in-between" and peripheral spaces, both real and conceptual, Integral Urbanism tends to them.

Perhaps this principle is illustrated by the vaccine that protects us from contracting an illness by introducing it into our system. Or by relaxation, which is best achieved through prior tension. Or by singing the blues to overcome them. Like the "integrated personality," Integral Urbanism acknowledges and accepts the urban shadow.

Irony is the response of the emotionally diminished, the expression of detachment and alienation; it is the opposite of home. Herb Childress

Who-ever attempts to solve the riddle of space in the abstract, will construct the outlines of emptiness and call it space...whoever attempts to meet men in the abstract will speak with this echo and call this a dia-logue. Aldo van Eyck

I've been guilty of irony and cynicism, those things that are symptomatic of our times. You can't really blame anybody, in the way irony and cynicism are pounded into everybody's heads in every TV commercial, as if we're all insiders on the big joke here. But there's got to be more than just the joke.
Beck

Authenticity

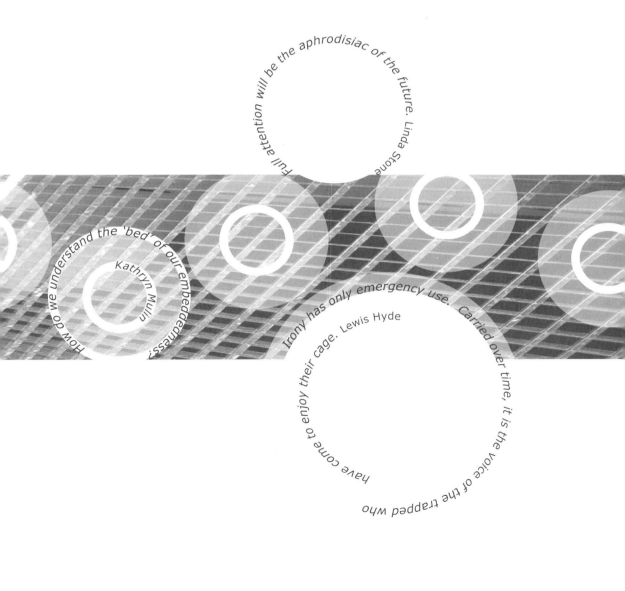

Full attention will be the aphrodisiac of the future. Linda Stone

How do we understand the 'bed' of our embeddedness? Kathryn Mulln

Irony has only emergency use. Carried over time, it is the voice of the trapped who have come to enjoy their cage. Lewis Hyde

AUTHENTICITY

THE BLASÉ COSMOPOLITAN

The German philosopher Georg Simmel wrote an essay about urban life in 1903, suggesting that the overstimulation of city living leads people to have a blasé attitude. The French word *blasé* is defined as "rendered indifferent due to the abuse one has sustained." As urbanization has proceeded apace over the last century, the blasé attitude has grown ever more pronounced. In addition, rapid globalization has increased the prevalence of the cosmopolitan, the person who feels equally at home everywhere … and nowhere.

Combining the two, we get the "blasé cosmopolitan" who is at home everywhere and nowhere; who believes everything and nothing; who is good at dispassion but not at involvement; who is rendered indifferent due to overstimulation; and who may feel numb much of the time, either afraid of or unaccustomed to feeling deeply.[1]

Certainly, much of our architecture could also be described as "blasé cosmopolitan." Instead of the vibrant, meaningful, and sacred spaces so characteristic of cities and towns prior to the twentieth century, we have the ubiquitous highway interchange, fast food restaurant, shopping mall, multiplex, suburban tract housing, big-box retail, gas station, international hotel, and corporate office building. These features of our global landscape are barely distinguishable from one another whether they are in London, Toronto, Chicago, or Singapore. Indeed, the words most commonly used to describe places today suggest an absence or aftermath: abandoned, vacant, generic, and anonymous. This loss of a sense of place contributes to feelings of emptiness, anxiety, and insecurity.

Over the last several decades, we have seen numerous efforts to rekindle a sense of place and with it a sense of interest, meaning, security, and community. Unfortunately, many of these efforts have only compounded the problems.[2]

FORM FOLLOWS FICTION, FINESSE, FINANCE, AND FEAR

One very prevalent response to rapid change and globalization in the western world has been a backlash: nostalgia for the clarity of the older boundary markers and efforts to resurrect them somehow. During the 1970s and 1980s, this was apparent in the desire to retribalize or to assert cultural distinctions. It was apparent in the search for "roots" through the tracing of family lineages, in the call to return to traditional values and institutions, in resurrecting old customs, and even inventing "new" traditions.

In architecture and urban planning, the nostalgic reflex has been apparent through ubiquitous references to past cities. The threat to previously clear boundaries incited an anxious effort to produce places that look as though they grew spontaneously over time without planning. There has also been a tendency to mask what is going on behind facades and escape into fantasy worlds, with the growth in the building of theme parks since the 1980s and of megastructures devoted to leisure and recreational activities. I call this desire to drag and drop forms from other places and other times into the present *form follows fiction.*[3]

Another prevalent defense mechanism for coping with change and uncertainty has been irony. With the challenge posed to beliefs in progress and to moral clarity, there is a lack of consensus and a loss of innocence. Ultrarelativity reigns, the view that all options are equally good or bad, or equally constructed, because there are no truths. The ironic response acknowledges that one's choices are just an arbitrary selection from things that have been done before; it is manifest through the tone of a voice, the wink of an eye, a tongue in a cheek. There is an emphasis on surface rather than substance; heroes have been replaced by celebrities; camp (self-conscious sentimentalizing) has become kitsch (bad taste).

But irony is a cop out. It is a way to hide and not take responsibility for improving the world. Irony precludes any deep commitments, convictions, or passions. It is too sophisticated to laugh aloud, to find something truly funny. It can lead to complacency and detachment. All that remains are images and texts, representations and discourses referring to each other. The ironic attitude says: "Nothing I do really matters. We can only live in and create fictions. So we may as well just distract ourselves with bread and circuses, with food and entertainment, rather than take care of our environment, others, and ourselves." The void created by this backseat position tends to be filled by the self-serving agenda of the market and sometimes of designers.

Architects who shirk from taking a stand and striving for betterment, striving instead to please themselves and impress colleagues, fall into the category I've described as *form follows finesse*.[4] Aiming to produce "star-chitecture" that will be profiled in the architectural press, the emphasis is on formalism and self-gratification. For finessers, architecture is primarily a personal expression rather than a social art, leading to what Fred Kent describes as a "crisis" in some contemporary cities. He observes that the new parks of Paris:

> ... are designed more as objects or icons than they are about public use. Park development is much less usable and much more playing to the design profession. [Similarly,] London and Barcelona are enamored with branded designers who have their own interests to protect. The new parks are unfit for human activity, and new buildings are stand alone icons drawing undesirable activity to their untended, unusable and isolated setting.

In the United States, Chicago's Millennium Park (2003) has been similarly criticized. One commentator wrote:

> Erecting attention-grabbing landmarks was the main point of Millennium Park's design; providing Chicagoans with a sense of contentment and wonder was a secondary consideration. Wandering through the park, as I did one beautiful evening in late summer, feels more like attending a splashy Pop Art exhibit than settling into a vital public place. Your eyes are dazzled by all the strange and shiny objects, but your soul feels a bit underfed.[5]

While garnering the lion's share of media attention, star-chitecture only accounts for a tiny fraction of what is built. Conversely, the vast majority of what is built receives the least attention. This is building undertaken by the private sector that is motivated principally by the bottom line, or *form follows finance*.[6] It is often manifest in the sprawling suburbs and the spread of transnational business operations housed in cookie-cutter forms or nondescript boxes repeated around the globe. Although divergent in their agendas, form follows finance and form follows finesse share a deep cynicism about the potential for improving the world through urban design.

The fourth response to rapid change, under which the other three might be subsumed, is *form follows fear*.[7] Along with historicism, nostalgia for traditional boundary markers has also been apparent in the retreat to one's own kind. "We want to be with people like us" is the common refrain. Segregated urbanism is most blatant in the growth of age-restricted (55 and older) communities, like Sun City in Arizona, but metropolitan areas are commonly segregated along ethnic and social class lines as well.

The impulse to retreat is epitomized by the growth of gated communities for all age and income levels. Currently, over eight million people in the United States live in gated communities and the number continues to grow, despite findings that gating communities has little impact on crime rates. If anything, gating may actually elevate crime rates, though the perception that it is safer to live in gated communities remains intact.

Outside of gated communities, the numbers of individually gated homes is increasing. For affluent clients, architects are increasingly requested to provide "safe rooms." Popularized by the movie *Panic Room* (2000) starring Jody Foster, these are security rooms concealed in the house plan and accessed by sliding panels and secret doors. More striking is that 52 million Americans (of a total population of 296 million) live in houses or condominiums governed by homeowners' associations. These private associations exercise a good deal of power, regulating house colors and additions, pets, basketball nets, lawn care, and much more. Although these "shadow governments" are not consensually supported, people who choose to join these associations submit to their rules in an effort to protect their property values and sometimes to be with others like themselves.[8]

The mentality of fear among homeowners of all kinds has led to a pronounced antigrowth movement. People who do not want development to occur near them are often described as NIMBYs (not in my back yard). Those who are opposed to growth of any kind are BANANAs (build absolutely nothing anywhere near anything). The mentality of fear has also led to a perceived need among many to carry guns. In the United States, there are currently more than 200 million guns in private hands and the number of women with guns has more than doubled over the last decade.

The popularity of the four-wheel drive sports utility vehicle, especially in cities, also suggests a desire to defend oneself. Although equipped for off-road driving, very few actually ever leave the roads. The appeal of this sort of vehicle is epitomized by the current vogue for the Humvee (the human military vehicle or high-mobility vehicle) which was released in a civilian edition called the Hummer, available for $65,000 and up. The cost of car insurance for these cars is exorbitant. Then actor, now Governor of California Arnold Schwarzenegger purchased the very first one back in the early 1980s. While the Hummer may be "the ultimate in body armor,"[9] the safety of all cars today is a major selling point, including a wide range of options from alarms to car phones, built-in car seats for children, air bags, bulletproof glass, and more.

As our private spaces have elevated in importance, our public spaces have been diminishing in quantity and quality. Those public spaces that remain often convey the messages, "Go away," or, "Don't linger long," since they have been stripped of public rest rooms, telephones, and even water fountains.

The escapist nature of these urban design and development trends — behind gates, away from our downtowns, into the past, other places, or fantasy worlds — may emit signals that the present is indeed unsavory. The rising tide of fear has led people to stay at home more. Activities that once occurred in the public realm are increasingly satisfied now in the private one via television or computer. Venturing out is increasingly restricted to the controlled settings of the shopping mall, theme park, or sports arena. Going out without a plan but merely to partake in the unpredictable and spontaneous public pageant, a characterizing feature of urban life, has grown increasingly rare. Rather, we tend to go out for specific purposes, with specific destinations in mind, and with a knowledge of where we will park and whom we shall meet.

All four of these tendencies are reactive. By responding to the anxiety wrought by rapid change through escapist and self-serving means, they are ultimately not sustainable. The proactive approaches of Integral Urbanism, in contrast, respond creatively and compassionately by remaining connected to our environment, to our communities, and to ourselves by being authentic.

THE AUTHENTI-CITY

We seek authenticity in a place just as we would rather slip between all cotton rather than polyester blend sheets at night. Moreover, as current sheet trends suggest, the higher the thread count the better. Just as higher thread count improves the comfort and quality of our sheets, so higher urban thread count — a fine as opposed to coarse-grained fabric — improves the comfort and quality of our cities.

How can we avoid the polyester blend environments and achieve this highly sought-after authentic urbanism? Should we step aside and allow the city to grow and change without any guidance whatsoever? No, that would simply allow market forces to drive urban development. Markets are only designed to allocate resources in the short term and without regard for things that do not have obvious financial value like the purity of our air and water or the quality of our communities. As Paul Hawken, Amory Lovins, and L. Hunter Lovins eloquently caution in *Natural Capitalism*, "Markets were never meant to achieve community or integrity, beauty or justice, sustainability or sacredness – and by themselves, they don't."

Rather, an authenti-city results from a combination of large-scale and small-scale interventions, both systematic and the serendipitous. How it happens is just as important – and goes hand in hand – with what happens. An authenti-city is responsive to community needs and tastes, which have to do with local climate, topography, history, and culture. It may not be best to demolish everything to start fresh upon a *tabula rasa*. Herbert Muschamp attributes the success of Diller + Scofidio's renovation of Lincoln Center in part to its "para-planning," an ability to reveal "latent qualities within imperfect spaces." He writes: "Feedback has entered the picture. Instead of tossing out entire categories of urban space in the name of ideology or for marketing purposes, architects are better off learning from concrete examples of performance. Goodbye, catastrophic planning."[10]

On the larger scale, the best urban plans contain both urban design *and* policy frameworks upon which a city can grow and change in a never-ending dynamic process. Like a good parent, a good plan nurtures healthy growth and change without being "over-involved," without determining everything, allowing the city to blossom and define itself. While providing some overall defining guidelines, these frameworks should not prescribe every land use and every architectural detail. Like all healthy organisms, an authenti-city is always growing and evolving according to new needs that arise, thanks to a self-adjusting feedback loop that measures and monitors success and failure. When people hatch an idea for improving the city such as a network of linear parks, a public market, better crime prevention and educational opportunities, or the development of small business incubators, an authenti-city has the ability to implement these.

REAL REALTY

This "search for the real" has been under way among urban designers over the last decade. A symposium on the topic stated: "In an age of simulation, cynicism, and self-absorption, western society at the end of the 20th century is obsessed with authenticity. For contemporary architectural critics, authenticity has replaced the Vitruvian triad of firmness, commodity, and delight as the primary standard of judgment."[11] In stark contrast to the excesses of irony, cynicism, and escapism characterizing Postmodern Urbanism, we have been witnessing a widespread and broad-based yearning for authenticity. Charlene Spretnak has described this as a "resurgence of the real."[12] In architecture and urbanism, clarion critiques of the collapse of reality[13] abound along with propositions for bringing it back such as Rem Koolhaas's advocacy of "Bigness" to "resurrect the Real."[14]

The quest for authenticity among urban designers has taken various directions. One is toward revealing undesirable aspects of our world that we have been hiding or denying. Those who take this tack might be described as "dirty realists," a term applied by Liane Lefaivre who notes similarities between some late 1980s architects and the school of literature that charts the "dirty realities" of late twentieth-century life rather than flee from them into escapism and narcissism as Postmodern literature had done. In literature and architecture alike, dirty realists engage in defamiliarization, seeking to make people aware of ordinary conditions in a new way. As Lefaivre explains, "The shock that sets off the critical judgment is sparked by the way in which dirty real architects, like dirty real novelists, slow down perception, jar conventions, and 'save things from obviousness.'"[15] In this dirty real category, she includes Koolhaas, Jean Nouvel, Bernard Tschumi, Zaha Hadid, and Nigel Coates. A younger generation has joined them such as Paul Lewis, Marc Tsurumaki, and David J. Lewis who seek to "exploit the potency of the unfamiliar that lurks behind the façade of familiarity".[16] This tendency might trace a lineage to the Situationists (1957–72) who, reacting to the Surrealists whom they criticized for not being real enough, used displacement and dislocation to generate new connections in search of an *urbanisme authentique* (authentic urbanism).

In contrast to the dirty realists, architects Deborah Berke and Steven Harris propose an "architecture of the everyday," while architects John Chase and John Kaliski along with urban theorist Margaret Crawford advocate "everyday urbanism," both referring to the work of French sociologist Henri Lefebvre. An architecture of the everyday "is blunt, direct and unselfconscious. It celebrates the potential for inventiveness within the ordinary and is thereby genuinely 'of its moment.' It may be influenced by market trends, but it resists being defined or consumed by them."[17] Everyday urbanism seeks inspiration from local cultures, environments, and spontaneous forms of popular expression. While corrective to the out-of-touch elitism characterizing much late twentieth-century architectural culture, everyday urbanism offers little in the way of informing interventions in the city. As Michael Speaks contends, it "is a commentator on the city, an interpreter rather than a force of transformation."[18]

Whereas dirty realists' transgressive approach implicitly critiques the manifestations of economic/social disparities in the landscape and everyday urbanism implicitly critiques the high/mass/popular culture divide, the New Urbanism claims to produce an "authentic urbanism" by learning from urban wisdom passed down through the ages. Considering the regional scale of urban design, the presumptive radical designers, whose interventions are largely at the building scale if not purely theoretical, may in fact be more conservative than the New Urbanists.[19]

Rather than the dirty realist emphasis on transgression, Integral Urbanism aspires to transformation and at times, transcendence. It does so by extending the everyday urbanists' respect for spontaneous expressions of popular culture and the New Urbanists' respect for urban traditions, while infusing these with local knowledge gained through attentive listening. While acknowledging a place for the defamiliarizing tactics of the dirty realists, Integral Urbanism does not consider these appropriate for large-scale interventions. It does not deny unpleasant social and urban conditions or retreat into formalism, nostalgia, fantasy, or cyberspace. In contrast to these escapist tendencies, it engages contemporary realities by honoring the local community and landscape as the greatest source of inspiration rather than hindrances to overcome or obstacles to surmount. It is sensitive to site and situation: the physical, political, economic, social, cultural, and historic contexts. Both a method and an attitude, Integral Urbanism is a "live theory"[20] for urban design, responsive to changing conditions and feedback, always with an eye toward application.

For urban integrity to flourish at the larger scale of districts or cities, there must be infinite opportunities for the "unofficial plans," developed by many different people with a wide range of ideas, described by Jane Jacobs above. These can only be effective, as Jacobs also points out, if certain tools are made available by the public sector. Redevelopment agencies, such as San Diego's Centre City Development Corporation (formed in 1975), and Tax Increment Financing[21] are essential to oversee and coordinate revitalization efforts that include important infrastructural improvements (especially transit) and to preserve social diversity. Initial public incentives to bring private development into targeted areas are also important for "priming the pump." Supporting local independent retail is critical for places to have a sense of distinctiveness and local character and for keeping money localized instead of sending it back to some remote (inter)national headquarters. Arts districts, as legislated in Maryland and in Providence, Rhode Island, are extraordinarily effective catalysts toward urban revitalization. It is also important to have programs to ensure affordable housing [e.g., San Diego's SRO (single-room occupancy) program and Seattle's taxpayer-approved low-income housing levy] and to ensure the preservation of buildings and neighborhoods that have value for the community. Finally, regulatory practices should support urbanism by requiring build-tos rather than setbacks and pedestrian-friendly uses on the ground level while determining maximum rather than minimum parking spaces.

Urban designer and critic Mark Hinshaw calls these places "True Urbanist" communities:

> Not the product of a singular vision, they emerge from the collective decisions of many organizations, associations, corporations and government bodies. They value the results of democracy – however messy, unpredictable, and uneven they may be ... They are constantly evolving, infilling, and re-developing, with a broad mixture of architectural styles and sensibilities ... They have a gritty urbanity that values variety over uniformity. Rarely are they subject to a highly prescriptive set of design standards; rather, they revel in the idea that everything need not fit an ideal. They may be subject to design guidelines and a design review process, but those techniques encourage creativity over conformity.

The International Making Cities Livable Movement promotes True Urbanism, enumerating its principles on their Web site. It advocates such generative design guidelines based upon the "DNA" of places. This DNA:

> ... is expressed in those architectural and spatial characteristics best loved by the city's inhabitants. These may consist of certain building materials and colors, a typical arrangement of scale and architectural forms, building lot size, rooflines, scale of public and semi-public spaces. In order to fit into the context, new buildings have respected this "genetic code," reflecting at least some existing patterns, or interpreting them in a contemporary idiom.

Pieces of True Urbanism have been emerging throughout the United States from Portland, Seattle, and San Diego to Baltimore, Pittsburgh, Denver, St. Paul, Kansas City, Dallas, Albuquerque, Minneapolis, Salt Lake City, Cleveland, Little Rock, Alexandria (Virginia), Missoula, Charlottesville, and elsewhere.

THIS TIME AROUND

Like the other qualities of Integral Urbanism, authenticity also had earlier incarnations. These include aspects of French nineteenth-century Realist painting and its architectural counterpart, which inspired Modernism, Louis Aragon's "marvelous quotidian" (1920s–30s Surrealism), Hans Hofmann's "search for the real" (1948) through the use of color in painting, Team 10's search for "ordinariness as opposed to order" (1950s–60s), Herbert Marcuse's "one-dimensional man" (1964), *cinema verité* (1960s), Henri Lefebvre's "real man" and attempt to reveal the "extraordinary in the ordinary," Heidegger's "authentic-agency-in-communion," which acknowledges mortality and finitude, and Charles and Ray Eames's effort to transform the ordinary into the extraordinary and find beauty in the commonplace.[22]

Current efforts to feel, experience, and express authentically recall these earlier ones but, like the other qualities, there is something different this time around. The search for authenticity appears to be unprecedented in its scope and reach, as a constellation of threats conspires to attenuate our grasp on reality.

The profusion of "themed" environments, not only in theme parks but also in shopping malls, schools, and neighborhoods, have, according to architectural critic Ada Louise Huxtable, rendered America "unreal" and suggest a preference for living in a fantasy world. Indeed, it has grown increasingly difficult to have an experience that has not been programmed and prepackaged. Emphasizing surface over substance, these hyperrealities and simulacra,[23] which may sometimes seem realer-than-real, challenge our perception and raise our expectations beyond the messiness and fallibility of real life.

In the architecture world specifically, the privileging of surface over substance has led to a preoccupation with image making that often becomes an end in itself. As Neil Leach argues in *The Anaesthetics of Architecture*, this can induce numbness in both designers and users, while obscuring deeper social and political concerns. Aesthetics threaten to become "anaesthetics," he maintains, as meaningful interventions are eclipsed by seductive images generated and displayed with technological finesse.

Our consumer-driven and media-dominated society has produced what Martin Pawley calls a "secondary reality," making the primary one ever more elusive. Meanwhile, business trends capitalize upon while exaggerating this tendency by purveying "experience" and "transformation" economies.[24] The Swedish documentary *Keeping It Real* by Sunny Bergman (2004) asks why so many people are in search of "authentic" experiences today, suggesting it is the inundation of media representations that makes us feel we are surrounded by artificiality and that renders us vaguely dissatisfied. The film suggests that authenticity has become a marketing ruse, or perhaps, a ruse that has become a new reality, a hyperreality.

Yet another source of our reality obsession is the intense blurring of real and fake enabled by new technologies. From digitally retouched photographs, we now create "synthespians," or "cyberstars," computer-animated human characters such as Dr. Aki Ross of *Final Fantasy*. The proliferation and intensity of online activities has generated a distinction between real life and virtual reality. In computer culture, the word "real" also refers to immediacy and sometimes engagement (interactivity). "Real technology," also described as streaming audio and video, is a medium allowing "real-time" – live not taped – Internet broadcasting. This medium has names such as "Real Networks" and "Real Play."

Also contributing to blurring real and fake are so-called "reality shows" that dominate television ratings, most with extensive Internet components so fans can follow these real people even when the show is not being aired. The executive producer of reality shows *Survivor* and *The Apprentice*, Mark Burnett, has described this genre as "dramality," a blend of drama and reality.

The blurring of real and artifice extends beyond film, television, and the Internet to the visual and performing arts, music, fashion, the built environment, and more. Uptown New York drag queens use the term "realness" to describe the quality of their impersonations. Retailers hawk prewashed (and often pretorn) jeans that appear already lived-in and imbued with sentimental value. New Urbanists say they are building new towns to look like old ones because people want authenticity.

Our growing interdependence with machines along with rapid change modulates the way we perceive ourselves and engage the world. As sociologist Robert Jay Lifton contends: "We are becoming fluid and many-sided. Without quite realizing it, we have been evolving a sense of self appropriate to the restlessness and flux of our time. This mode of being differs radically from that of the past, and enables us to engage in continuous exploration and personal experiment."[25]

These are popular themes among human potential and business management gurus. As David Whyte, poet and Fortune 500 consultant, maintains:

We are moving from a familial, parent-child relationship in the workplace to an adult-adult relationship with our organizations, with all the shock, difficulties, triumphs, and fear that entails. Unknown hands and as yet barely articulated tidal forces, are molding and scouring not only the ground on which we stand but the very shape of our identities.[26]

In the bestseller *The Circle of Innovation*, Tom Peters describes how businesses can prosper in this contemporary permanent state of flux.

The feeling that our grasp on reality may be slipping also derives from our increasingly sophisticated defense mechanisms, the blasé attitude that protects us from the uncomfortable bombardment of our senses. The toppling of New York City's twin towers on September 11, 2001, the 2004 tsunami, Hurricanes Katrina and Rita in 2005, and other tragic events are so horrific that the lure of distractions tugs and pulls while the defense of numbness beckons. The casualty is that as we shut out the unpleasant, we may also shut down. We may lose the ability to respond proactively to these conditions while also shutting out the pleasant. To counter the ensuing lack of feeling, we may yearn intense feeling through evermore extreme experience.

This desire to feel things along with the fluidity characterizing contemporary Western society has led to "trying on" identities as never before. The phrase "crossing over" is used to suggest a deliberate shift from one identity (ethnic, sexual, and so forth) to another, or from one musical genre or other form of expression to another. Crossing over implies an ability to express oneself freely as well as the freedom to change. It also, though, bespeaks a gnawing sense of dissatisfaction with who we are while magnifying the anxiety associated with lack of stability. This dissatisfaction derives in large part from the market. Ads never say, "You are okay just the way you are." Instead, they fabricate discontent to sell products.

Increased difficulty with having an authentic experience has gone hand in hand with increased inability to feel and express oneself authentically. Psychologists trace this to the inability to express feelings and thoughts as a child, either because one is not listened to or is made to feel ashamed. If people cope by building a wall of protection around themselves and distrusting others, they may even distrust their own feelings, not recognize them, or feel embarrassed by them. Rather than embrace their whole selves – good and less so – and see things for what they are, they may instead deny, negate, project, inscribe, intellectualize, and idealize. This lack of self-awareness and self-respect may lead to depression or more extreme, "splitting" and borderline personality syndrome, a separation of mind and body, a separation from one's true self.[27] If the building of walls – real and metaphorical – is an urban and societal manifestation of this lack of connection with self and others, perhaps it can be similarly healed by learning to listen to oneself and others and, thereby, developing compassion and respect.

Another way of coping is to fill our lives to the brim and beyond with work, other activities, and possessions that wind us up faster and faster. As Aldo van Eyck once said, "We rush to forget our loss of being, to forget our lost sense of dwelling, to forget our homelessness and our alienation."[28] In reaction, global grassroots efforts such as the Slow Movement and the Simplicity Movement have been attempting to step off the treadmill, slow down, pare down, and smell the flowers. Beginning in Italy with the Slow Food movement a decade ago, a Slow City Movement has recently emerged with its first conference in a Norwegian slow city in 2005.[29] "Slow is the new fast," according to Carl Honoré, who describes this larger movement in his book *In Praise of Slowness*.[30]

In highbrow culture, it has grown hopelessly unfashionable to presume there is a reality. In part, this reflects a sensitivity toward cultural diversity and a respect for the wide range of worldviews. However, it can also be a pretext for self-absorption and not recognizing the plight of those less fortunate. The popular hand gesture mimicking quotation marks is an ironic mannerism that calls into question the validity or sincerity of the words referenced, ultimately assuring your listeners that what you are saying does not have gravity. Similarly, the qualifier "like," initiating with teenage girls but extending far beyond, similarly diminishes our commitment to what we are saying. "She's like 50 years old" or "It lasted like two hours" allow a vagueness, some wiggle room for plausible deniability. In the world of academia, the Poststructuralist vogue of the 1980s and 90s insisted there is no "real," only individual perceptions and interpretations. The most Poststructuralists could usually muster was to say that something is "highly suggestive" and recommend that more research be done.

These attitudes contributed to a pathological relativism that discouraged taking a stand and acting upon one's convictions. From the Greek word for dissembling, irony opposes integrating. The ironic attitude, writes Jedediah Purdy in *For Common Things*, bespeaks "a quiet refusal to believe in the depth of relationships, the sincerity of motivation, or the truth of speech." It can, he warns, become a substitute for action and thought, leading to indifference and alienation. By default, it accepts the status quo. Against irony, Purdy urges us to rediscover civic values, to reintegrate ourselves into the larger civic fabric.

THE QUEST MANIFEST

All of these threats to our grasp on reality today have incited a widespread and far-reaching search for distinction and validation, for intense feeling, for sincerity and honesty, and for meaningful connections. This search is manifest in a myriad of ways, both proactive and reactive, from extreme sports to Internet dating, brand loyalty, the attempts to slow down and simplify our lives, moving to New Urbanist communities, and more.

Since people crave distinctiveness today, places can no longer promote themselves through familiarity, as the Holiday Inn did with its successful 1975 campaign, "The best surprise is no surprise." Instead, places must emphasize their uniqueness. This has amplified the demand for "branding," essentially an attempt to convey a sense of uniqueness about a product or service. People want to feel that it will distinguish them or offer them an authentic or distinct experience.

This demand from the business world to brand goods and services has led to an explosion in the design professions. The Berlage Institute reported: "In today's design paradise there is more work than ever for the architect. These days everything in the experience economy – from fashion brand to urban concept – must be designed ... This demand upon architecture, in which culture has been folded into economy, represents a new challenge."[31] Over the last decade, the number of graphic designers has greatly increased and design schools have opened in places they did not exist previously, including Japan, Singapore, and South Korea. Following Harvard's lead, other universities have been renaming their schools to make design the umbrella rubric under which architecture, planning, landscape architecture, graphic design, product design, and fashion design become subsets.[32]

Likewise, as cities seek to promote urban and economic revitalization, they now focus on developing aspects that are unique to the place and on turning these cultural assets to economic advantage.[33] For instance, a citizens' group in Seattle met to discuss the following issue:

With so many of Seattle's neighborhoods undergoing changes, it's easy to wonder if we're going to be happy with what we get. How would you feel if the new Seattle waterfront was a copy of the Embarcadero in San Francisco or Tom McCall Park in Portland? We all want our neighborhoods to be authentic to Seattle, but what is authentic? Does authentic mean historic? If so, when did the city's authenticity start? Join us as we explore Seattle's authenticity and apply it to the design of Seattle's next great civic space, the Central Waterfront.[34]

The search for authenticity is also apparent in other forms of expressive culture. Art critic Richard Nilsen eloquently pleaded in 1999 that art offer us genuine experience and, thereby, assist us to reconnect with the world. He said:

> ... we must reacquaint ourselves with experience, and our art must not explain us to ourselves, but offer us experiences. Please, let's end the PC moralizing and instead discover what it feels like to bite into a crisp apple, what it feels like to dance. What it feels like to give birth, or raise a child. Or get old, or fear death ... Art should show us things, make us hear things, make us touch things and recognize the body we inhabit.

Five years hence, Nilsen happily reported that "The tide is finally receding. And what is replacing the Pomo blip is art that once more gives its audience an experience: visual, emotional, tactile, intellectual. It is art once more connected to the experience of being alive, connected to the wider world." He cites as examples the work of James Turell, Bill Viola, Kiki Smith, Peta Coyne, and Andy Goldsworthy. This art, he said, "is less likely to preach to us and more likely to engage us."

An entire literature has emerged on the search for authenticity. Albert Borgmann applies the phrase "focal reality" to describe the "encounters each of us has with things that of themselves have engaged mind and body and centered our lives." Signs of focal reality, he says, include "commanding presence, continuity with the world, and centering power."[35] Neil Everden speaks of "radical astonishment,"[36] the intensity of presentness and intense sense of self sometimes experienced in the natural environment.[37]

Engaged in the search for authenticity, Westerners have been turning to non-Western traditions as well as older wisdom traditions.[38] Hence, the popularity of yoga, martial arts, bioenergetic forms of healing, the Kabbalah, the mandala, the labyrinth, the feather circle, and others, many of which address the issue of authenticity directly. The American Indian notion of "original medicine," for instance, holds that each of us has our own unique personal talents and challenges and that people should be "in their medicine." For some American Indians, the term "Sacred Hoop" means "authenticity" or being connected with one's spirituality. When we are ourselves, they maintain, we are "in our sacred hoop."[39]

In sum, the authenticity quest – a search for self and meaning – continues to intensify. It is double-sided, leading to intense alienation and all its accompanying psychological and social ills on the one hand or to emancipation from oppressive situations and unprecedented creative solutions on the other. Insecurity and anxiety have been mounting proportionate to opportunities to develop innovations for improving the human condition.

GETTING A GRIP

All of this begs the question: *What is authentic?* Though a particular concern of the moment, this existential question it not a new one. A story many of us were read as children explores this question. In *The Velveteen Rabbit*, written by Margery Williams in 1922, the Rabbit asks the Skin Horse: "What is REAL?" The Skin Horse responds, "When a child loves you for a long, long time, not just to play with, but REALLY loves you, then you become Real." Asked whether it hurts, the Skin Horse replies "Sometimes," but "When you are Real you don't mind being hurt." Asked how it happens, the Skin Horse explains:

> "It takes a long time. That's why it doesn't often happen to people who break easily, or have sharp edges, or who have to be carefully kept. Generally, by the time you are Real, most of your hair has been loved off, and your eyes drop out and you get loose in the joints and very shabby. But these things don't matter at all, because once you are Real you can't be ugly, except to people who don't understand.'"

Like the Skin Horse, a city becomes and stays real through ongoing meaningful connections, not through cosmetic quick fixes or through massive razing and rebuilding of large swaths of the existing urban fabric. Becoming real signals a transformation from isolation to integration, from numbness to feeling, from boredom to excitement, from cynicism to caring, and from complacency to engagement. It occurs when, to paraphrase George Carlin, we are making a life, not just a living, and when we add life to years, not just years to life.

At the risk of being reductive, I would say, very simply, that our search for the real reflects a desire for interconnectedness with the places we live and with a community of people.[40] In the headlong rush not to fall off the treadmill of progress, these most obvious of qualities have become increasingly elusive. Though integral to most prewar landscapes, it will not do to copy older buildings and cities, for we have changed. What we need to recover is our "urban instinct," the ability to satisfy this desire for interconnectedness today through design and other means. Such an ethic of taking care — of self, others, and the environment — calls for a shift in emphasis and attitude, the subject of the next chapter.

Le coeur a ses raisons que la raison ne connaît pas.
Pascale

Zig zag is the way to success. A straight line leads to failure.
Masai proverb

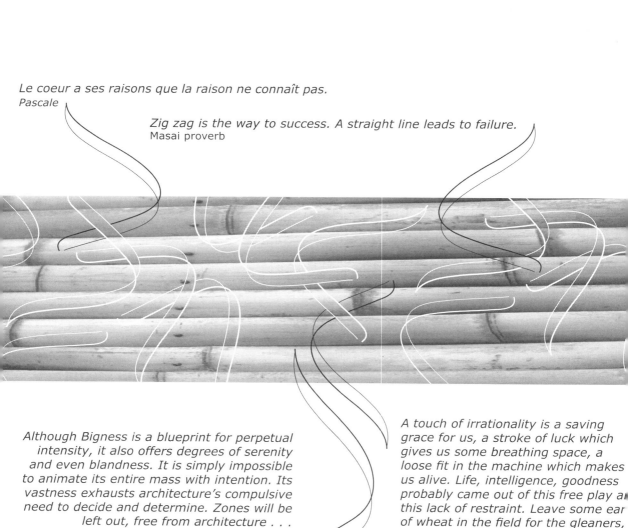

Although Bigness is a blueprint for perpetual intensity, it also offers degrees of serenity and even blandness. It is simply impossible to animate its entire mass with intention. Its vastness exhausts architecture's compulsive need to decide and determine. Zones will be left out, free from architecture . . .
Rem Koolhaas

A touch of irrationality is a saving grace for us, a stroke of luck which gives us some breathing space, a loose fit in the machine which makes us alive. Life, intelligence, goodness probably came out of this free play and this lack of restraint. Leave some ear of wheat in the field for the gleaners, he said. Perhaps we shall learn one day that the most reliable machines leave room for the unexpected.
Michel Serres

Vulnerability

The Next Big Thing may be a whole lot of little things - call it economic pointillism.
Richard D. Parsons

Designing is like improvisation, finding a sound for each place.
Walter Hood

*When the world was created,
God made everything a little bit
incomplete. Rather than making
bread grow out of the earth, God
made wheat grow so that we might
bake it into bread. Rather than
making the earth of bricks, God
made it of clay so that we might
bake the clay into bricks. Why?
So that we may become partners
in completing the work of creation.*
The Midrash

VULNERABILITY

THE DUAL TEMPTATION

Prometheus was bound to a rock for stealing fire from the gods and giving it to people. Adam and Eve were banished from the Garden of Eden for eating fruit from the Tree of Knowledge. The Babylonians were forced to speak mutually unintelligible languages and were scattered across the earth for attempting to build a tower to heaven and to achieve notoriety. These cautionary tales describe punishments inflicted and suffered for the crimes of wanting to know, explain, create, and obtain recognition. As allegories about our desire for control, they advocate against rationality and for wonder, awe, mystery, and sanctity. They advocate against hubris and for humility. They serve as reminders to acknowledge and celebrate our human qualities in contrast to the dual temptation to become godlike or machinelike.

This dual temptation is endemic to architects and planners. The last century particularly was dominated by attempts to plan cities and design buildings that would be "machines for living"[1] through the omnipotent application of master planning and by adhering to the tenet of "form follows function."[2] Master planning and Modern Urbanism ultimately have fallen short in achieving their goals, however, because they are too inclusive and utopian to be realized fully. Realized only partially, they produce fragments of cities that do not congeal into an urban fabric. In addition, the segregation and rigidity of master planning and Modern Urbanism run counter to the integration and dynamism of the life lived in them.[3]

Widespread dissatisfaction with these efforts has been inspiring alternative approaches that do not forgo technological advances but relinquish, nonetheless, some of the control that twentieth-century planning and architecture presupposed. In addition to emphasizing *relationships* rather than isolated objects, *complementarity* rather than opposition, and *substance* rather than surface (as described in the preceding chapters), these approaches and the landscapes they generate also emphasize *process* rather than product.[4]

FROM PRETENSE OF PERMANENCE TO PROCESS

If the city is to survive, process must have the final word.
SPIRO KOSTOF[5]

We cannot think of planning in static terms, in three-dimensional space, when we live in a four-dimensional world.
SHADRACH WOODS[6]

Life is movement — road is architecture.
NORIAKI KUROKAWA[7]

Time is the greatest innovator.
FRANCIS BACON 1665

As the rate of change has been accelerating, we can no longer sustain our pretense of permanence. With time more integral to space than ever before, the process becomes as important as the product. In fact, it becomes part of a product that is never completed. As novelist John Barth declared in *Tidewater Tales*, his ode to minimalist literature, "The key to the treasure may be the treasure itself." The journey and the destination become inseparable. As do the means and the ends. Therefore, it can no longer even be a question of the end justifying the means, itself a Modernist notion. Without the pretense of permanence, everything becomes contingent, provisional, even fleeting. The distinction between permanent and impermanent dissolves. Buildings and the city are always works in progress, always drafts.

This has implications for how we think about design, what we design, the role of clients and users, and how we teach design. Regarding process as paramount, rather than the finished product, Integral Urbanism veers away from master planning's comprehensiveness, aiming to master everything including nature. Instead, as described above, it proposes more punctual interventions that contribute to activating places through the creation of thresholds[8] or places of intensity.[9]

As process becomes product, so the journey becomes as important as the destination — or becomes the destination itself — in terms of how a designer approaches and conceives a given project. In contrast to the modern preoccupation with getting from point A to point B as quickly as possible, designers are beginning to pay more attention to the quality of the journey itself. Graphic designer Bruce Mau contends, "When the outcome drives the process we will only ever go to where we've already been. If process drives outcome we may not know where we're going, but will know we want to be there."[10] Moreover, we may go somewhere never gone before. As the means converge with the ends, clients and users also become active collaborators. Similar to the shift from passive television watching to interactivity, the distinction between creator and audience blurs as the client or audience becomes more engaged.

The inextricability of space and time is recognized in the definition of space as "an interval of time" and in the commonly interchangeable locution, "This is where/when …" Modernity, however, both separated the categories of space and time and "emptied" them.[11] Rendering space and time universal, neutral, abstract, and homogenous allowed for and justified imperialism and the imposition of standards and norms. As sociologist Anthony Giddens explains, "Once time and space have become emptied, and disentangled, they can be systematically reappropriated."[12] The reappropriation of these spaces proceeded to suppress or devalorize specificity, the local, the anomaly, the irregular, the fragment, and the other.

Over the last several decades, the shortcomings of Modern Urbanism along with the need to contend with rapid change have been prompting a welcome reunion of space and time along with their "re-filling." Rather than neutralize and normalize, Integral Urbanism is keenly aware of specific places while incorporating time, along with its unpredictable outcomes, into the design brief.

INSIGHT IN SITE

In urban design theory, the reintegration and refilling of space and time are apparent in attention toward the vernacular and the everyday, chance and serendipity, the "space-time continuum,"[13] and in multiple efforts to realize critical regionalism. In urban design practice, this is apparent in the shift from emphasizing typologies and formal concerns to infrastructures and flows.[14] Like space, time is no longer considered empty, nothingness, infinite, or homogenous. Explaining this shift, Ben van Berkel and Caroline Bos contend:

> The postindustrial, global urban conglomerate is a topology of networks; an open, dynamic structure of interconnected nodes in which expansion depends upon communication. Access is defined as the distance between nodes, measured in time. Structuring such models of urban growth implies incorporation of time into architecture and planning.[15]

As we incorporate time into our proposals, we inevitably consider how places are used (over time), or human behavior. To express dynamic systems, architect Kristina Hill suggests that "a process language, rather than a pattern language, is what's missing in our current era of priorities." She proposes combining words referring to forms with words referring to actions, thereby "generating a new functional poetry," e.g., "rain gardens."

Integral Urbanism thus features a willingness to relinquish control, to let things happen, and to play – a vulnerability. This translates into a shift from the all-inclusive master plan (in which land use considerations are primary) to a more project-oriented, site- and client-specific, incremental, catalytic, and tentacular form of intervention.

Numerous designers have described this attitude. Stan Allen, for instance, says that in order to map the complexity of the contemporary city, "some measure of control may have to be relinquished."[16] Steven Holl maintains, "Working with doubt allows an acceptance of the impermanence of technological change while opening up to metaphysical particularities of place."[17] Jusuck Koh explains that "Accepting the inevitability of change in use and users requires architects to forego their own Egos and desires to imprint, and to place emphasis on processes of adaptation and adjustment rather than products."[18] Rem Koolhaas advocates an urbanism that:

> … will not be based on the twin fantasies of order and omnipotence; it will be the staging of uncertainty; it will no longer be concerned with the arrangement of more or less permanent objects but with the irrigation of territories with potential; it will no longer aim for stable configurations but for the creation of enabling fields that accommodate processes that refuse to be crystallized into definitive form; … it will no longer be obsessed with the city but with the manipulation of infrastructure for endless intensifications and diversifications, shortcuts and redistributions.[19]

A vulnerable urbanism allows things to happen, things that may be unforeseen. Gilles Deleuze and Felix Guattari might describe this process as liberating the natural flows of desire (which perpetually seek connections and syntheses) from the repressive and hierarchical modern city.[20] This approach might also be regarded as a form of "urban acupuncture"[21] that liberates *chi*, or the life force. Applied to existing built environments as well as new development, these interventions may have a tentacular[22] or domino effect by catalyzing other transformations. Since the process of building continues with inhabitation and appropriation, a vulnerable urbanism highlights the role of users who become collaborators rather than passive recipients.

Like flow and the other four qualities, vulnerability describes the nature of Integral Urbanism as well as a means of achieving it. A vulnerable urbanism is dynamic, improvisational, and always unresolved in contrast to the Modernist obsession with control, completeness, fixing things, designing all, contempt for client (e.g., Frank Lloyd Wright's "client-proof" architecture), cleanliness, and utopia. In contrast to what appears in retrospect as an anxiety related to rapid change and desire for control characterizing much of the twentieth century, a vulnerable urbanism embraces change; it surrenders to it. In contrast to the modern clean-it-up and fix-it mentality, there is acceptance of the dirt, the broken, the imperfect.

A vulnerable urbanism is soulful and poetic. It combines system with serendipity[23] and intellect (or spirit) with "subtlety, complexity, ripening, worldliness, incompleteness, ambiguity, wonder."[24] As psychologist Thomas Moore maintains:

> The intellect wants a summary meaning ... but the soul craves depth of reflec-
> tion, many layers of meaning, nuances without end, references and allusions
> and prefigurations ... It likes persuasion, subtle analysis, an inner logic, and
> elegance ... Relatedness is a signal of soul. By allowing the sometimes vulner-
> able feelings of relatedness, soul pours into life.[25]

Just as the nests of birds are part of nature, so are the structures we create. Integral Urbanism does not regard landscape as an afterthought, token, antidote, distraction, or mere decoration, what Richard Ingersoll has described as "landscapegoat."[26] Rather, landscape and buildings are fully inte-grated. The same applies to "art" or "public art." The city itself is a work of art, not only isolated pieces of it. Likewise, the process of creating the city, and of community building, is a collective work of art.

The Japanese tradition of understanding humanity as part of nature, in con-trast to the Western tradition that has opposed people to nature, allows for an easy and natural accommodation with the site. Tadao Ando, for instance, main-tains, "The architectural pursuit implies a responsibility to find and draw out a site's formal characteristics, along with its cultural traditions, climate, and natu-ral environmental features, the city structure that forms its backdrop, and the living patterns and age-old customs that people will carry into the future."[27] Yoshio Taniguchi, who designed the addition to the Museum of Modern Art

(MoMA) in New York City, similarly explains, "The site is the point of departure, the most basic issue in architecture. I visit the site to assure that I do not succumb to abstract theories and a vision of style that applies only to the work's surface, so that I arrive at architecture in its true and full form."[28]

Deep awareness of nature in design respects the "natural laws" of the universe including internal laws of growth along with shared external forces generated by the sun, wind, and water. The Fibonacci series, named after the medieval Italian mathematician who identified it, is the infinite sequence of numbers, each one a sum of the two preceding it, that governs phyllotaxis (the arrangement of leaves on a stem to give optimum chlorophyll production) as well as the spiral (found in sunflowers, pinecones, seeds, climbing plants, animal horns, the nautilus shell, and more). This series of numbers also generates the Golden Section and the Golden Rectangle, characterized by a ratio considered to define harmonious proportions by Classical and Renaissance architects. Fractal geometry describes the self-similarity of forms and rhythms found in nature from snowflakes to leaves, branches, mountains, waves, and coastlines. No matter the scale, these forms and rhythms will be similar, though never identical. When architects seek to harmonize with and express the fractal self-similar patterns of nature in their design, they seek iterative "textural progression."[29]

Rather than devise solutions that will only become tomorrow's problems, designing in flow with nature produces solutions that are as efficient and synergetic as nature itself. Industrial and software designer Jim Fournier contends:

> If one looks into the behavior of natural systems ... there is a synergy which human technological systems have not even begun to aspire to. It is as if every element serves multiple purposes and solves multiple problems at once, and the net result is that the whole system functions harmoniously. As a designer, one sometimes has moments in a design process where this seems to happen. It is as if one is in the final stages of untangling the Gordian knot and the more one undoes one problem the more it frees up others and the whole solution just unfolds as if it is doing itself ... Contrast this with the apparent state of the world in late modern/post-modern times. It is as if all of the problems are intractable and the more we do one thing to attempt to solve one problem the more it throws three others into a deeper state of crisis ... It is just the opposite of what happens in a successful design flow state, and very much the opposite of what seems to be apparent in the design of all of nature's systems.

The successful design flow state, according to Fournier, feels "as if one is discovering a solution, which was already present in potential and had to be teased out, discovered, in order to be brought into manifestation. It is very much an experience of humility and awe rather than intellectual triumph and control."[30]

Acknowledging that we are part of nature, a vulnerable urbanism attempts to partner with it rather than master it. Attuned to the deep interrelationships through space and time, it understands how all affects us and how our actions, in turn, may affect all else. It presumes that we belong to the land rather than the land belonging to us. Rather than seek freedom from nature, a vulnerable urbanism seeks freedom in nature.

POINTS OF PRESENCE: FROM MEGAPOPS TO PITAPOPS

Integral Urbanism offers punctuation marks or reference points to "inflect" (change of word by tense, mood, gender, etc.) the landscape and our experience in it. These interventions activate "dead" or neutral spaces. They acknowledge and care for abandoned and neglected spaces. By increasing density of activity and perhaps building mass, they make connections between places, people, and experiences.

There are numerous expressions of this attitude toward intervention. Architect and theorist Christopher Alexander advocates piecemeal growth with each intervention having a healing effect on the landscape.[31] The redevelopment of Barcelona during the 1980s, with architect Mayor Oriol Bohígas at the helm, emphasized "projects, not planning," realizing a network of discrete outdoor spaces, each one contextual with its surrounding neighborhood. Ignasi de Sola-Morales's "urban acupuncture" involves catalytic small-scale interventions with potentially wide-ranging impact.[32] Bernard Tschumi's "events"[33] are intended to punctuate space and time, as demonstrated by the *"folies"* at the Parc de la Villette in Paris. Dan Hoffman's Cool Connectors for Phoenix (2001) introduce "luscious places" that can be quickly implemented, provide comfort and connectivity, and serve as catalysts for urban revitalization. Michael Gamble and Jude LeBlanc have described their method for large-scale suburban strip retrofitting as "incremental urbanism."

Borrowing from computer culture, we might call these catalytic punctual interventions "points of presence," or "pops," which are the physical nodes or hubs for computers, the buildings housing the mainframes that enable computers to function. To ensure clear connections, it is good for computers to be in physical proximity to a pop. Therefore, it is good for pops to be in places of high computer density (even though these buildings are only entered by a few systems operators and, therefore, are not themselves urban nodes or hubs). Currently, these are megapops (using megabytes). In time, they will be gigapops, followed in turn by terrapops and pitapops with the ability to serve as hubs for increasing numbers. Along with the urban analogues of "pops" described above are numerous efforts to design the links between these, or infrastructures (see pp. 42–7).

SOFT URBANISM

This focus on interventions that have a catalytic but unprogrammed effect departs dramatically from the master planning that dominated the twentieth century. In contrast to that rigid or "hard" urbanism, Michael Speaks describes this approach as "soft urbanism" because it is dynamic and flexible.[34]

The national call for building a lot rapidly in the Netherlands in the 1990s led Dutch architects and planners to focus on large-scale interventions and phasing.[35] Emphasizing interactive and time-driven processes, they have applied "scenarios" (from military strategists) to visualize "plausible spaces."[36] Architect Winy Maas of MVRDV has developed software to generate "scenarioscapes," not unlike *Sim City*.[37] The Berlage Mixer, for instance, developed by Maas and his students, variously combines three components – units, envelopes, and sliders – to generate possible urban scenarios. Andreas Ruby explains:

> Contrary to the plan and its inclination to streamline the real according to its will, the scenario tries to tempt it into a reflective process of stimulus and response. Thus, the scenario frees itself from the logic of domination which is inherent to the concept of the plan. Instead it opens a mode of intervention which is based on play and dialogue with the field of intervention itself.[38]

Another scenario-based technique developed with Berlage students is the Urban Gallery of Raoul Bunschoten (of Chora). Whereas, Maas focuses on quantitative data for his scenarioscapes, Bunschoten uses more qualitative information based on fieldwork. Stage One of the Urban Gallery involves gathering information that reveals something about the dynamics of a particular place at a particular time. This information is often notated in a haiku-like fashion with an eye toward four basic processes: erasure (what is taken away), origination (emergence of something new), transformation, and migration (things moving through). Analyses based on these miniscenarios are called "operational fields" describing the underlying processes and mechanisms in three categories: scale (from local to global), impact (environmental, social, etc.), and involvement (actors, agents, and target groups). Stage Two of the Urban Gallery involves the development of a prototype that draws from the latent potential of Stage One. The prototype mediates between two or more operational fields and reweaves them, producing new conditions. A prototype responds to four layers of action: branding (identity formation, scripting), earth (referring to land, water, air, ecological issues, biodiversity and landownership), flow (movements through a site including traffic, people, goods, information, money, air, water, and waste), and incorporation (altering legal, managerial, social, political frameworks). This prototype is tested in Stage Three through "scenario games," simulations of possible realities. Stage Four is the action plan that seeks to implement the prototype and unfolds indefinitely through time.[39]

The Netherlands has provided fertile ground for soft urban approaches. The firms Crimson and max.1, for instance, incorporated a temporally driven feedback mechanism into the Rotterdam Harbor plan, so that the plan can adapt to new conditions like a living organism.

In the United States, landscape architect Walter Hood advocates incremental transformations for the design of public space that blend old and new as well as the surrounding sites and the various constituencies using the public space. Hood phased the redesign of Lafayette Square Park in Oakland, California (1994), so that the transients who frequented it would not be displaced. Rather than gentrify the park, he chose to improve the park for those already using it while also making it welcome to others. For Splash Pad Park (2003), located at an intersection beneath a freeway, also in Oakland, Hood created a "hybrid landscape" in an attempt to satisfy its diverse constituency. Drawing from the pattern of the freeway pylons, narrow sidewalks crisscross the site; an existing street is converted into a popular weekly farmers market; and a long wavy bench upon sand allows water from an underground creek to seep through. The park has become the social center of the neighborhood. Andrew Blum observed that, "the design is open-ended, even confusing and messy. No one would mistake it for minimalism – and no one would say people's behavior here is minimized... They inhabit the space fully, bringing life to it..." Blum describes Hood's formula for designing public space as "rooted in the tangible past, enlivened by the public, and integral to the community."

Along with these catalytic and incremental approaches, form-based coding (see pp. 38–41) offers another example of a vulnerable urbanism. Just as the rich urban fabric of traditional cities was not a product of zoning regulations, but of a few accepted rules regarding access to light and air, climatic comfort, accessibility, and privacy and community, so form-based coding attempts to veer away from the ultracontrolled master plan without stepping aside and allowing the market to hold sway. All of these approaches propose a "kit of parts" that can be variously assembled by others to produce original combinations that nonetheless share common elements, offering variation within a larger unity.

Sometimes attempts at vulnerability go awry, particularly if relinquishing control is merely feigned or if control is simply displaced to another arena. For instance, efforts to experiment with designing only the space between buildings, have met with mixed results. Identifying flaws in the conventional Modernist approach of designing the "solids," these experiments reverse that formula, focusing instead on the "voids." For "Les Figures" in the French town of Jouy-le-Moutier, architect Jean-Paul Girardot, inspired by the work of Kevin Lynch, designed only the public space (1978).[40] This "public" space was built, but no one ever came (see Figure 52). After lying vacant for almost a

Figure 52

decade, a homebuilder purchased the land and built conventional housing. Rem Koolhaas similarly proposed designing only the space between future buildings for the French new town of Melun-Sénart (1987 competition, not awarded).

A vulnerable urbanism is responsive rather than resistant. It occurs when cities, cultural institutions, or neighborhoods "go with the flow" and graciously accommodate activities that have been taking place spontaneously (or would take place if allowed). For instance, the director of Brooklyn Museum of Art, Arnold Lehman, renovated the museum's forecourt to better accommodate the spontaneous gatherings occurring there in the evenings, instead of fending them off with walls and surveillance. Another example is First Friday in downtown Phoenix when the streets transform into a celebration of art and performance for one evening a month that regularly draws crowds of 10,000 people.

Rather than ply the scientific method in search of mastery and control, a vulnerable urbanism requires attentive listening and observing. Many designers have thus been adopting ethnographic or therapeutic approaches,[41] adding these to their methodological toolboxes.

Like the other qualities, vulnerability is characterizing expressive forms of culture outside urban design from film to painting, photography, dance, television, music, fashion, and performance art.[42] It is also apparent in the social sciences, biological sciences, and humanities.

PRECEDENTS

Once again, there are precedents. Valuing process, incompleteness, ambiguity, dynamism, serendipity, and improvisation have all appeared before in various guises. Paul Klee maintained that art should be experienced as a process of creation, not just a product (1944). Heidegger defined the work of art's very nature as unconcealment, revealing, unfolding, or emerging from hiddenness to reveal truth (1954). Charles Eames asserted, "Art is not a product. It is a quality" (1977). For the Japanese Metabolists, change and flexibility were central to their view of architecture as well as designing with regard for the city as a whole.[43] Although concerned more with buildings than the larger urban scale, Robert Venturi proclaimed in his "gentle manifesto" (1966): "I am for messy vitality over obvious unity ... Blatant simplification means bland architecture."[44] Henri Lefebvre wrote longingly of the premodern "residue resisting analysis" (1968) and later developed the method of "rhythmanalysis" (1992) that takes its cue from the rhythms of the body in space.

Satirizing the all-controlling architect, architect Adolf Loos told the story of "The Poor Little Rich Man" (1908) whose completely designed home was so oppressive that he became deeply unhappy. The story ends with the man declaring, "Now I have to live with my own corpse. Yes, I am finished. I am complete." Permitting people to be and express themselves in their surroundings, Team 10's "open aesthetic" (1950s and 1960s) aspired to indefinite growth and change. Shadrach Woods, for instance, conceived of the Berlin Free University, "as an object in flux, transforming itself in relation to people's changing needs and aspirations."[45] During the 1960s and 1970s, there were many such efforts including the "open architecture" of Lucien Kroll, "supports" of Nikolaas Habraken, open or "unfinished" urban systems of Hans Scharoun, and Charles Moore and William Turnbull's "Process Architecture."[46] In planning and urban design, Cedric Price proposed the "Non-Plan" (1969) and Christopher Alexander rejected the master plan, proposing instead a "pattern language" based on traditional typologies (1977 and 1987).

The call for regaining our innocence or the child within, along with valuing play, has also recurred. Fifteenth-century theologian Nicolas of Cusa said we must "unlearn" that which screens us from perceiving truth in order to achieve the "child's unknowing."[47] Zen similarly recommends not losing the "beginner's mind." John Keats recommended a state of "negative capability," which is described as "being in uncertainties, mysteries, doubts, without any irritable reaching after fact and reason."[48] The value of play was apparent in the Surrealist's "exquisite corpse," the Situationists' *dérive* and *détournement*, and in Nietzche's critique of negativity and cultivation of joy. In design education, the Bauhaus *Vorkurs* (preliminary course) sought to cleanse minds and bring students back to kindergarten through Zen, Tao, and the philosophy of Eckhart. The goal was "to return incoming students to the noble savagery of childhood."[49]

What a vulnerable urbanism asks us to "unlearn," in contrast to the Modern period, is the part that privileges reason over intuition and experience, "expert knowledge" over our own feelings and opinions, and static discrete objects over contexts, relationships, and processes. Rather than privilege one over the other, it values – and integrates – all ways of knowing from the tactile, to intuition, to reason. A vulnerable urbanism does not advocate the *tabula rasa*, ultimately just a veiled attempt to impose someone else's vision, whether it is an architectural vision on a bladed site or an ideological vision on a "cleansed" mind. The emphasis on process rather than product suggests that education be context-based and self-reflective rather than object-centered,[50] valuing subjective knowledge and qualitative methods as well as scientific and technical knowledge and quantitative methods.[51]

With regard to educating designers, David Orr maintains:

> Design is not just about how we make things, but rather how we make things that fit harmoniously in an ecological, cultural, and moral context. It is therefore about systems, patterns, and connections ... At its best, design is a field of applied ethics that joins perspectives, and disciplines that otherwise remain disparate and often disjointed.

Karsten Harries asserts that we need to know how to dwell in order to build.[52] Referring to Heidegger's notion of dwelling,[53] Harries makes the obvious, yet somehow long overlooked, observation that integrated buildings can only be designed by people with integrated lives. Therefore, he suggests, a part of design students' education should be devoted to learning how to understand themselves, their community, and their place in the larger world.

At the Post–St. Joost Academy of Design in the Netherlands, all students spend the first trimester studying *I* (identities), the second *We* (public sphere and urban space), and the third *They* (proposal-counterproposal). Rather than offer a "medium-specific education," the school "attempts to introduce a methodology that is both resistant and open to technological, economic and cultural innovation."[54] The core course for Ph.D. design students at ASU is similarly organized into Me-Search, We-search, and Research, asking, respectively: Who am I? What is the nature of community and culture? What are my particular areas of interest and how might I contribute?[55]

This kind of education elevates goals such as environmental sustainability and respecting the human dignity of all people over power, prestige, and profits. While contributing significantly to enhancing the environment, it also contributes to enhancing the credibility of architects and other urban design professionals.[56]

SYSTEM AND SERENDIPITY

Listening to the minute differences noticed by my then-six-year-old daughter Theodora between her *Star Wars* Legos and the characters from the movie, I remarked that she remembered many more details from the movie than I did. Theodora responded, "Children who found the beauty of being a child when they were a child remember these things. I guess you didn't find the beauty of being a child when you were a child. Or you lost it." Struck by the painful recognition of my innocence lost, I asked, "Is there anyway I could get it back?" She thought for a moment and replied, "If you lose the beauty of the child, it's very hard to get it back. You get it by playing a lot. Maybe if you have lots of fun as a grown-up, you can get it back." After a brief pause, she added, "Once you've got your child back, there's nothing that can stop you from doing anything."

Just as the "beauty of the child" may get buried beneath the responsi-bilities of adulthood, so the vitality of a city — its soul and character — can disappear if squeezed into a rational and overly prescribed master plan. Rather than throw any discipline or planning to the wind, perhaps we might rethink how and when to apply them. Keeping a place's "child" alive, or bringing it back to life, would not mean zero intervention but instead a gentle guidance that is responsive, flexible, playful, and nurtur-ing, permitting self-realization.

To achieve the aforementioned qualities of hybridity, connectivity, porosity, and authenticity, we have been reconsidering our approach and attitude toward architecture and urban design. Rather than solely analyze and dissect, or alternatively opt to be artist and poet, a vulnerable urbanism does not regard these conventional dichotomies as antagonistic. Instead, it plies them both without erasing their distinction: system and serendipity, rational and romantic, principle and passion, the Apollonian and the Diony-sian, spirit and soul, and the striated and smooth as well as molar and molecular lines (of Deleuze and Guattari). Rather than go the route of binary oppositions, a vulnerable urbanism takes another path, one that occupies the slash between them, like the bamboo reed that is deeply rooted and firm while also yielding.[57]

Vulnerability does not denote weakness, indifference, apathy, or anarchy. Rather, it bespeaks an awareness and acceptance of our human qualities along with a certain relinquishing of control, an embracing of our shadows (personal, collective, and urban), and recognizing change as the only constant. For designers, it translates into an enhanced receptivity toward the client, the site, and culture, as well as logistical issues. Rather than constraints, these become opportunities and sources of inspiration.

The stories of Prometheus, Genesis, and the Tower of Babel all tell about an initiation into complementarity: good and evil, joy and suffering, success and defeat, pride and shame, harmony and conflict, knowledge and ignorance, vulnerability and control. If we truly wish to heal our landscapes and the design professions while improving our quality of life, we must not forsake our vulnerability.

SLASH CITY (/CITY)

We might say that Integral Urbanism produces the Slash City (/city) or Slash Architecture (/architecture) because of the hybrid programs (this-slash-that). It is also "slashy" because of the emphasis on the slash itself, the porous membrane, the boundary and its occupation. To slash something implies bringing it together with something else and, thereby, transforming it in some way while also retaining its integrity. In addition to slashing the city, Integral Urbanism is also slashing — or bringing together in new ways — the professions that have divided and subdivided over the last century: architecture, planning, landscape architecture, engineering, interior design, industrial design, graphic design, and so forth. In the process, we are also perhaps slashing some conventional ways of thinking, acting, and building featuring permeable membranes (the slash itself) that become thresholds of diversity (biodiversity, social and cultural diversity, diversity of creative expression, functional diversity, and commercial diversity).[1]

The popular culture trend to "slash" television programs involves rewriting them or writing into them. This literary genre (which appears in "slash zines" and on numerous Web sites) is a subgenre of "fanfic." Writers of fanfic rework primary texts, "repairing or dismissing unsatisfying aspects, developing interests not sufficiently explored."[2] They may do this by recontextualizing (filling in gaps between episodes), altering the historical period or location in which a show takes place, refocusing (shifting attention from main characters to secondary ones), moral realignment (for instance, transforming villains into protagonists), personalization (inserting oneself in the program), emotional intensification, eroticization,[3] genre shifting, and crossing over (combining programs).

Engaging with and rewriting these programs might reflect a desire to engage with and rewrite other conventions of mass culture, a desire to enjoy the offerings of mass culture and not receive them passively. By reworking these, and in the process expressing fantasies while also subverting their messages, subcultures of like-minded people develop, offering mutual validation. Fanfic writers describe their interactivity with and appropriation of television programs as a project of "real-making" of both programs and themselves.

Applied to architecture and urban design, we "slash" the city when we challenge conventions regarding dichotomies and hierarchies and become actively involved in transforming them. We apply similar techniques to those of fanfic writers by rewriting the city and creating intensities in places where they had only been suggested, or were absent, previously. We may do this by filling in gaps (in urban fabrics), "crossing over" or combining programs, and other means. By thus occupying the boundary, we shift from being blasé to feeling, from isolation to integration, realizing both ourselves and the city in the process.

CONCLUSION

We are re-defining the edge and entering a complex world of new paradigms.
A new worldview is forming. At its core is the interconnectedness of sun, sky,
land, you, me, and the myriad creatures and resources of the Earth ... Should
you choose to accept the challenge, architects and designers can be at the
leading edge of positive change.

SUSAN S. SZENASY[1]

CONVERGENCE

The urban and environmental challenges of the last century have led to a
reconsideration of values, goals, and a means of achieving them, particularly
over the last decade. In contrast to the fast-paced more-is-more mentality, the
appeals of simplicity, slowness, spirituality, sincerity, and sustainability are
clearly on the rise. Side by side with the still prevalent reactive tendencies of
form to follow fiction, finesse, finance, and fear, myriad proactive initiatives
from a wide range of participants in shaping the environment are shifting the
paradigm toward integration.

Integral Urbanism runs counter to prevailing urban development
(particularly in the United States) characterized by freestanding single-use
buildings connected by freeways along with rampant (sub)urban sprawl
and the attendant environmental, social, and aesthetic costs. In contrast to
the master-planned functionally-zoned city, which separates, isolates,
alienates, and retreats, Integral Urbanism emphasizes connection, communication, and celebration. While integrating the functions that the modern
city separated, this approach also seeks to integrate conventional notions
of urban, suburban, and rural to produce a new model for the contemporary city. In doing so, it considers the means of integrating design with
nature, the center with the periphery, the process with the product, local

character with global forces, and people of different ethnicities, incomes, ages, and physical abilities.

These various integrations are achieved through hybridity, connectivity, porosity, authenticity, and vulnerability with the goal of achieving flow. *Hybridity* and *connectivity* are about bringing activities and people together at all scales (from local to global). *Porosity* is about the nature of the relationships between these. *Authenticity* is about engaging real social and physical conditions with an ethic of care, respect, and honesty. *Vulnerability* is about relinquishing control while remaining engaged, valuing process as well as product, dynamism, and reintegrating space and time. These qualities describe the approach or attitude of Integral Urbanism as well as the form it takes and the way it is lived.

In contrast to the modern view of space as objective, homogenous, and neutral, Integral Urbanism acknowledges and celebrates subjectivity, heterogeneity, and meaning. It rejects the purely functional (in the mechanistic sense) understanding of architecture and city planning in favor of making places that satisfy other kinds of needs as well.

Integral Urbanism activates places by creating thresholds, or places of intensity, where diversity thrives. Interventions respond to current needs and desires, while also allowing for new ways of being and thinking as people and activities converge. Integral Urbanism allows greater self-determination and empowerment because it offers more opportunities for people to come together and more time and energy to envision better alternatives and to implement them. By enabling efficiencies and synergies, it allows us to move toward greater conservation and less waste, more quality time, and less distrust, paranoia, and fear. Translated into the language of business, greater optimization enhances effectiveness.

Convergences in space and time (of people, activities, businesses, and so forth) generate new hybrids. These hybrids, in turn, allow for new convergences and the process continues. This is, in fact, the definition of development.[2] While the modern paradigm discouraged convergences through its emphasis on separation and control, this new paradigm encourages them. Indeed, the diversity of actors involved in producing this big picture demonstrates the principle of ecodiversity along a threshold of time.

In brief, Integral Urbanism is about:

- Networks not boundaries
- Relationships and connections not isolated objects
- Interdependence not independence or dependence
- Natural and social communities not just individuals
- Transparency or translucency not opacity
- Permeability not walls
- Flux or flow not stasis
- Connections with nature and relinquishing control, not controlling nature
- Catalysts, armatures, frameworks, punctuation marks, not final products, master plans, or utopias

CLEARING BLOCKAGES

Despite the momentum toward integration, there remain numerous obstacles along the course. One of these is the lure of the familiar, even if unsatisfactory. Our tendency to stick with the tried – even when not true – renders change difficult even if the change would be beneficial. Indeed, the decline of meaningful public space along with the narrowly defined identities people have been constructing thanks to information technologies may be contributing to widespread xenophobia[3] leading, in turn, to more privatization, continuing the downward spiral. Combating this fear along with the fear of change, people are joining in large numbers to form powerful, often global, coalitions based on interests and place. These groups include Livable Places, Making Cities Livable, Project for Public Spaces, the Learning Communities Catalyst, and the Slow City Movement (see p. 110), along with a wide array dedicated to sustainability, local enterprise, and social equity.

A deeply engrained source of the problems in our environment and in the architectural profession is the perceived need to protect turf for fear of losing control, jobs, and recognition. This problem is not unique to architects. Attorney John F. Molloy, in his book *The Fraternity* (2004), observes that, "By complicating the law, lawyers have achieved the ultimate job security. Gone are the days when American courts functioned to serve justice simply and swiftly … Surely it's time to question what has happened to our justice system and to wonder if it is possible to return to a system that truly does protect us from wrongs." Though it is a popular pastime in American culture to make jokes at the expense of lawyers, architects have evaded this fate, probably because people are not required to make recourse to architects as they are to lawyers and because most architects do not command the fees of lawyers. The architectural profession has, nonetheless, like the legal one, strayed from its mission. By complicating and isolating the task of providing the best possible physical environments for people in an effort to protect turf, the architectural profession has ironically grown less relevant to the contemporary world than it could – and certainly should – be.[4]

The Modernist emphasis on distilling and separation has influenced the way architects understand and describe their task. Ellen Dunham-Jones observes a tendency among architects to "present [buildings] in terms of professional or theoretical discourse rather than in terms of their participation in a specific urban or regional context." She points out that "Not only does this disengagement reinforce the common perception of architects as elitist, it also guarantees the marginalization of the profession."[5] For the well-being of both the architectural profession and the built environment, this must change. As Vincent Pecora has emphasized, as long as architects insist that economic, political, and social issues are irrelevant, "architecture finally succeeds in making itself irrelevant."[6] The Berlage Institute initiated an International Forum of Architecture and Mediation in 2005 to address this tendency explaining: "Architects are famously unable to communicate, or even to explain themselves. They are myopic, selfish, and arrogant; driven by their own obsessions; megalomaniac; and unequipped to listen to a public that is increasingly eager to talk to them."

Efforts are also being made to correct this isolationist tendency through architectural education. The widely hailed Carnegie Foundation report of 1996 called for more interdisciplinarity as well as a greater symbiosis between school curricula and professional practice.[7] Although resistance to such change is endemic to both academia and the profession, cross-fertilizations are, nonetheless, occurring.[8] In both teaching and practice, attention is being increasingly paid to process as well as product, to human experience and use, and to what has been described as "designing without boundaries,"[9] or rethinking the organization and task of the design professions. Within academia, this is apparent in the rise of Landscape Urbanism programs, the increase in Urban Design programs and transdisciplinary centers devoted to enhancing the environment and quality of life, and the introduction of issues about place and sustainability into curricula.[10] Pedagogy generally is moving to surmount these obstacles; "Instead of a one-way information flow – typified by broadcast TV or a teacher addressing a group of passive students – new teaching techniques are, like the Internet, two-way, collaborative, and interdisciplinary."[11]

In the architectural profession, there has been a clarion call for boundaries to become more porous and statements about variously "integrating" the practice of architecture are ubiquitous. One of these maintains:

> The integrated design process is one in which all technical aspects of a design situation are brought to bear during all stages of the design process from conceptualization of form and systems to realization of the physical, constructed architecture. By definition then, the design process is one in which there is no conceptual separation between notions and propositions of the form of architecture and the performance aspects of its systems – structure, enclosure, mechanical services, and other traditionally "technical" aspects of a building.[12]

Richard Hobbs, vice president of professional practice for the American Institute of Architects (AIA), asserted, "There is an unlimited need for the integrated design approach" involving "the integration of skill sets to achieve an overall goal of integrated design, construction, and operation of a facility." Examples of this "new integrated profession of architecture" are documented in *AIArchitect* as well as *AIAOnline*.

The designer-builder-developer hybrid is increasingly popular as designers take a more proactive and collaborative approach. Another popular practice is the flexible firm that may have only one or several members who take on work of all types and contract the appropriate people for each job, much the way the film industry functions.[13]

In product design:

> Integrated Innovation compels business, design and engineering teams to confront the real challenge facing 21st century product development – namely, to design products that people want and need while, at the same time, creating measurable value in the marketplace, and improving society and the environment.[14]

Integrated Innovation aims toward a more sustainable future through direct interaction with users, market research, sensitive application of technology and materials, and an understanding of relevant social, political, and environmental issues.

These efforts in architecture – as well as other design practices – to become more flexible, responsive, and inter- or transdisciplinary have produced wide-ranging positive results. The task of designing well at the scale of the neighborhood, city, and region, however, remains underserved in the United States since the profession of urban design still lacks a solid academic and professional foundation. As Peter Calthorpe contends:

> There is a profession waiting to be born, that is not a kind of catchall. Sometimes people slip out of architecture and become urban designers, but that's pretty rare because they are so fascinated with the building. Sometimes good landscape designers become urban designers, but they are not trained to. There is a lot of empathy in the planning field, but very little talent or skill for it because they have no design training... We don't have a profession to address these problems in the way they need to be addressed ... There is no profession of urban designers. There is a profession and license for landscape design, for planners, for civil engineers, for traffic engineers but not for the most important profession, urban design ... That's the missing link.[15]

ALIGNMENT

Although there remain social and professional obstacles impeding the flow of integration, we are nonetheless passing through a rare historical moment when urban design theory is fortuitously aligned with political, economic, and social trends. In some cases, these trends have been supporting the propositions set forward by designers, but in other instances, Integral Urbanism is being realized without the input of designers at all. Some of the most powerful trends supporting Integral Urbanism include concern for protection of the environment and the conservation of historic urban fabrics, the rise of regional governments, the renaissance of central cities, the emphasis on bioregions, the growth of regional or metropolitan governments, discussions about "smart growth" and the creation of quality public spaces and public transit, favoring of urban infill, brownfield and grayfield conversions, the revitalization of postwar housing projects, transit-oriented and pedestrian-oriented development, and the exponential growth of neighborhood associations and community gardens along with the important establishment of community land trusts.

After centuries of increasingly dividing labor; cataloguing things and knowledge; segregating the landscape according to function as well as social class, age, and ethnicity; objectifying nature and people and fetishizing objects; we are now witnessing concerted efforts to dealienate by reintegrating these, albeit in a new way. Some of the manifold ways in which this reintegration is apparent are a shift back from monoculture to polyculture and from functional zoning to mixed use, massive restructurings of the labor force (initiated from above as well as below); reenvisioning the purpose and structure of urban institutions such as museums, schools, libraries, and zoos; increased participation in local politics, in urban development, and in what we consume from food, to goods, advertising, and information; and in new collaborations among professions and between the professions and academia.

All of this is occurring, in part, because knowledge has become a more significant commodity than goods. Since knowledge is everywhere and unpredictable, designer Francis Duffy contends,

> ... the *modus operandi* of the Knowledge Economy has to be systemic, open ended, longitudinal, interdisciplinary, creative, dealing as much with values and judgment as with facts. The social conventions, the intellectual disciplines, the technologies, and the environments that the Knowledge Economy demands are certain to be very different from the formulaic and homogenised ways of working that so called "modern" societies have inherited.

With knowledge as the key driver in the information age, people become the most important resource. As Charles Landry emphasizes, "Human cleverness, desires, motivations, imagination and creativity are replacing location, natural resources and market access as urban resources. The creativity of those who live in and run cities will determine future success."[16]

Economic trends associated with this shift to a knowledge economy include e-commerce, partnering, and technological convergences, all translating into greater convenience for consumers and profits for purveyors. From the corporate end, mass customization and the targeting of niche markets (market segmentation) are countering standardization and lack of choice. At the same time, there has been an exponential increase in small independent businesses, a large proportion of which are women- and minority-owned, enabled in large part by the Internet.

This historic moment is rarer still thanks to the conspiring of new technologies. Instead of offering prosthetic devices to combat the natural environment while sometimes alienating us from it, technology is corroborating, elaborating upon, and implementing this new integration. Because refusal to change or adopt new technologies is no longer an option, the question is not whether but how best to proceed. This phenomenon may in itself illustrate the proposition that our universe is self-organizing on ever higher levels.

Parallel developments in astronomy, physics, and the biosciences suggest new ways of conceiving centrality, order, complexity, and chaos. The pursuit of integration is perhaps epitomized by the contemporary search for a "theory of everything" or a coherent cosmology.[17]

These shifts translate into valuing interdependence over independence and challenging other dualisms that characterize the western philosophical tradition such as mind/body, reason/emotion, spirit/flesh, masculine/feminine, and culture/nature.[18] It is a shift from binary oppositions, from a paradigm of competition (win/lose), and from either/or to the slash itself: a paradigm of synthesis (win-win) and integration through interdependence. Interdependence does not mean eliminating boundaries but allowing them to be permeable. Mary Catherine Bateson describes this sensibility saying, "Instead of concentration on a transcendent ideal, sustained attention to diversity and interdependence may offer a different clarity of vision, one that is sensitive to ecological complexity, to the multiple rather than the singular."[19]

Although Integral Urbanism pertains specifically to urban design, its five qualities might effectively apply to governance, homeland security, management, business, education, mediation, technology, the healing arts and sciences, and the other expressive forms of culture. Hybridity, connectivity, porosity, authenticity, and vulnerability might serve as litmus tests and bywords for a wide range of contemporary endeavors. Applied to other realms, these qualities translate into acknowledging the primacy of relationships and process over products (community-, capacity-, and trust-building); regarding organizations as dynamic networks formed of hubs, nodes, and connectors (built-in flexibility with a feedback mechanism); maintaining an ethic of care and respect for people and the environment; and bringing people and other resources together to achieve efficiencies (optimization). Applying these qualities brings a deep shift from competition to synergism (which is different from the kind of collaboration that produces the lowest common denominator).

There are numerous instances where this is occurring. In education, an emphasis on building relationships instead of focusing exclusively on learning outcomes is growing. This is apparent in the widespread development of "learning communities" for all age groups and in efforts to transform urban schools through building strong relationships.[20] Information technologists have been designing "complex adaptive systems," software programmed to build itself through a process that mimics naturally occurring mutation and natural selection.[21] Systems thinking is applied extensively in business and management. Complementary, alternative, integral, and other kinds of holistic healing are widely replacing or joining traditional forms of allopathic medical practices. In the field of psychology, the notion that psychotherapy should protect the separation between an autonomous self and the external world has largely been supplanted by an effort to nurture connectedness. Other arenas still mired in the modern focus on hierarchies, competition, and outcomes could benefit from similar shifts to integration.

Those taking the contemporary world pulse, like Susan Szenasy quoted above, feel the beat of change and transformation. Industrial and software designer Jim Fournier contends that time is (like space) variable and textured and we have arrived at an "inflection point" in time, the point when something changes dramatically.[22] Japanese architect and planner Kisho Kurokawa observes an increasingly symbiotic attitude around the world in shifts toward democracy, the growing emphasis on pluralism and multiculturalism, and especially on interreliance and ecology, a shift he describes as "the symbiosis of diverse species."[23] With regard to shaping our environment, Steven Holl has observed that "paradigm shifts comparable to those of the beginning of the twentieth century seem imminent" because of the electronic connection of "all places and cultures in a continuous time-place fusion" and the simultaneous "uprising of local cultures and expression of place."[24]

We have been coming full circle or, more accurately, full spiral. Learning from the inherent wisdom of nature and of cities and city builders of the past, we are infusing this wisdom with contemporary sensibilities arising from new technologies, expectations, and sensibilities. Rather than choosing to continue or abandon the modern project,[25] our hyperrational reliance upon computer technologies along with the simultaneous revalorization of process, relationships, and complementarity is conspiring to eradicate the either/or proposition. We are doing both simultaneously, each providing feedback for and adjusting the other accordingly, holding potential for achieving integration at another level.

In the process, the modern project is revised, or perhaps supplanted by an integral process. The modern project sought liberation through scientifically and creatively controlling nature and the irrational. The integral process cultivates liberation (from oppression, inequality, ignorance, pain, and discomfort) by understanding our place in nature, including the irrational, and drawing upon science, technology, creativity, and our own deep empathy or greater intelligence in pursuit of the common good, personal fulfillment, and world peace.[26]

As our connections to the environment and other people grow increasingly tenuous – a condition commonly described as the breakdown in community and the family as well as the ecological crisis – efforts to rethink urban design have been seeking to reconnect or provide places allowing connections to occur. Rather than respond to specific problems with piecemeal solutions that only exacerbate the problems or push them elsewhere (reactive solutions), the emphasis on holism and seeing or forging connections at a higher and more complex level is leading to a wide range of proactive interventions.

ACROSS THE FISSURES

The Modern era divided the world and our thinking about it into fragments and our landscape followed. We are suffering the results. To bring it back together, we need to overcome the divisions in our thinking, so we can envision the integration and implement it. Not the way it used to be, but a new integration.

A decade ago, Herbert Muschamp described the "Urban Revisions" exhibition at the Los Angeles Museum of Contemporary Art as "a sprawling mess of undigested ideas." He also remarked, "so is the field of urbanism that it sets out to survey." Muschamp concluded that "If nothing else, the show exposes the need for a new vocabulary of urbanism – a language capable of bridging the differences among those who shape the public realm." He maintained, "if designers want to reinforce the connective tissue of cities, they will have to speak across the fissures that have opened up among themselves."[27]

Integral Urbanism aspires to speak across these fissures. It offers an alternative to the tired and unproductive opposition between radical high designers and traditionalists, whom Robert Campbell calls the "rads" and the "trads":

> The rads and the trads are the same. They're much more like each other than they are different. That's because they both seek to substitute a utopia of another time for the time we actually live in. The trads find utopia in the past; the rads find it in the future … What both the rads and the trads ignore, in their love of utopias of the past and the future, is the present. They both try to elbow aside the real world we live in and substitute a world of another era. It's a lot easier to design a utopia than to deal with the complex reality of a present time and place. You don't have to deal with the tension between memory and invention. You just take one or the other. If you do that, you inevitably create architecture that is thin, bloodless, weak, and boring.[28]

Instead of posing yet another contender for the war-banism, Integral Urbanism draws from the most compelling aspects of all contemporary trends from dirty realism to everyday urbanism, soft urbanism, authentic urbanism, true urbanism, incremental urbanism, her-banism,[29] reurbanism,[30] posturbanism,[31] market urbanism, the New Urbanism, and more. To clearly transmit these keys to best practices, it distills this synthesis into the constituent five qualities. These five qualities offer a harbor or point of departure, like the basic chord structure in jazz from which musicians improvise, or any set of technical skills (artistic, technological, business, sports, culinary, and so forth) essential for generating something of value.

Without shifting into reverse, Integral Urbanism seeks to put a brake on the continual fragmentation of our landscapes and our lives through proactive design solutions. Resolutely refusing to idealize the past or to escape the present, it seeks to mend seams in the urban and social fabrics by acknowledging contemporary challenges and by formulating inspired alternatives for an enriched future.

If our places are to sustain us, they must, of course, offer clean air and water along with other essentials for survival. However, if that is all they offer, we will only survive. Applying the five qualities of Integral Urbanism can offer the soul food necessary for our cities and communities to blossom and truly thrive.

If the 1960s produced the We generation emphasizing peace and love, the 1970s the Me generation emphasizing self-awareness and self-actualization, the 1980s the Whee generation emphasizing materialism and escapism, then the 1990s may have been the Whoa generation, placing a self-imposed brake upon the rapid changes which have been wreaking havoc upon our landscapes and our well-being. This new millennium could — with a clear wide-angled vision and the courage to implement it — spawn the Re-generation. Let us not forsake this opportunity to rebuild our towns and cities, revitalize our communities, restore what has been taken from the earth, and realign design with the goal of supporting humanity.

ILLUSTRATIONS

20. East River Esplanade SHoP Architects, Richard Roger Partnership and Ken Smith. Courtesy of SHoP Architects with permission.
21. Rio Salado Habitat Restoration, City of Phoenix Parks and Recreation with Ten Eyck Landscape Architects.
22. Rio Salado Habitat Restoration, City of Phoenix Parks and Recreation with Ten Eyck Landscape Architects.
23. Portals and Loops, Papago Salado Trail (Phoenix, Scottsdale, Tempe, AZ), Studio Ma. Courtesy of Studio Ma with permission.
24. Shared street at Good Shephard, UACDC. Courtesy of UACDC with permission.
25. V-Mall, SHoP Architects. Courtesy of SHoP Architects with permission.
26. Wal-Mart retrofit, UACDC. Courtesy of UACDC with permission.
27. Wal-Mart ecotones, UACDC. Courtesy of UACDC with permission.
28. Concrete block walls, ASU, Tempe, AZ.
29. Concrete block walls, ASU, Tempe, AZ.
30. Kunsthal, Rotterdam, OMA (Rem Koolhaas).
31. Kunsthal, Rotterdam, OMA (Rem Koolhaas).
32. Public art installation, Seattle.
33. Stone Pavillon, Phoenix Zoo. Swaback Architects.
34. Salt Lake City Public Library, Children's section, Moshe Safdie.
35. Translucent concrete by Bill Price. Courtesy of Bill Price with permission.
36. Translucent concrete by Bill Price. Courtesy of Bill Price with permission.
37. San Jose Hotel, Austin, Lake/Flato Architects.
38. San Jose Hotel, Austin, Lake/Flato Architects.
39. Desert Broom Library, Cave Creek, AZ. Richärd + Bauer. Courtesy of Richärd + Bauer Architecture with permission.
40. Desert Broom Library, Cave Creek, AZ. Richärd + Bauer (2005). Courtesy of Richärd + Bauer Architecture with permission.
41. Papago Arroyo Wildlife Corridor Restoration for Sunstate Builders implemented under the City of Tempe's Art in Public Development (AIPD) mandate by Laurie Lundquist. Courtesy of Laurie Lundquist with permission.
42. Papago Arroyo Wildlife Corridor, Laurie Lundquist. Courtesy of Laurie Lundquist with permission.
43. Dia Beacon pervious paving, Beacon, NY, Robert Irwin.
44. Waterfire panorama, Providence, Rhode Island, Barnaby Evans. Courtesy of Barnaby Evans with permission.
45. Waterfire stokers of fires, Providence, Rhode Island, Barnaby Evans. Courtesy of Barnaby Evans with permission.
46. Target, Albany, RSP. Courtesy of RSP with permission.
47. Target, Minneapolis, RSP. Courtesy of RSP with permission.
48. Blur Building, Diller + Scofidio. Courtesy of Diller + Scofidio with permission.
49. Blur Building, Diller + Scofidio. Courtesy of Diller + Scofidio with permission.

50. Petrosino Park model, Pollak and Marpillero. Courtesy of Pollak and Marpillero with permission.
51. Cool Connectors, Dan Hoffman. Courtesy of Dan Hoffman with permission.
52. Les Figures, Jouy-le-Moutier, France, Jean-Paul Girardot.

ADDITIONAL ILLUSTRATIONS IN PRÉCIS

x-xi Hybridity: Left: (Untitled) courtesy of Mike Berkow with permission. Top Right: courtesy of ImageAfter.com. Small image L to R: (Blur) courtesy of Theodora Ballew, (Stairs) courtesy of Mahesh Senagala, (Outdoor children's section of Phoenix Central Library designed by Will Bruder Architects) courtesy of Nan Ellin.

xii-xiii Connectivity: Top Left: courtesy of ImageAfter.com. Bottom Left: ("Amonia Blue") courtesy of Toni Gentilli with permission. Top Right: (Esplanade) courtesy of SHoPArchitects with permission. Small images L to R: (Blurs) courtesy of Theodora Ballew with permission, (Kite) courtesy of Mahesh Senagala with permission.

xiv-xv Flow: (Untitled) Courtesy of Mike Berkow with permission.

xvi-xvii Patterns: Top Left: (Blur) courtesy of Theodora Ballew. Bottom Left: courtesy of ImgeAfter.com. Top Right: (Primary School Children School Playground) courtesy of Adobe Stock Photos. Small images L to R: (Sculptured House 1, 2) courtesy of Sherab Koppenburg with permission, (Sculptured House 3) courtesy of Paul Norquist with permission.

xviii-xix Convergence: Bottom Left: (Highway 9B) courtesy of UACDC with permission. Top Right: (Phoenix Central Library) courtesy of Will Bruder Architects with permission. Bottom Right: (Untitled) courtesy of Mike Berkow with permission. Small images L to R: (Phoenix Central Library 1, 2, 3) courtesy of Will Bruder Architects with permission, (Lights) courtesy of Mahesh Senagala with permission, (Phoenix Central Library 4) courtesy of Will Bruder Architects with permission.

xx-xxi Porosity: Top Far Left: (Sand being sifted through hands) courtesy Adobe Stock Photos. Top Near Left: courtesy of Ellin. Bottom Left: courtesy of Ellin. Top Right: courtesy of ImageAfter.com. Small images L to R: (South Mountain Community College by Jones Studio, San Jose Hotel by Lake/Flato Architects, Kunstahl by OMA, Public Art Seattle, James Hotel by Deborah Berke Architects) courtesy of Ellin, (Sculptured House 4) courtesy of Paul Norquist, (Ten Eyck Office) courtesy of Ellin.

xxii-xxiii Authenticity: Top Left and Right: (The Hague Square) courtesy of Ellin. (All small images) courtesy of ImageAfter.com.

xxiv-xxv Vulnerability: Bottom Left: (Ecotone Matrix) by UACDC, courtesy of UACDC with permission. Top Right: (Untitled) courtesy of Mike Berkow with permission. Mid Right: ("Asphalt") courtesy of Toni Gentilli with permission. Small

Images L to R: (Leaf) courtesy of ImageAfter.com, (City View Marker) courtesy of Barbara Ambach with permission, (Rope) courtesy of Mahesh Senagala with permission, (Phoenix Central Library) designed by Bruder and Burnette, courtesy of Ellin, (Nautilus) courtesy of ImageAfter.com.

xxvi-xxvii Integration: Top Left: (Steps) courtesy of Mahesh Senagala with permission. Top Right: ("Cienfuegos") by José Parla, courtesy of José Parla with permission.

xxviii ("Love") by José Parla, courtesy of José Parla with permission.

OTHER ILLUSTRATIONS

All unattributed illustrations courtesy of Nan Ellin.

NOTES

PREFACE

1. Max Weber, *The Protestant Ethic and the Spirit of Capitalism* (New York: Penguin, 2002) (1st edition 1905).

INTRODUCTION

1. This phrase, "more from less," first applied by Buckminster Fuller, is now finding a much broader constituency, e.g., Ian Ritchie.

2. Some Modernists, particularly those described by Lefaivre as the "postwar humanist rebellion," also understood functionalism with more subtlety. Josep Lluis Sert, for instance, maintained, "We should understand that functionalism does not necessarily mean that only the functional has a right to exist: The superfluous is part of our system — it is as old as man" (Lefaivre, 1989). About contemporary understandings of function, Susan Yelevich, assistant director of Cooper Hewitt Design Museum, suggests that "Functionality has become more dimensional. Function now embraces psychology and emotion." (cited by Frank Gibney, Jr., and Belinda Luscombe. "The Redesigning of America," in *Time*, March 20, 2000, 70). Describing his own shift from 1930 to 1998, Philip Johnson recounts that in 1930, Alfred Barr's (of MoMA) attitude toward art and his own "came from rational, Cartesian, enlightenment thinking, and especially from Plato. Alfred's foreword to 'Machine Art' quoted Plato: 'By beauty of shapes I do not mean, as most people would suppose, the beauty of living figures or of pictures, but, to make my point clear, I mean straight lines and circles, and shapes, plane or solid, made from them by lathe, ruler and square. These are not, like other things, beautiful relatively, but always and absolutely...' What Alfred Barr and I did not know at that time was that our belief in absolute functionalism was subjective — all in our minds. In the same way, when I built the glass house in 1949, I accepted that glass could be the savior material for mankind. But we can change our minds. That's reality. Neither Mies van der Rohe nor Alfred would have believed that. The Weltanschauung has shifted from Platonic absolutism to a more relativist position, in art as in other disciplines. Architecture and design are inevitably affected by such change. I have changed." (Philip Johnson, "How the Architectural Giant Decided that Form Trumps Function," *New York Times Magazine*, December 13, 1998, 77–78).

3. Michael Hough, *Cities and Natural Process* (New York: Routledge, 1995), 6.

4. Ken Wilbur, *A Brief History of Everything* (Boston: Shambhala, 2000). Here I cite the 1996 edition.

5. Beck's work [Don E. Beck, *Spiral Dynamics: Mastering Values, Leadership, and Change* (Malden, MA: Blackwell, 1996)] is based on Clare Graves' "value systems" theory of human development. Beck and Wilbur have joined forces to form SDi (Spiral Dynamics integral).

WHAT IS INTEGRAL URBANISM?

1. Spiro Kostof, *The City Assembled* (London: Thames & Hudson, 1992), 305.

2. Mihaly Csikszentmihalyi, *Flow: The Psychology of Optimal Experience* (New York: HarperPerennial, 1990).

3. In landscape ecology, these are described as disturbances: "Disturbances tend to stimulate innovations. More broadly, disturbances stimulate ecological and human adaptations. Species without adaptations, and people that are not sufficiently adaptive, are apt to be bypassed by others in the long run … External and internal changes are the norm, and therefore, a key attribute of a sustainable environment is adaptability, a pliable capacity permitting a system to become modified in response to disturbance" [Richard T. T. Forman, *Land Mosaics: The Ecology of Landscapes and Regions* (New York: Cambridge University Press, 1995), 502, 504].

4. Applying psychological concepts to the city recalls the city as organism metaphor that was predominant until the early decades of the twentieth century when it was superceded by the predominant machine metaphor [see Nan Ellin, *Postmodern Urbanism, Revised Edition* (New York: Princeton Architectural Press, 1999) (1st edition 1996), Ch. 8].

FIVE QUALITIES OF AN INTEGRAL URBANISM

1. Jane Jacobs, *The Death and Life of Great American Cities* (New York: Vantage, 1961).

2. Spretnak, *States of Grace* (New York: HarperCollins, 1991), 135.

3. Ibid., 260.

4. Ibid., 260–61.

5. Ibid., 219.

6. Spretnak, *States of Grace* (New York: HarperCollins, 1991), 19.

7. Ibid., 4.

8. Barbara Crisp, *Human Spaces* (Gloucester, MA: Rockport Publishers, 1998), 6.

9. Sim Van Der Ryn and Sterling Bunnell, "Integral Design," in *Theories and Manifestoes of Contemporary Architecture,* ed. Charles Jencks and Karl Kropf (London: Academy Editions, 1997).

10. Jane Jacobs, *The Nature of Economies* (New York: Modern Libraries, 2000) and Janine M. Benyus, *Biomimicry: Innovation Inspired by Nature,* (New York: Perennial, 1998).

11. James Wines, John Todd, and others share this view, which evolved from earlier discussions of Aldo Leopold (1949), Ian McHarg (1968), Gregory Bateson (ecology of mind), Charles and Ray Eames (powers of 10), E. F. Schumacher (1973), Ivan Illich, Murray Bookchin, and others. It is also an extension of Jane Jacobs's understanding of the city as a "problem of organized complexity" (Jacobs, *The Death and Life of Great American Cities*) as well as Robert Venturi's discussion about complexity [Robert Venturi, *Complexity and Contradiction in Architecture* (New York: Museum of Modern Art, 1966). Buckminster Fuller, whose motto was "We can't put it together; it is together," emulated nature with the geometry of synergetics using octet trusses and geodesic domes with intelligent membranes that are self-correcting and can change their properties as conditions change. Calling for integration of people and the city through understanding natural processes, Frei Otto contends: "The youngest ecological system within evolution is the big human city which has probably never been genuinely healthy since it came into existence. Not blind conservation of nature, but integration of the natural individual into his environment, into the world in which he lives, is our new task. And this means achieving greater knowledge of the natural processes which lead to the forms of objects which, in turn, form the overall picture of nature" [Frei Otto, "The New Plurality in Architecture," in *On Architecture, the City, and Technology,* ed. Marc Angelil (London, Butterworth Architecture, 1990), 14]. In architecture specifically, there is a long tradition of seeking inspiration from nature: Frank

Lloyd Wright's organic architecture; Bruno Zevi's "Towards an Organic Architecture" (1945), which regarded the organic as a social ideal; Kenzo Tange and the Metabolists; and Richard Neutra's "Human Settings in an Industrial Civilization" (1958) on "bio-realism." Although emphasizing formal attributes and individual buildings, these sometimes included larger processes and sites.

12. In nature, scientists Tilman and McCann, in separate articles, have confirmed that the stability of an ecosystem is directly related to species richness.

13. Biochemist John Todd advocates such living machines and along with ecological designer Jay Baldwin, he created a house with its own metabolism.

14. Carl Steinitz, "What Can We Do?," *Harvard Design Magazine* 18 (Spring/Summer 2003).

15. Ken Yeang, *The Green Skyscraper* (New York: Prestel, 1999), 38.

16. Yeang, *The Green Skyscraper*, 57. Yeang also writes: "Maintaining the integrity of the web of species, functions, and processes within an ecosystem and the webs that connect different systems is critical for ensuring stability and resilience. As ecosystems become simplified and their webs become disconnected, they become more fragile and vulnerable to catastrophic, irreversible decline" (36). "Ecological design must seek to repair and restore ecosystems" (38). "Ecological design seeks a symbiosis between manmade systems and natural systems" (38). "In the long term, it must be acknowledged that at the global and national level, changes in the economic, social and political systems based on holistic ecological principles are crucial if the objectives of a sustainable future for mankind are to be met" (35). We "can define ecological design as the prudent management of the holistic connections of energy and materials used in the built system with the ecosystems and natural resources in the biosphere, in tandem with a concerted effort to reduce the detrimental impact of this management, thus achieving a positive integration of built and natural environments. In addition, we need to ensure that this endeavor is not a once-only effort; the interactions of building and nature have to be monitored and managed dynamically over time" (57).

17. Cultural theorist Catherine Roach, for example, argues "against the idea that nature and culture are dualistic and opposing concepts," suggesting that this idea is "environmentally unsound and [needs] to be biodegraded, or rendered less harmful to the environment" (1996, 53). The common colloquialism "it's second nature" bespeaks an understanding that we are a part of nature.

18. Nicolas Wade, "Life's Origins Get Murkier and Messier." *New York Times*, June 13, 2000.

19. Dennis Overbye, "The Cosmos According to Darwin." *New York Times Magazine,* July 17, 1997.

20. John R. Logan and Todd Swanstrom, eds. *Beyond the City Limits* (Philadelphia: Temple University, 1990), 21.

21. Rachel Sara, "The Pink Book," EAAE Prize (2001–2002), 130. She also writes: "There is a new epoch dawning for the architectural profession. The present model values competition, isolation, the individual, esoteric professional knowledge bases, and singular, one-size-fits-all education paths. But this model is now seen to be problematic. Current literature all points in the same direction: architecture needs to give voice to 'other'; to value collaboration, compromise and communication, team-working and co-operation and new models of teaching and learning; to re-position process and product, re-emphasize context, and erode the myth of the genius" (130).

22. Alison Dunn and Jim Beach, personal communication.

23. James Stewart Polshek, "Built for Substance, Not Flash," *New York Times,* January 22, 2001. I have suggested that we call this valuing of the feminine in architecture and urban planning "her-banism."

24. According to Kenda, The Renaissance doctrine of anima mundi understood there to be a soul in nature and all else, as described particularly by Pico della Mirandola, Marsilio Ficino, and Lorenzo di Medici. The city should therefore breathe (it has pneuma). Feng shui and renaissance views both emphasize that the life force should be liberated in building. [Barbara Kenda, "On the Renaissance Art of Well-Being: Pneuma in Villa Eolia." *Res* 34 (Autumn 1998), 109–11].

25. Metabolist Kiyonori Kikutake explained that "contemporary architecture must be metabolic. With the static theory of unsophisticated functionalism, it is impossible to discover functional changes. In order to reflect dynamic reality … we must stop thinking about function and form, and think instead in terms of space and changeable function … unity of human space and of service functions … to serve free human living" [cited by Alexander Tzonis and Liane Lefaivre. "Beyond Monuments, Beyond Zip-a-ton." *Le Carré Bleu* 3–4 (1999): 4–44].

26. Dennis Crompton wrote, "The city is a living organism, it divides and multiplies" (in "City Synthesis," 1964, cited by Tzonis and Lefaivre, "Beyond Monuments," 1999).

27. Advanced by British biologist James Lovelock in 1969.

28. Inspired by the theoretical contributions of Gilles Deleuze (on "le pli"), examples are found in the work of Daniel Libeskind, Greg Lynn, Jeffrey Kipnis, Zaha Hadid, the Ocean Group, and Dagmar Richter.

29. Fritjof Capra describes this "paradigm shift" in *The Web of Life* (New York: Anchor, 1997).

30. Jacobs, *The Nature of Economies*.

31. These were talks given in 1985–86.

32. Italo Calvino, *Six Memos for the Next Millennium* (New York: Vintage, 1988), 51.

33. Kelbaugh advances yet another formulation of five, suggesting that repairing the American metropolis should focus on place (local inspiration, not imitation); nature (biomimicry); history (successful typologies); craft (detail, craftsmanship, quality of construction); and limits (scale and boundaries) [Douglas Kelbaugh, *Repairing the American Metropolis* (Seattle: University of Washington, 2002)].

34. Anita Berrizbeitia and Linda Pollak, *Inside Outside: Between Architecture and Landscape* (Gloucester, MA: Rockport, 1999).

35. Jonathan Barnett, *Redesigning Cities* (Chicago: American Planning Association, 2003).

36. I borrow this phrase from designer Shashi Caan who maintains that live theory "is about deeply thinking, re-assessing and setting forth ideas that are pertinent to our current cultural milieu" in contrast to theory that may be less directly relevant to contemporary issues. I believe that ideas do not exist in isolation from people but are developed by people and transmitted among people through a wide range of communication channels from speaking to writing, singing, painting, dancing, the Internet, and many more. Our attitudes toward the ideas we receive grow from these contexts, and we proceed to appropriate the ideas and retransmit them and so forth. Ideas thus circulate the globe and are passed down through time, inextricably intertwined with the people who shape and communicate them. In other words, live theory is lived.

HYBRIDITY & CONNECTIVITY

1. "Megalopolitan development" is Ken Frampton's term.

2. As architect Vernon Swaback explains, "Starting in the 1960s, suburban developments began to associate separation with the creation of value. We created stratified housing projects, some of which have been abandoned, and we created office parks and big box shopping centers. Everything was put neatly in its place. For the future, a far more complex integration of uses will be necessary to create sustainable value. The urban fabric will become not only more efficient, but more alive. It is another opportunity to do more with less" [Vernon Swaback, *Designing the Future* (Tempe, AZ: Herberger Center for Design Excellence, 1996), 92].

3. Forman, *Land Mosaics*, 515.

4. Jacobs, *Death and Life*, 241.

5. Ibid., 150–51. Robert Venturi was another early proponent of hybridity, stating "I like elements that are hybrid rather than 'pure'" (*Complexity and Contradiction in Architecture*, 1966), but he was more interested in buildings than the city as a whole.

6. See Ellin, *Postmodern Urbanism*, 1999.

7. The Modernist drive to cleanly and neatly separate the world may have underlain and been a reaction to actual hybridization, particularly cultural hybridization, which is the thesis of Patricia Morton's *Hybrid Modernities* (Cambridge, MA: MIT Press, 2003). While claiming authenticity, accuracy, and objectivity as well as the separation of France from its colonies, Morton proposes that the 1931 International Colonial Exposition in Paris exhibition actually demonstrated their intense cross-fertilization from expressive forms of culture to lifestyle and more.

8. Hybridization, Steven Holl contends, "would be a general consequence in seeking a new unity of dissociated elements in architecture" and it would fuse "the worlds of flow and difference" (Holl Web site).

9. Rem Koolhaas, "The Generic City," in *SMLXL* (New York: Monacelli, 1996), 1254.

10. Ibid. Koolhaas describes the Singapore model in terms of "thematic intensification," as soft authoritarian control and freedom with urban form or organization, taking programming to its limits.

11. Koolhaas, "Bigness: or the Problem of Large" in *SMLXL*.

12. Marc Angelil and Anna Klingmann, "Hybrid Morphologies: Infrastructure, Architecture, Landscape," *Daidalos* 73 (1999): 24.

13. Roger Trancik, *Finding Lost Space* (New York: Van Nostrand Reinhold, 1986), 220.

14. Robert Putnam, *Bowling Alone* (New York: Simon and Schuster, 2000), 93.

15. Fred Kent, "Great Public Spaces by Project for Public Spaces — Instructive Lessons from Here and Abroad," project for *Public Spaces Newsletter* (2005).

16. The acronym cc has a double entendre: Children's Center or cubic centimeters.

17. Where does the New Urbanism fit into this? While taking a step toward integration, it only steps forward if this integration acknowledges contemporary needs and tastes.

18. Ellen Dunham-Jones, "Seventy-Five Percent," *Harvard Design Magazine* (Fall 2000): 10.

19. E.g., Northrup Commons over a medical center and Macadam Village over grocery store (both in Portland), Tribeca over a Safeway in Seattle.

20. http://www.transcond.com/us_pavilion/biennale2004/bien_yu.html.

21. Kenneth Frampton, "Toward an Urban Landscape," in *Columbia Documents for Architecture and Theory: D4* (New York: Columbia University Press, 1995).

22. Dunham-Jones, "Seventy-Five Percent." 6.

23. Due to home shopping and big-box stores, it is predicted that 20 percent of the existing shopping malls from 1990 will be out of business by the end of 2000. Some of these are being retrofitted such as a Pasadena mall dating from the 1960s, which will have small shops at the ground level and four hundred "lofts" above them. In Los Angeles (Fairfax and 3rd), a mall of discount stores has been replaced by small shops, cafes, and more than six hundred condos. Other mall conversions include Aventura Town Center (2003) where Loehmann's Fashion Square in Aventura, Florida added 655 condos (which all sold in one day!), a ten-story office tower, pedestrian arcades lined with restaurants and shops, and a piazza; Village of Merrick Park and Douglas Grand in Coral Gables, Florida; the Downtown Wisconsin Rapids conversion of an abandoned Wal-Mart into retail space, a Montessori school, a senior center, a hospital clinic, and community access television; the Glendale Shopping Center in Bayshore, Wisconsin, conversion of a 1950s strip mall into a "town center" using ecological design principles; Freestate Mall in Bowie, Maryland (by Oxford Development); Paseo Colorado in Pasadena, California; and Santana Row in San Jose. See "Greyfields into Goldfields: Dead Malls become Living Neighborhoods" by Lee Sobel et al.; "Sprawl and Public Space: Redressing the Mall" by National Endowment for the Arts; www.icsc.org; and www.deadmalls.com.

24. Supporting efforts to revitalize older suburbs, groups have emerged such as the Michigan Suburbs Alliance (MSA). MSA has already drafted standards and lobbied the U.S. Congress. In addition to its own team of real estate professionals, it partners with Michigan State University whose grad

students get assigned to specific communities to provide planning studies and develop urban design solutions, http://www.michigansa.org/redev.htm. In addition, incentives have been offered, such as New Jersey's seed money "for the establishment of a town center within a community that has no such center and no distinct identity at present" in Dunham-Jones (2000: 12). See Dirk Johnson, "Town Sired by Autos Seeks Soul Downtown," *New York Times*, August 7, 1996.

25. Herbert Muschamp, "The Polyglot Metropolis and Its Discontents," *New York Times*, July 3, 1994.

26. Elaine Heumann Gurian, "Function Follows Form: How Mixed-Used Spaces in Museums Build Community," *Curator* 44 (1) (2001): 87–113.

27. Lewis Mumford, *The City in History* (New York: Harcourt Brace Jovanovich, 1961). Michael Speaks describes this potential saying, "Somewhere between the besieged territories of urbanism and the immense arteries and non civic territories of the conurbation lay the hunting grounds for another urbanism. It is here that we find the most maddening sedimentations of power disguised as power-lessness, and the most exciting collection of possibilities disguised as impossibilities. Between the clear-cut territories of the refinery and the middle class neighborhood lay areas that do not derive their logic and filling from one single authority or owner but from the fact that they are filled to the brim with political, functional, and physical leftovers of the city" [Michael Speaks, "Big Soft Orange," in *Archi-ecture of the Borderlands,* ed. Cruz and Boddington (New York: John Wiley & Sons, 1999), 90–92].

28. Elizabeth A. T. Smith, comp., *Urban Revisions: Current Projects for the Public Realm* (Cambridge, MA: MIT Press, 1994), 6.

29. *Arizona Republic*, December 26, 2001.

30. The Silverleaf Club was designed by Don Ziebell of Oz Architects.

31. Jacobs coined this phrase in *The Death and Life of Great American Cities*.

32. In a *New Yorker* essay, Malcolm Gladwell noted similarities between these new workspaces and the organic urban vitality theories of Jane Jacobs.

33. The TBWA\Chiat\Day offices were designed by Clive Wilkinson Architects.

34. See, e.g., Frances Anderton "'Virtual Officing' Comes In from the Cold" in *New York Times*, December 17, 1998.

35. Richard Florida, *The Rise of the Creative Class* (New York: Basic Books, 2002), 122.

36. Other office furniture companies followed suit with Steelcase producing Personal Harbors (late 1990s), Blue Space (developed with IBM), and Knoll producing the A3.

37. The Mainspring squash court/conference room was designed by Beth Katz and Robert Caulfield of Visnick and Caulfield (Boston).

38. Smith, *Urban Revisions*, 14.

39. Mark Lee, "The Dutch Savannah: Approaches to Topological Landscape," *Daidalos* 73 (1999): 13–14. Lee explains, "This involves the production of an artificial terrain where the flowing, contin-uous, pliant space of landscape is constantly calibrated by the definitive, enclosing qualities intrinsic to architectural spaces" (10).

40. *Encyclopedia Brita*nnica, www.eb.com.

41. Marion Roberts, et al., "Place and Space in the Networked City: Conceptualizing the Integrated Metropolis," *Journal of Urban Design* 4 (1) (1999): 52. They maintain that urban design and city management should support such "networks of movement and communication … paying particu-lar attention to the nodal connections" (51).

42. Ibid., 63.

43. Ibid., 52.

44. Ibid., 62.

45. Ibid., 64. These views are similar to the Dutch authorities' urban hierarchy proposal and to Friends of the Earth (1994) document Planning for the Planet.

46. This proposal vindicates the findings of Kevin Lynch in *The Image of the City* (Cambridge, MA: MIT Press, 1960) that paths, nodes, districts, landmarks, and edges are the organizing principles of our mental maps. The most significant of these, Lynch found, is usually paths. Second in importance is the place where paths intersect, or nodes, to create points of intensity or convergence. Charles Moore and Donlyn Lyndon, in *Chambers for a Memory Palace* (Cambridge, MA: MIT Press, 1996), maintain that the art of successful place-making relies upon "axes that reach/paths that wander."

47. See Ellin, *Postmodern Urbanism*, 1999.

48. Calthorpe in Douglas Kelbaugh, series ed., *Michigan Debates on Urbanism I, II, and III: Everyday Urbanism (Margaret Crawford v. Michael Speaks)*, ed. Rahul Mehrotra, *New Urbanism (Peter Calthorpe v. Lars Lerup)* ed. Robert Fishman, *Post Urbanism and ReUrbanism (Peter Eisenman v. Barbara Littenberg and Steven Peterson)*, ed. Roy Strickland (Ann Arbor: University of Michigan Press, 2005), 36.

49. Ibid.

50. Peter Calthorpe, William Fulton, and Robert Fishman, *The Regional City: Planning for the End of Sprawl* (Washington, D.C.: Island Press, 2001).

51. For less salutary impacts of "bundling" networks of infrastructures together at large scales, particularly social polarization, see Stephen Graham and Simon Martin, *Splintering Urbanism* (New York: Routledge, 2001).

52. www.doa.state.wi.us/olis.

53. Neil Peirce, "Megalopolis has Come of Age," *Arizona Republic*, July 29, 2005.

54. Peter Katz, "Form First: The New Urbanist Alternative to Conventional Zoning," *Planning* (November 2004).

55. This occurred in Contra Costa County, California, where Geoffrey Ferrell developed a FBC in 2001 for a $200 million mixed-use development.

56. Governor Schwarzenegger signed Assembly Bill 1268 facilitating form-based development in the state. This bill reads, "The text and diagrams in the land use element [of the general plan] that address the location and extent of land uses, and the zoning ordinances that implement these provisions, may also express community intentions regarding urban form and design. These expressions may differentiate neighborhoods, districts, and corridors, provide for a mixture of land uses and housing types within each, and provide specific measures for regulating relationships between buildings and outdoor public areas, including streets" (cited by Katz, "Form First").

57. Muschamp, "The Polyglot Metropolis."

58. *PPS Newsletter*, November 2004.

59. Peter Lindwall, "Impact of the Strand on the Townsville Community," *Queensland Planner* 44 (2) (2004): 18–19.

60. Peter V. McAvoy, Mary Beth Driscoll, and Benjamin J. Gramling, "Integrating the Environment, the Economy, and Community Health: A Community Health Center's Initiative to Link Health Benefits to Smart Growth," *American Journal of Public Health* 94 (2) (2004): 525–27.

61. Smith, *Urban Revisions*, 7.

62. Nicolai Ouroussoff, "Sobering Plans for Jets Stadium," *New York Times*, November 1, 2004.

63. The High Line is scheduled to open in Fall 2007.

64. SHoP architects is a partnership of William Sharples, Coren Sharples, Chris Sharples, Kimberly Holden, and Gregg Pasquarelli.

65. Nicolai Ouroussoff, "Making the Brutal F.D.R. Unsentimentally Humane," *New York Times*, June 28, 2005.

66. Alex Wall, "Programming the Urban Surface," in *Recovering Landscape*, ed. James Corner (New York: Princeton Architectural Press, 1999), 234.

67. Ben Van Berkel and Caroline Bos, "Rethinking Urban Organization: The 6th Nota of the Netherlands," *Hunch 1 — The Berlage Institute Report 1998/1999* (Rotterdam: Berlage Institute, 1999), 73.

68. Herbert Muschamp, "Woman of Steel," *New York Times*, March 28, 2004.

69. See www.maricopa.gov/parks and www.valleyforward.org.

70. The Rio Salado Habitat Restoration project along with the Rio Oeste extension was undertaken by the Phoenix Parks and Recreation Department with Ten Eyck Landscape Architects.

71. The team contributing to the Papago Salado Trail proposal includes Christopher Alt, Dan Hoffman, Christiana Moss, Michael Boucher, Laurie Lundquist, B. J. Krivanek, Nancy Dalett, Harvey Bryan, and consulting engineers at Entellus.

72. Whereas Jonathan Bell uses "car-chitecture" to demonstrate the impact of actual car design on the design of buildings and cities [Jonathan Bell, *Carchitecture* (Cambridge, MA: Birkhauser Boston, 2001)], I use it somewhat differently to describe the rethinking of architecture and urban design to incorporate car spaces.

73. See Ben Hamilton-Baillie, "Home Zones, Reconciling People, Places and Transport : A Study Tour of Denmark, Germany, Sweden and The Netherlands," http://www.gsd.harvard.edu/professional/ loeb_fellowship/sponsored_sites/home_zones/index.html.

74. As Kathryn Milun writes, "These are zones of urban life where walking sets the pace for an awareness of surroundings whose most significant orienting device comes not from rational planning which seeks to segregate and control from the top down, nor from commercial directives which overwhelm the senses, but from the individual's participation in an open yet small-scale community that can still surprise the self" [Kathryn Milun, *Pathologies of Modern Space* (New York: Routledge, forthcoming)].

75. Wall, "Programming the Urban Space," 242; Berrizbeitia and Pollak, *Inside Outside.*

76. Rather than describe the contemporary period as post-industrial, sociologist Manuel Castells identifies a restructuring in the 1980s to "informational capitalism" or "informationalism," a global economy dependent upon technological development, which in turn depends on knowledge [Manuel Castells, *The Rise of the Network City*, (Cambridge, MA: Blackwell, 2000); Manuel Castells, *The Network Society*, (North Hampton, MA: Edward Elgar Publishing, 2004]. Replacing hierarchical and bounded models of the industrial society, this informational one is not bounded in time or space and follows a "new spatial logic" characterized by networks. He calls this the "space of flows" (*The Rise of the Network City*, 408).

77. George Johnson, "First Cells, Then Species, Now the Web," *New York Times*, December 26, 2000.

78. *Six Degrees of Separation* was based on a 1998 article by Duncan Watts and Steven Strogatz who looked at the nervous system, the power station web forming the electrical grid, and the social web of actors.

79. The "rich get richer" effect was proposed by Albert-Lazlo Barabasi and Reka Albert, *Science* 286, (1999).

80. G. Johnson, "First Cells."

81. Hillier and Penn describe a "movement economy" in cities, characterized by a network of origins and destinations (cited in Roberts, et al., "Place and Space").

82. Describing the importance of flows in the urban network, Van Berkel and Bos contend: "The contemporary urban network is a material organization of time-sharing social practices that work through flows. Flows are sequences of exchange and interaction in the economic, political, and symbolic structures of society. The space of flows is made up of specific, localized networks that link up with global networks" ("Rethinking Urban Organization," 73).

83. Undercurrent stabilization has been successfully applied to restore the shoreline at Najmah Beach in Saudi Arabia.

84. As Jim Fournier has pointed out, when we build things that approach the elegance of nature, such as photovoltaics, they can stick around for a long time (1999).

85. According to Larry Santoyo, "Permaculture is the art and science that applies patterns found in nature to the design and construction of human and natural environments. Only by applying such patterns and principles to the built environment can we truly achieve a sustainable living system. Permaculture principles are now being adapted to all systems and disciplines that human settlement requires. Architects, planners, farmers, economists, social scientists, as well as students, homeowners and backyard gardeners can utilize principles of Permaculture Design" (http://www.bfi.org/ Trimtab/ spring02/permaculture.htm).

86. See Ellin, *Postmodern Urbanism*, Ch. 8.

87. Or perhaps not so ironic. The originator of the modern computer, Charles Babbage, believed that such technological advances provided "some of the strongest arguments in favor of religion" and David F. Noble, in *The Religion of Technology* points out that the technological enterprise has always been "an essentially religious endeavor" (both cited by Edward Rothstein in "The New Prophet of a Techno Faith Rich in Profits," *New York Times*, September 23, 2000).

88. Expressing this shift from the ideal and static to the diverse and dynamic, Hani Rashid and Lise Ann Couture (Studio Asymptote) included a video in their installation at the Venice Biennale (2000) of a moving person vis-à-vis the still Vitruvian Man who was the classical measure of all things. A Platonic figure inscribed inside a perfect square and a perfect circle, the Vitruvian Man was placed on land and aligned with cardinal points to create colonial towns in the United States.

89. Italo Calvino, *Invisible Cities* (New York: Harvest/Harcourt Brace Jovanovich, 1978).

90. Saskia Sassen, *Cities in a World Economy* (Thousand Oaks, CA: Pine Forge Press, 1994); Saskia Sassen, *The Global City* (Princeton, NJ: Princeton University Press, 2001).

91. Trancik, *Finding Lost Space*, 219–34.

92. Stan Allen, "Logistical Activities Zone: Users' Manual," stanallenarchitect.com.

93. According to Allen, "The variables in organizational diagrams include formal and programmatic configurations: space and event, force and resistance, density, distribution and direction. Organization always implies both program and its distribution in space, bypassing conventional dichotomies of function vs. form or form vs. content … Unlike classical theories based on imitation, diagrams do not map or represent already existing objects or systems but anticipate new organizations and specify yet to be realized relationships. They are not simply a reduction from an existing order; their abstraction is work as 'abstract machines' and do not resemble what they produce." Regarding the score, Allen explains: "The score is not a work itself, but a set of instructions for performing a work. A score cannot be a private language. It works instrumentally to coordinate the actions of multiple performers who collectively produce the work as event. As a model for operating in the city, the collective character of notation is highly suggestive. Going beyond transgression and cross-programming, notations could function to map the complex and indeterminate theater of everyday life in the city. The use of notation might provoke a shift from the production of space to the performance of space" (Web site).

94. Jusuck Koh, "Success Strategies for Architects through Cultural Changes Leading into the Post-Industrial Age," in *Environmental Change/Social Change, Proceedings of 16th EDRA Conference*, ed. S. Klein, R. Wener and S. Lehman (Washington, D.C.: EDRA, 1985), 13.

95. Use of the term smooth is a reference to Gilles Deleuze and Felix Guattari, *A Thousand Plateaus* (Minneapolis, MN: University of Minnesota Press, 1980), implying that the space connects differences and is ever changing.

96. Rem Koolhaas, "Pearl River Delta, The City of Exacerbated Difference" in *Politics-Poetics Documenta X — the Book*, ed. Jean-François Chevrier (Kassel, Germany: Verlag, 1997).

97. SCAPE Web site: www.kostudio.com.

98. www.uacdc.uark.edu.

99. See Alison Smithson's essay "Mat Buildings" in *Case: Le Corbusier's Venice Hospital and the Mat Building Revival* (Case Series), ed. Hashim Sarkis, Pablo Allard, and Timothy Hyde (New York:

Prestel Publishing, 2002). Le Corbusier's Venice Hospital was designed "to extend the city's roads and canal networks, while simultaneously turning in on itself to create flexible, quasi-urban interior environments in the form of endlessly repeating courtyards." The Team 10 diagrams can be understood more as representations of process rather than urban. Their approaches shared a search for patterns of "association," the network of human relations.

100. As Jonathan Barnett points out, these efforts, such as the Mechanic Theatre district in Baltimore, offered examples of cross programming, but turned their backs to existing city by suppressing streets and creating superblocks with a public plaza in the interior, accessed primarily via underground parking structures.

101. Josep Lluis Sert is often considered to be the person who coined the term "urban design" and he created the first degree program in urban design in 1959 at Harvard University.

102. Lewis Mumford, *The Culture of Cities* (New York: Harcourt Brace and Co., 1938).

103. Angelil and Klingmann, "Hybrid Morphologies," 21–22.

104. Gerrit Confurius, "Editorial," *Daidalos* 72 (1999): 4.

105. Wall, "Programming in Urban Surface," 235.

106. Alexander Tzonis, "Pikionis and the Transvisibility," *Thresholds* 19 (1999): 15–21. Doxiadis was a student of Pikionis.

107. Tzonis and Lefaivre trace this to the Bible. They also remind us that "Artists, architects and urbanists have for a long time sought to capture movement within the spatial framework of design. One approach to achieving this has been to emphasize the expressive visual-spatial qualities of the design object, arranging its masses in controlled disequilibrium so as to anticipate a future state. (Elsewhere, in relation to the work of Santiago Calatrava, we have called this the 'aesthetics of the pregnant moment.' Prior to the Second World War the word used to describe this strategy was 'plasticity,' relating the iconic likeness of the artefact to an organism which moves or grows" ("Beyond Monuments," 1999).

108. Tzonis, "Pikionis and the Transvisibility," 1999.

109. Liane Lefaivre, "Critical Domesticity in the 1960s: An Interview with Mary Otis Stevens," *Thresholds* 19 (1999): 22–26. Stevens explains, "We were interested in how it allowed growth and change and variation. We designed the building from the inside out ... It was the result of a process, not the application of preset notions."

110. All from Tzonis and Lefaivre, "Beyond Monuments," 1999.

111. Tzonis and Lefaivre, "Beyond Monuments," 1999.

112. Ibid. Woods advocated "the creation of environment at every scale of human association" appropriate for a "society ... entirely new ... a completely open, non-hierarchical co-operative in which we all share on a basis of total participation and complete confidence" (Tzonis and Lefaivre, "Beyond Monuments," 1999). He tried to accomplish this in the new town prototype he designed with Candilis and Josic.

POROSITY

1. Roland Barthes defines "readerly" texts as quick easy reads versus "writerly" texts that conceal and reveal and are, therefore, more satisfying. See *The Pleasure of the Text (1975, translated by Richard Miller, NY: Hill and Want* and *S/Z (1970, Paris: Editions du Seuil).*

2. For Herbert Muschamp, the veil has become a prevalent graphic device in contemporary design, symbolizing the contemporary condition between the industrial and information ages. As a subset of translucency, as I'm conceiving it, the veil, according to Muschamp, "conveys the conflicting desire to conceal and reveal." "Shadow, translucency, reflection, refraction, dappling, stippling, blurring, shimmering, vibration, moiré, netting, layering, superimposition: these are some of the

visual devices used to render the veil in contemporary design. Recent examples include the Apple G4 Power cube; shadow niches in the walls of the British architect John Pawson; the spring 2001 collection by the fashion designer Helmut Lang; curtains by the Dutch designer Petra Blaisse; a new book Life Style by the Canadian graphics designer Bruce Mau" (Herbert Muschamp, "A Happy, Scary New Day for Design," *New York Times*, October 15, 2000). In architecture, Muschamp contends "Modulating the visual texture of glass with reflectivity, fretted patterns, screened-on images, blurring, veiling, coloration, support systems and other techniques, these projects summon forth states of narcissism, exhibitionism, voyeurism, veiling, vamping, elusiveness, disconsolation, Hitchcock's blonde" (Herbert Muschamp, "Architectural Trendsetter Seduces Historic Soho," *New York Times*, April 11, 2001).

3. Ken Shulman, "X-Ray Architecture," *Metropolis* (April 2001).

4. As Hartman explains, "The translucent blocks are made by mixing glass fibers into the combination of crushed stone, cement and water, varying a process that has been used for centuries to produce a versatile building material ... Load-bearing structures can also be built from the blocks as glass fibers do not have a negative effect on the well-known high compressive strength of concrete. The blocks can be produced in various sizes with embedded heat isolation too." These walls of light-transmitting concrete can be very thick since the fibers work without any loss in light up to 20 meters, according to Losonczi. (Carl Hartman, "Seeing the Future of Construction through Translucent Concrete," Associated Press, July 8, 2004.)

5. Robert Scully, "Systems of Organized Complexity," *Arcade* 21 (4) (Summer 2003).

6. Herbert Muschamp, "Forget the Shoes, Prada's New Store Stocks Ideas." *New York Times*, December 16, 2001.

7. Seventy percent of the world's drylands are degraded or desertified. Desertification results from loss of biodiversity and productivity due to unsustainable human activities (overcultivation, overgrazing, deforestation, and poor irrigation practice) or climate change.

8. Calthorpe, Fulton, and Fishman, *The Regional City*; Patrick Condon, presentation at "Urbanisms: New and Other," University of California at Berkeley, 2001.

9. Kenneth Frampton, *Modern Architecture: A Critical History* (London: Thames and Hudson, 1985) (1st edition, 1980).

10. Mark Wexler, "Money Does Grow on Trees — And So Does Better Health and Happiness," *National Wildlife* (April–May 1998): 70.

11. Ian McHarg, *Design with Nature* (Garden City, NY: Natural History Press, 1969).

12. http://www.communityschools.org.

13. For instance, a planning exercise in Los Angeles hosted by Livable Places (2004) envisioned a new high school and middle school combined with a mix of housing, parks, and other civic/community uses.

14. James Traub, "This Campus Is Being Simulated," *New York Times*, November 19, 2000.

15. Cited in Christopher Hawthorne, "Captain Koolhaas Sails the New Prada Flagship," *New York Times*, July 15, 2004.

16. Rowe and Slutsky's phenomenal transparency might fall into the category of symbolic porosity, though they were referring specifically to the scale of buildings, not the urban scale. Phenomenal transparency produces an experiential tension by implying depth and inciting the viewer to perceive places simultaneously and to mentally reconstruct, e.g., the layered facades of Le Corbusier's villas.

17. Julie V. Iovine, "An Avant-Garde Design for a New-Media Center," *New York Times*, March 21, 2002.

18. Forman, *Land Mosaics*, 84.

19. Jacques Derrida, *The Truth in Painting* (Chicago: University of Chicago Press, 1987).

20. In mathematics, there is a class of propositions considered to be independent because they can neither be proved true nor false.

21. This quest for separateness was one offshoot of the "project of modernity" (coined by Jurgens Habermas) that emerged during the Enlightenment and grew dominant throughout the Western world. This project sought to discover that which is universal and eternal through the scientific method and human creativity, in order to dominate natural forces and, thereby, liberate people from the irrational and arbitrary ways of religion, superstition and our own human nature [David Harvey, *The Condition of Postmodernity* (Malden, MA: Blackwell, 1989), 12–13]. See Ellin, *Postmodern Urbanism*, 125.

22. Spretnak, *The Resurgence of the Real*, 77.

23. See Ellin, *Postmodern Urbanism*, Ch. 8; Nestor Garcia Canclini and Silvia Lopez, Hybrid Cultures (1995); Robert J. C. Young, *Colonial Desire: Hybridity in Theory, Culture and Race* (1995); Ruth Behar and Deborah Gordon, eds. *Women Writing Culture* (1995); and Anna Lowenhaupt Tsing, *In the Realm of the Diamond Queen* (Princeton, NJ: Princeton University Press, 1992). Cultural theorist Homi Bhaba introduced the term "the third space" [Homi Bhaba, *The Location of Culture* (New York: Routledge, 1994)] to describe people located between or among cultural identities. This "third space," according to Bhaba, is emancipating in that cultural meanings "can be appropriated, translated, rehistoricised and read anew." While emphasizing the possibilities generated by the new hybrids, others suggest that pluralism and multiculturalism may not be emancipating, e.g., AlSayyad's "third place" [Nezar AlSayyad, *Hybrid Urbanism: On the Identity Discourse and the Built Environment* (Westport, CT: Greenwood, 2001)]. As a method, George E. Marcus recommends "multi-sited ethnography" [George E. Marcus, *Ethnography through Thick and Thin* (Princeton, NJ: Princeton University Press, 1998)]. See also Artur Aldama on "cultural hybridity" and Daniel Arreola on "border cities."

24. Anna Lowenhaupt Tsing, *In the Realm of the Diamond Queen*, 37.

25. Michel Serres, *The Natural Contract*, trans. E. MacArthur and W. Paulson (Ann Arbor, MI: University of Michigan, 1995).

26. Renato Rosaldo, *Culture and Truth* (New York: Beacon, 1989), 208.

27. bell hooks, "Choosing the Margin," in *Yearning* (Toronto: Between-the-Lines, 1990), 152.

28. German sociologist Ulrich Beck raises similar issues in his discussions of "second modernity" and "reflexive modernity" [Ulrich Beck, *Risk Society: Towards a New Modernity*, Trans. Mark Ritter (London: Sage Publications, 1992) (1st edition, 1986); Ulrich Beck, Wolfgang Bonss, and Christoph Lau, "The Theory of Reflexive Modernization," *Theory Culture & Society*, 20 (2) (April 2003): 1–34].

29. Frampton, *Modern Architecture*, 327.

30. Frampton, "Toward an Urban Landscape," 91.

31. Richard Sennett, "The Powers of the Eye," in *Urban Revisions: Current Projects for the Public Realm*, comp. Elizabeth A. T. Smith (Cambridge, MA: MIT Press, 1994), 59–69.

32. This attention to the edge has nothing to do with the building of "edge cities," which instead of breaking down barriers, create new ones.

33. Deleuze and Guattari, *A Thousand Plateaus* and *Anti-Oedipus*.

34. From *Anti-Oedipus*.

35. Charlene Spretnak (*States of Grace*. New York: HarperCollins, 1991), 19–20.

36. Cited in Michael Kimmelman, "Interview with Howard Gardner," *New York Times*, February 14, 1999.

37. Arthur Erickson, "Shaping," in *The City as Dwelling*, ed. Arthur Erickson, William H. Whyte, and James Hillman (Dallas: Dallas Institute of Humanities and Culture, 1980): 23, emphasis mine.

38. Quantum mechanics, developed during the first half of the twentieth century by Einstein and others, produced a revolution in thinking about cosmology, from a cause and effect machinelike universe to an understanding that all things are related and interconnected.

39. Manuel De Landa, *One Thousand Years of Nonlinear History* (New York: Zone Books, 1998).

40. Steven Johnson, *Emergence: The Connected Lives of Ants, Brains, Cities and Software* (New York: Penguin, 2001).

41. Among urban developers, this threat to previously clear boundaries has incited an anxious effort to obscure "an increasingly pervasive pattern of hierarchical relationships among people and order-ings of city space" with "a cloak of calculated randomness," as demonstrated by the plan to revital-ize New York City's Times Square [Peter Marcuse, "Not Chaos, But Walls: Postmodernism and the Partitioned City," in *Postmodern Cities and Spaces*, ed. Sophie Watson and Katherine Gibson (Oxford, UK: Blackwell, 1995), p. 243]. Among the public at large, a reflex has been the atavistic marking of one's turf with walls, gates, and prohibitions, lending a new and eerie resonance to Max Weber's "iron cage" metaphor (*The Protestant Ethic and the Spirit of Capitalism*). These are both clearly reactive responses.

42. Steven Holl, for instance, asserts: "A new architecture must be formed that is simultaneously aligned with transcultural continuity and with the poetic expression of individual situations and communities. Expanding toward an ultra-modern world of flow while condensed into a box of shadows on a particular site, this architecture attempts William Blake's, 'to see the universe in a grain of sand.' The poetic illumination of unique qualities, individual culture and individual spirit reciprocally connects the transcultural, transhistorical present" (Web site).

43. See Ellin, *Postmodern Urbanism*, Ch. 7.

44. Project for Public Spaces, "Letter to the *New York Times*," July 2004.

45. Heidegger (1971: 356), originally delivered to a group of architects after the Second World War.

46. Jacobs and Appleyard, 114.

47. Gordon Cullen, *The Concise Townscape* (New York: Reinhold, 1961).

48. "Postwar humanist rebellion" is Tzonis and Lefaivre's term ("Beyond Monuments").

49. Bakema (1946), cited in Tzonis and Lefaivre, "Beyond Monuments."

50. At a 1955 CIAM gathering, cited in Tzonis and Lefaivre, "Beyond Monuments."

51. See Ellin, *Postmodern Urbanism*.

52. Paralleling the shift from "ego boundaries" in understanding ourselves, this concept of the urban boundary as connector rather than divider, as the place where relationships take place, is variously articulated. For landscape architect James Corner, "rather than separating boundaries, borders are dynamic membranes through which interactions and diverse transformations occur. In ecological terms, the edge is always the most lively and rich place because it is where the occupants and forces of one system meet and interact with those from another." Corner's method of "field operations," his alternative to the master plan "enable alternative ideas and effects to be played out through con-ventional filters" and provide "ways in which borders (and differences) may be respected and sus-tained, while potentially productive forces on either side may be brought together into newly created relationships. Thus, we shift from a world of stable geometric boundaries and distinctions to one of multidimensional transference and network effects" [James Corner, "Field Operations," in *Architecture of the Borderlands*, AD 69, ed. Teddy Cruz and Anne Boddington (New York: John Wiley & Sons, 1999), 53–55].

53. Angelil and Klingmann, "Hybrid Morphologies," 24.

54. Pollak maintains: "Conceiving of landscape as layers rather than an unbroken surface supports the construction of an urban landscape as an overlay of scales that is understood in section as well as plan and in time as well as space. Cutting through multiple layers of urban information supports a project whose formal result is not a stylistic signature, but an intersection of concerns, intensities and modes of inhabitation," [Linda Pollak, "City-Architecture-Landscape: Strategies for Building City Landscape," *Daidalos* (1999): 48–59].

55. Berrizbeitia and Pollak, *Inside Outside*.

56. Allen Web site. Allen elaborates: "Its primary modes of operation are: 1. The division, allocation and construction of surfaces; 2. The provision of services to support future programs; 3. The establishment of networks for movement, communication and exchange … Infrastructures allow detailed design of typical elements or repetitive structures, facilitating an architectural approach to urbanism. Instead of moving always down in scale from the general to the specific, infrastructural design begins with the precise delineation of specific systems within specific limits. Unlike other models (planning codes or typological norms for example) that tend to schematize and regulate architectural form, and work by prohibition, the limits to architectural design in infrastructural complexes are technical and instrumental."

57. Ibid. Allen elaborates: "Although static in and of themselves, infrastructures organize and manage complex systems of flow, movement and exchange. Not only do they provide a network of pathways, they also work through systems of locks, gates and valves — a series of checks that control and regulate flow … Infrastructural systems work like artificial ecologies. They manage the flows of energy and resources on a site, and direct the density and distribution of habitat. They create the conditions necessary to respond to incremental adjustments in resource availability, and modify status of inhabitation in response to changing environmental conditions … In infrastructural urbanism, form matters, but more for what it can do than for what it looks like."

58. In 1997, Charles Waldheim mounted a Landscape Urbanism exhibition and launched a Landscape Urbanism program at University of Illinois in Chicago. The description of this program reads: "Dialectical oppositions of city and nature are critiqued in favor of an understanding of both 'natural' and 'built' environments as networks of socially constructed and culturally relative representations." Landscape Urbanism programs have also been developed at Notre Dame University and the Architectural Association (London). Issues of *Daidalos* 73 (1999), "Landscapes," *Praxis* 4 (2002), and *Architectural Design* (March/April 2004) have been devoted to this topic.

59. As Graham Shane recounts, "Landscape ecology grew up as an adjunct of land planning in Germany and Holland after the Second World War, reaching America only in the 1980s … In America during the 1990s, European land management principles merged with post-Darwinian research on island biogeography and diversity to create a systematic methodology for studying ecological flows, local biospheres, and plant and species migrations conditioned by shifting climatic and environmental factors (including human settlements). Computer modeling, Geographic Information Systems, and satellite photography formed a part of this research into the patches of order and patterns of "disturbances" (hurricanes, droughts, floods, fires, ice ages) that help create the heterogeneity of the American landscape" [Graham Shane, "The Emergence of 'Landscape Urbanism," *Harvard Design Review* 19 (Fall 2003/Winter 2004): 13–20].

60. Many aspects of landscape ecology have been adopted and adapted to urban design. Drawing from Forman's *Land Mosaics*, these include the notion that "Like all living systems (those containing life), the landscape exhibits structure, function, and change" (5). Adopted words and phrases include *corridor*, a strip of a particular type that differs from the adjacent land on both sides that may serve as conduit, barrier, or habitat (38) and *boundary*, a zone composed of the edges of adjacent ecosystems (85). In contrast to the gradient, an *ecotone* features a "sharp change in species distributions, or a congruity in the distributional limits of species. Species present in an ecotone are intermixed subsets of the adjacent communities." (85). The portion of an ecosystem near its perimeter where influences of the surroundings prevent development of interior environmental conditions is an *edge*. An edge effect refers to the distinctive species composition or abundance in this outer portion. Forman distinguishes edge, boundary, and ecotone, saying: "Each landscape element contains an edge, the outer area exhibiting the edge effect, i.e., dominated by species found only or predominantly near the border [which is] the line separating the edges of adjacent landscape elements. The two edges combined compose the boundary or boundary zone. When species distributions within the boundary zone change progressively or from side to side, analogous to a compressed gradient, this describes an

ecotone" (85). The word *connectivity* is defined in landscape ecology as a measure of how connected or spatially continuous a corridor, network, or matrix is. The fewer gaps, the higher the connectivity. Functional or behavioral connectivity refers to how connected an area is for a process, such as an animal moving through different types of landscape elements. A *matrix* is the background ecosystem or land-use type in a mosaic, characterized by extensive cover, high connectivity, or major control over dynamics. *Mosaic* refers to the spatial heterogeneity found at all spatial scales from submicroscopic to the planet and universe. Land mosaics are at the human scale: landscapes, regions, and continents. Mosaics are patterns of patches, corridors, and matrix, each composed of small similar aggregated objects, forming distinct boundaries. Without energy input, a landscape becomes disorganized (second law of thermodynamics). But thanks to solar energy, land is always organized by spatial heterogeneity of different adaptive land forms. It may consist entirely of patches or of patches and corridors, but not of only corridors. The alternative to a mosaic is a *gradient*, where there is gradual variation over space in the objects present with no boundaries, patches or corridors, as in a rainforest. But this is rare (pp. 4 and 38). A *network* is an interconnected system of corridors. *Patch*: "an ecologically optimum patch shape usually has a large core with some curvilinear boundaries and narrow lobes, and depends on orientation angle relative to surrounding flows" (515). *Nodes* are patches attached to corridors. *Sustainability* is the condition of maintaining ecological integrity and basic human needs over human generations.

61. James Corner, "Highline/Fresh Kills and Other Projects," in *Landscape Urbanism* (Institute of Urban Design, New York, 2004).

62. Jacques Derrida, *Margins of Philosophy*, trans. A. Bass (London: Harvester Press, 1982), 14 (1st edition, 1972).

63. See Capra, *The Web of Life*, and Center of Ecoliterary Web site.

64. Preface to *Obra poetica* (Emece Editores, 1989).

65. Josef Albers, *Interaction of Color* (New Haven: Yale University Press, 1975) (1st edition, 1963).

66. Karsten Harries, *The Ethical Function of Architecture* (Cambridge, MA: MIT Press, 1998).

67. See Ellin, *Architecture of Fear.*

68. Lars Lerup, *After the City* (Cambridge, MA: MIT Press, 2000).

69. Charles Landry, *The Creative City* (London: Earthscan, 2000).

70. Louis Sullivan's "form follows function" (1896) seems to be widely interpreted instrumentally although it appears he understood function more subjectively. For Sullivan, form was the language or means to express the infinite creative spirit.

71. Paul Lewis, Marc Tsurumaki, and David J. Lewis. *Situation Normal*, Pamphlet Architecture 21 (New York: Princeton Architectural Press, 1998), 12–13.

AUTHENTICITY

1. Pico Iyer has described the cosmopolitan as follows: "Seasoned experts at dispassion, we are less good at involvement, or suspension of disbelief … We are masters of the aerial perspective, but touching down becomes more difficult." ("Nowhere Man: Confessions of a Perpetual Foreigner" Utne Reader May-June 1997, 78–9.)

2. This is the subject of my book *Postmodern Urbanism*.

3. Ellin, *Postmodern Urbanism*.

4. Ibid.

5. Jay Walljasper, *Project for Public Spaces Newsletter*, September 2004.

6. Ellin, *Postmodern Urbanism*.

7. This is the subject of Ellin, *Architecture of Fear.*

8. Neil Peirce, "Neighborhoods Closing Doors," *Washington Post Writers Group*, July 15, 2005.

9. Ralph Rugoff, "L.A.'s New Car-tography," *LA Weekly,* October 6, 1995.

10. Herbert Muschamp, "You Say You Want an Evolution? OK, Then Tweak," *New York Times,* April 13, 2004.

11. This symposium took place in Savannah, Georgia.

12. Spretnak, *The Resurgence of the Real.*

13. See, e.g., Ada Louise Huxtable, *The Unreal America: Architecture and Illusion* (New York: Penguin, 1997) and Neil Leach, *The Anaesthetics of Architecture* (Cambridge, MA: MIT Press, 1999).

14. Rem Koolhaas, "Bigness: or the Problem of Large" in *SMLXL.*

15. Liane Lefaivre, "Dirty Realism in European Architecture Today," *Design Book Review* 17 (Winter 1989): 18.

16. Lewis, Tsurumaki, and Lewis (Situation Normal, 8). They apply Michel de Certeau's idea of tactics from *The Practice of Everyday Life* (1970s), which "turn the logic of the strategy against itself within the space established by that strategy" (5), i.e., they conspire with reality.

17. Deborah Berke, "Thoughts on the Everyday," in *Architecture of the Everyday,* ed. Steven Harris and Berke (New York: Princeton Architectural Press, 1997), 226.

18. In Kelbaugh, *Michigan Debates on Urbanism I,* 36.

19. A point made by Robert Fishman in Kelbaugh, *Michigan Debates on Urbanism.*

20. See definition of live theory in Rem Koolhaas, "Bigness: or the Problem of Large" in *SMLXL.*

21. When municipalities create Tax Increment Financing Districts, they can retain a portion of property or sales tax (or both) from new development within that district for a predetermined number of years and use this revenue for new development in the district.

22. Eames's *Powers of 10* documentary (1977) powerfully demonstrated the relation between everyday picnics and cosmic mystery.

23. See Ellin, *Postmodern Urbanism,* 126–29.

24. B. Joseph Pine, II, and James H. Gilmore, *The Experience Economy: Work Is Theatre and Every Business a Stage* (Cambridge, MA: Harvard Business School, 1999).

25. Robert Jay Lifton, *The Protean Self: Human Resilience in an Age of Fragmentation* (Chicago: University of Chicago Press, 1993), 1.

26. David Whyte, *Crossing the Unknown Sea: Work as a Pilgrimage of Identity* (New York: Penguin, 2002), 24–25.

27. Psychologist Alice Miller contends that such self-deception has dangerous social implications saying, "Individuals who do not want to know their own truth collude in denial with society as a whole, looking for a common 'enemy' on whom to act out their repressed rage." She maintains, "The future of our democracy and democratic freedom depends on our capacity to … recognize that it is simply impossible to struggle successfully against hatred outside ourselves, while ignoring its messages within … *Consciously experiencing our legitimate emotions is liberating,* not just because of the discharge of long-held tensions in the body but above all because it opens our eyes to reality (both past and present) and frees us of lies and illusions" [Alice Miller, *The Drama of the Gifted Child: The Search for the True Self* (New York: Basic Books, 1997), 114–16 (1st edition 1979)].

28. Cited by Liane Lefaivre and Alexander Tzonis, *Aldo van Eyck Humanist Rebel.*

29. Città Slow or the Slow City Movement grew out of and extends the Slow Food movement (in reaction to "fast food") both starting in Italy. A Cittaslow is one where there is a desire to implement an environmental policy that nurtures the distinctive features of that town or city and its surrounding area, and focuses on recycling and recovery; put in place infrastructure that will make environmentally friendly use of land, rather than just put up buildings on it; encourage the use of technology that will improve the quality of air and life in the city; support the production and consumption of organic foodstuffs; eschew genetically modified products; put in place mechanisms to help manufacturers of distinctive local produce that get into financial difficulty; protect and promote products

that have their roots in tradition; reflect a local way of doing things; help to make that particular area what it is; facilitate more direct contact between consumers and quality producers through the provision of designated areas and times for them to come together; remove any physical obstructions or cultural obstacles that might prevent full enjoyment of all that the town has to offer; make sure that all inhabitants — not just those involved in the tourist trade — are aware of the fact that this is a Cittaslow, focusing particularly on the next generation by encouraging learning about food and where it comes from; encourage a spirit of genuine hospitality toward guests of the town. The Mayor of Oriveto, Stefano Cimichchi, is president of the Slow City movement. In Italy, eighteen towns and cities have been certified as Città Slow and many others are awaiting certification. See http://www.cittaslow.net/world/ and www.cittaslow.com.

30. Carl Honoré, *In Praise of Slowness* (New York: HarperCollins, 2004): 146. For more on slowness and simplicity, see Ellin, *Postmodern Urbanism*, 1–2.

31. Berlage Institute, "What Will the Architect Enact Tomorrow?" *Public Events* (Autumn 2002/03).

32. For example, University of Pennsylvania's PennDesign and ASU's College of Design.

33. Landry, *The Creative City*, 7.

34. Spacecity listserv, 2005, space-city-events@space-city.net.

35. Albert Borgmann, *Crossing the Postmodern Divide* (Chicago: University of Chicago Press, 1993), 119–20. He also refers to "eloquent reality": "On the other side of hyperreality and its supporting mechanical and marginal reality lies eloquent reality. It speaks in its own right and in many voices. It speaks in asides and in sermons. At times it troubles and threatens, at other times it consoles and inspires. An approximate and familiar appellation for 'eloquent' is 'natural' or 'traditional.' Premodern reality was entirely natural and traditional, and typically it was locally bounded, cosmically centered, and divinely constituted. Postmodern reality is natural and traditional only in places where hyperreality and its mechanical supports have left openings. On closer inspection, the line between hyperreality and eloquent reality turns out to be heavily reticulated. Hyperreality is like a thickening network that overlies and obscures the underlying natural and traditional reality … There are yet generous openings for eloquent reality" (119).

36. Neil Everden in *The Natural Alien: Humankind and the Environment* (1985), cited by Dennis Doordan, "Simulated Seas: Exhibition Design in Contemporary Aquariums," *Design Issues* 11 (2) (Summer 1995).

37. Architect Dennis Doordan attempts to enable this experience through design.

38. Spretnak suggests turning to wisdom traditions such as Buddhism, Native American spirituality, Goddess spirituality, and the Semitic traditions, which can "help us to nourish wonder and hence to appreciate difference, the unique subjectivity of every being and community, thereby subverting the flattening process of mass culture. Such awareness keeps hope alive. It protects consciousness from becoming so beaten down that it loses a grasp of what is worth fighting to defend" (Spretnak, *States of Grace*, 223).

39. Angeles Arrien, *The Four-Fold Way* (San Francisco: Harper, 1993).

40. Beatley offers numerous suggestions for reconnecting with places and people including natural guidebooks offered to new residents, place-based celebrations and art, and neighborhood tool banks [Timothy Beatley, *From Native to Nowhere: Sustaining Home and Community in a Global Age* (Washington, D.C.: Island Press, 2004)].

VULNERABILITY

1. Le Corbusier's "*machines à habiter.*"

2. See page 2 about Louis Sullivan's true meaning of "form follows function." There were exceptions over the last century found, for instance, in the work of Aldo Van Eyck, Constantinos Doxiadis,

Shadrach Woods, and the Situationists. See Lefaivre and Tzonis, *Aldo van Eyck Humanist Rebel* "Beyond Monuments," and Tzonis, "Pikionis and the Transvisibilty."

3. Pat Morton explains in "Getting the 'Master' Out of the Master Plan" [*Los Angeles Forum of Architecture and Urban Design* (October 1994): 2]: "The 'Master Plan' is designed by a 'master,' always a male in the canonical conception of the phrase, who single-handedly envisions a brave new world, conceived in largely formal terms that can be uniformly applied to all sectors of the city. The masculinist construction of urban design as the production of a solitary genius is embedded in this phrase. There are many problems with this conception of planning. First, the Master Plan presupposes that a city can be designed like a building; that is, that urban forms are equivalent to architectural form, on a larger scale. Second, the Master Plan presumes that a single person or group of people can produce forms that anticipate or allow for the city's future and meet the needs of its inhabitants. And, last, the Master Plan is predicated on the idea that the city must be controlled in this overarching manner, that overall urban planning is necessary both to solve the city's problems and to provide for its future." Kathryn Milun reminds us that we were warned over one century ago by George Simmel that "the metropolitan citizen's need to make rationality the dominant approach to all social encounters in public space would produce its own pathology" (manuscript of Milun).

4. Jusuck Koh also emphasizes the importance of process and complementarity in design [Jusuck Koh, "Ecological Reasoning and Architectural Imagination," Inaugural Address, Wageningen University, The Netherlands, November 11, 2004].

5. Kostof, *The City Assembled*, 305.

6. Shadrach Woods (1964), cited by Tzonis and Lefaivre, "Beyond Monuments."

7. Noriaki Kurokawa (1964), cited by Tzonis and Lefaivre, "Beyond Monuments."

8. The ecological threshold as metaphor for urban interventions has been suggested by Sennett ("The Powers of the Eye," 69), Berrizbeitia and Pollak, and Corner, among others.

9. The Project for Public Spaces articulates this attitude saying: "instead of approaching the city through the lens of a complex, heavy-handed one-size-fits-all master plan, we should view it as an agglomeration of neighborhoods, each of which contains key places that can have a substantial impact in improving quality of life" (*Project for Public Spaces Newsletter*, November 2004).

10. Bruce Mau, "An Incomplete Manifesto for Growth," *I.D.* (March/April 1999).

11. This point is eloquently made by Milun in *Pathologies of Modern Space*.

12. Cited by Milun, from "Preface" to Roger Friedland and Deirdre Boden, eds., *Nowhere: Space, Time, and Modernity (University of California, 1994).*

13. Space-time as a single entity developed as a twentieth-century modern concept (in physics), with points of space-time referred to as "events." Tschumi was referring to this at La Villette with his "evenements."

14. See, e.g., the work of Linda Pollak, Mark Angelil and Anna Klingmann, Raoul Buschoten, Winy Maas of MVRDV, Ben van Berkel and Caroline Vos, and Rem Koolhaas. Describing this shift to viewing places dynamically, Alex Wall says, "familiar urban typologies of square, park, district, and so on are of less use or significance than are the infrastructures, network flows, ambiguous spaces, and other polymorphous conditions that constitute the contemporary metropolis" (Wall, "Programming the Urban Space").

15. Van Berkel and Bos, "Rethinking Urban Organization," 73.

16. Allen Web site.

17. Holl Web site.

18. Koh, "Success Strategies for Architects," 14.

19. Koolhaas, "Whatever Happened to Urbanism?" *SMLXL*, 969.

20. Deleuze and Guattari, *A Thousand Plateaus*.

21. Ignasi de Sola Morales describes "urban acupuncture" as catalytic small-scale interventions that are realizable within a relatively short period of time and capable of achieving maximum impact on

immediate surroundings [Kenneth Frampton, "Seven Points for the Millenium: An Untimely Manifesto," *Architectural Record* (August 1999): 15].

22. Tom Wiscombe, "The Haptic Morphology of Tentacles," in *BorderLine,* ed. Woods and Rehfeld (Austria: Springer-Verlag/Wien and RIEAeuropa, 1998).

23. This distinction resembles those made by Deleuze and Guattari (*A Thousand Plateaus*) between "striated" and "smooth" or "molar" and "molecular" lines.

24. Thomas Moore, *Care of the Soul* (New York: HarperCollins, 1992), 247.

25. Moore, *Care of the Soul,* 92, 94, 235, 246–47.

26. Richard Ingersoll, "Landscapegoat," in *Architecture of Fear,* ed. Nan Ellin (New York: Princeton Architectural Press, 1997), 253–59.

27. Tadao Ando (1991) acceptance speech for Arnold W. Brunner Memorial Prize.

28. Yoshio Taniguchi cited by Suzannah Lessard, in *New York Times Magazine* April 12, 1998.

29. David Pearson, *New Organic Architecture* (London: Gaia Books, 2001). A charter for organic architecture and design proposed by David Pearson holds that it should be inspired by nature and sustainable, healthy, conserving, and diverse; unfold, like an organism, from the seed within; follow flows and be flexible and adaptable; satisfy social, physical, and spiritual needs; "grow out of the site" and be unique; celebrate the spirit of youth, play, and surprise; and express the rhythm of music and the power of dance.

30. Jim Fournier, "Meta-Nature," Fournier Web site, 1999.

31. Christopher Alexander, *A New Theory of Urban Design* (New York: Oxford University Press, 1987).

32. De Sola-Morales's "urban acupuncture" is referred to by Frampton, "Seven Points for the Millenium."

33. See Bernard Tschumi, *Architecture and Disjunction* (New York: Princeton Architectural Press, 1994).

34. Speaks, "Big Soft Orange." The compilation *Breathing Cities* profiles architectural practices engaged in designing for dynamism, sometimes regarding the city as a living and breathing organism [Nick Barley, ed., *Breathing Cities: The Architecture of Movement* (Cambridge, MA: Birkhauser, 2000)].

35. See Bart Lootsma, *SuperDutch* (New York: Princeton Architectural Press, 2000).

36. Speaks, "Big Soft Orange," 92.

37. Ruby.

38. Andreas Ruby, "The Scene of the Scenario," *hunch* 8 (2004): 95–96.

39. This paragraph draws from Ruby, "The Scene of the Scenario." Summarizing Bunschoten and students' approach, Ruby says, "They use a descriptive parameter of the existing situation for the latter's future transformation."

40. See Nan Ellin, "In Search of a Usable Past: Urban Design and Society in a French New Town" (Ph.D. dissertation, Columbia University, 1994).

41. Kathryn Milun (acknowledging Leonie Sandercock) maintains: "Instead of managing fear as urban reformers have for the past century and a half, since Haussmann, by rendering the city transparent and orderly, creating parks and playgrounds and other 'civilizing urban facilities' (as if by controlling space we could control the subjectivities produced in that space), these critics propose a 'therapeutic approach' (in the psychoanalytic sense of creating a dialogue) wherein a city planner begins by acquiring a deep understanding of the cultural differences that are behind projections of urban fears. The therapeutic approach asks the urban planner to work as an anthropologist would, hanging out, talking with people and generally studying the cultural differences that have provoked fear in dominant groups and anger, mistrust and misunderstanding among minority groups. With the aim of enabling cross-cultural understanding, the city planner then creates safe spaces for antagonistic parties (the 'strangers' and the dominant others) to discuss their concerns and negotiate a solution. Different communities will negotiate different solutions and a city planned in these bottom up ways where middle-class, majority values do not silence the differences of the 'strangers' will be a city of great diversity, fostering cross-cultural awareness, tolerance and, importantly, new kinds of zoning, new kinds of public spaces"

(Milun, *Pathologi*). There are many examples. Television programs and movies often feature the process of making them (in the opening credits, throughout, or as a separate product). The British- produced *1900 House*, a four-part miniseries tracking a real family selected from four hundred applicants to live a Victorian lifestyle for three months, devoted its first episode to the process of selecting the family and refurbishing the house. Movies are devoted to the process of making movies. Performance art shuns the material products or object in favor of the experienced process.

42. There are many examples. Television programs and movies often feature the process of making them (in the opening credits, throughout, or as a separate product). The British-produced *1900 House*, a four-part miniseries tracking a real family selected from four hundred applicants to live a Victorian lifestyle for three months, devoted its first episode to the process of selecting the family and refurbishing the house. Movies are devoted to the process of making movies. Performance art shuns the material products or object in favor of the experienced process.

43. Maki, for instance, sought to achieve a dynamic equilibrium between the "parts" and the "whole."

44. Venturi, *Complexity and Contradiction in Architecture*, 22.

45. Tzonis and Lefaivre, "Beyond Monuments."

46. See Ellin, *Postmodern Urbanism.*

47. In Thomas Moore, *Care of the Soul*, 258.

48. Ibid., 262.

49. Reyner Banham, *Theory and Design in the First Machine Age* (Cambridge, MA: MIT Press, 1980) (1st edition 1960).

50. There have been earlier versions of this discussion. Paul Klee maintained that art should be experienced as a process of creation, not just a product (1944). Hans Scharoun considered open systems or the "unfinished" essential in designing cities that should be responsive to prevalent tendencies (Angelil and Klingmann, "Hybrid Morphologies," 21–22). Charles Eames asserted that "Art is not a product. It is a quality" (1977). Millennia prior, Heraclitus contended that reality is ever-changing while Parmenades argued that all change is illusory.

51. John Friedmann, *Planning in the Public Domain: From Knowledge to Action* (Princeton, NJ: Princeton University Press, 1987), 413–15.

52. Harries, *The Ethical Function of Architecture*, 264.

53. Martin Heidegger, "Building, Dwelling, Thinking," in *Poetry, Language, Thought*, trans. A. Hofstadter (New York: Harper and Row, 1971).

54. Gert Staal, "Introduction," in *Copy©Proof: A New Method for Design and Education*, ed. Edith Gruson and Gert Staal (Rotterdam: 010 Publishers, 2000), 17.

55. I first taught this in 2005 after using variations on this format for a Community Works (service learning) seminar at the University of Cincinnati (1996–98) and for a course called Culture of Space (2003–present).

56. Supporting all of these points, the American Institute of Architects Student Chapter advanced "A New Program for the Design of Studio Culture" in 2002. It asserted that studio culture should promote design-thinking skills; design process as much as design product; collaboration over competition; meaningful community engagement and service; the importance of people, clients, users, communities, and society in design decisions; interdisciplinary and cross-disciplinary learning; confidence without arrogance; oral and written communication to complement visual and graphic communication; healthy and constructive critiques; healthy and safe lifestyles for students; balance between studio and nonstudio courses; emphasis on the value of time; understanding of the ethical, social, political, and economic forces that impact design; clear expectations and objectives for learning; an environment that respects and promotes diversity; successful and clear methods of student assessment; and innovation in creating alternative teaching and learning methodologies.

Speaking more generally about architectural education, Rachel Sara reiterated some of these concerns and expressed others in "A Manifesto for Architectural Education." Sara recommends that we conduct ongoing reviews after the criticism; develop communication and interpersonal skills; diminish the power of teacher over student; promote cooperative learning; introduce others into the studio; prioritize inclusive design; educate critical thinkers; allow for self-responsibility in learning; prioritize learning over teaching; value students prior experience; implement interdisciplinary learning; allow students to move into other careers; enable critical reflection; value process as well as product; value the everyday; promote empathy; provide a nurturing environment; counter the genius myth; introduce context and contingency; acknowledge the role of values and ethics; and study in spaces which reflect the pedagogy.

57. Michel Serres calls our understanding of the world in terms of binary oppositions the "dualistic hell" (1995b). Niels Andersen, a former student from Denmark, wrote (in a paper for Beyond Postmodern Urbanism seminar, Fall 2002): "We have, in other words, failed to see that without the evil sisters, there would be no Cinderella, and therefore obviously no fairytale ... the design process grows from the problem, and the beauty of the blooming flower can only be articulated from the potentials within."

SLASH CITY (/CITY)

1. Given the importance of new information technologies for this moment in urbanism, we might be inclined to describe it as the "backslash" city or architecture.

2. Henry Jenkins, *Textual Poachers: Television Fans and Participatory Culture* (New York: Routledge, 1992), 162, cited in www.chisp.net, "In Defense of Slash."

3. Slashing often supposes a homoerotic relationship between characters intended to be heterosexual. Probably the most slashed couple of all is *Star Trek*'s Spock and Kirk.

CONCLUSION

1. Susan S. Szenasy, "(Re)defining the Edge," Bruce Goff Lecture, University of Oklahoma, September 8, 2004.

2. Jacobs, *The Nature of Economies*.

3. As suggested by sociologist Manuel Castells, *The Network Society*.

4. See Ellin, "Crisis in the Architectural Profession," in *Postmodern Urbanism*.

5. Dunham-Jones continues: "Is it a coincidence that while the suburbs have been experiencing tremendous expansion, architectural discourse shifted from the 1950s and '60s focus on practice to the 1970s and '80s focus on theory? ... Theory-oriented designers claimed the high road as they declared their autonomy from context and commerce, staking positions from which to critique the wider culture. Architectural theorists, in particular, have become increasingly isolated from both practice and the dominant landscape of everyday life" ("Seventy-Five Percent").

6. Vincent Pecora, "Towers of Babel," in *Out of Site*, ed. Diane Ghirardo (Seattle: Bay Press, 1991), 48.

7. Lee Mitgang and Ernest Boyer, *Building Community: A New Future for Architectural Education and Practice* (Pittsburgh, PA: Jossey-Bass, Carnegie Foundation, 1996).

8. As Szenasy says, "The university ought to be on the leading edge of collaborative work, but for that to happen, the silos of academia must fall" ["(Re)defining the Edge"].

9. Benzel, 1997.

10. See David Orr ["The Education of Designers," *ACSA Newsletter* (January 2001)], Timothy Beatley (*From Native to Nowhere*), and Richard Louv [*Last Child in the Woods: Saving our Children from Nature-Deficit Disorder* (Chapel Hill, NC: Algonquin Books, 2005)].

11. "New Ways to Learn" in *Byte*, March 1995.

12. *ACSA Newsletter*, October 1999, 18, call for submissions to ACSA Technology Conference July 2000, "Emerging Technologies and Design: The Intersection of Design and Technology," Co-Chairs, William Mitchell and John E. Fernandez.

13. The Shashi Caan Collective is one example. The Collective is structured to allow talent of all disciplines to come together when the individuals are available in order to address specific design goals. Caan is involved with every project and constitute teams to optimize and actualize the full potential of the opportunity, similar to how a film is made.www. innovationspace.asu.edu.

14. From Web site for InnovationSpace at Arizona State University.

15. In Kelbaugh, *Michigan Debates on Urbanism II*, 68.

16. Landry, *The Creative City*, xiii. Although Jacobs' "human capital theory" posited that people drive economic growth decades ago, it is only with Florida's "creative capital theory" that this notion has become more widely accepted.

17. See Smolin. (Referenced in Overbye.)

18. Art critic Suzi Gablik, for instance, observes a "change in the general social mood toward a new pragmatic idealism and a more integrated value system that brings head and heart together in an ethic of care" (1993: 11).

19. Mary Catherine Bateson, *Composing a Life* (New York: Grove Press, 1990).

20. See, e.g., the Comer School Development Program.

21. Schwartz on James Rutt [John Schwartz, "Internet 'Bad Boy' Takes On a New Challenge" *New York Times*, April 23, 2001].

22. Jim Fournier, presentation at Paradox III conference at Arcosanti, 2001.

23. Kisho Kurokawa, *Intercultural Architecture: The Philosophy of Symbiosis* (Washington D.C.: AIA, 1991).

24. Holl Web site.

25. See Ellin, *Postmodern Urbanism*, Ch. 6.

26. This greater intelligence can also be described as our cosmic empathy or anima mundi, nurturer of life in the cosmos (Spretnak, *The Resurgence of the Real*, 78).

27. Muschamp, "The Polyglot Metropolis."

28. Robert Campbell, "Why Don't the Rest of Us Like Buildings that Architects Like?" *Bulletin of the American Academy* (Summer 2004), 22–26.

29. See note 23 in "Five Qualities of an Integral Urbanism" above.

30. Reurbanism is a broad category covering everything from high-end examples of "positive redevelopment and revitalization of American cities that is now happening piecemeal" to local architecture with its default urbanism" (Kelbaugh, *Michigan Debates on Urbanism III*, 8–10).

31. Posturbanism is avant-garde and "driven by aesthetics" (Kelbaugh, 2005). Michael Speaks suggests calling it "Not Urban" (Kelbaugh, *Michigan Debates on Urbanism I*, 35).

ADDITIONAL NOTES FOR CHAPTER HEADINGS

Hybridity & Connectivity

Calvino, Italo. *Six Memos for the Next Millennium*, 52.

Carson, Scott. Former Arizona State University student, and currently an architect at George Christiansen Associates, Arizona.

Koolhaas, Rem. cited in *Vogue Magazine*.

Smithson, Alison and Paul Smithson. *The Charged Void: Urbanism*. New York: Monacelli, 2005.

Van Eyck, Aldo. Cited by Tzonis and Lefaivre, "Beyond Monuments," 1999.

Porosity

Alaimo, Stacy. Lecture at Arizona State University, February 6, 2004.

Forster, E. M. *Howard's End*. New York: Modern Library, 1999 (1st edition, 1910).

Hill, Kristina. "A Process Language for Urban Design." *Arcade* 21 (4) (Summer 2003).

Kahn, Louis. Cited by Charles Moore, "Foreward" in *Praise of Shadows*, Jun'chiro Tanizaki. Stony Creek, CT: Leete's Island Books.

Kraft, Sabine. "The City upon the City," Trans. (from German) by Irina Mack (personal translation).

Miyake, Issey. "Issey Miyake: Sewing a Second Skin," *Artforum*, February 1982.

Yamamoto, Akira. *Culture Spaces in Everyday Life: An Anthropology of Common Sense Knowledge*. Lawrence, KS: University Press of Kansas, 1979.

Authenticity

Beck. Quoted by Jon Pareles, "A Pop-Postmodernist Gives Up on Irony" in *New York Times*, November 8, 1998.

Childress, Herb. "Review of Architecture of Fear" in *Environmental and Phenomenology Newsletter*, v. 9, no. 3 (Fall 1998): 7–8.

Hyde, Lewis. Cited by David Foster Wallace cited by Joe Hagan in *New York Times*, March 25, 2001. "Music: A Thinking Slacker's Rock Hero."

Milun, Kathryn. *Pathologies of Modern Space: Empty Space, Urban Anxiety, and the Recovery of the Public Self*. New York: Routledge, 2006.

Stone, Linda, former Microsoft techie. Cited by Ellen Goodman in "The Art of Living Slowly," *Arizona Republic*, August 12, 2005.

Van Eyck, Aldo. Cited by Liane Lefaivre and Alexander Tzonis, *Aldo van Eyck Humanist Rebel: Inbetweening in a Postwar World* (Rotterdam: Uitgeverig, 1999).

Vulnerability

Hood, Walter. "The Hybrid Spaces of Walter Hood," *Land Online*, American Society of Landscape Architects, May 2, 2005.

Koolhaas, Rem. "Bigness: or the Problem of Large" in *SMLXL*.

Serres, Michel. "China Loam," in *Detachment*, trans. Genevieve James and Raymond Federman. Athens, OH: Ohio State University Press, 1989, 11 (1st edition 1986).

Midrash. A Jewish commentary on the Scriptures.

Parsons, Richard D. "Connecting Dots," *New York Times*, June 12, 2005.

Pascal, Blaise. *Pensées and Other Writings*, translated by Honor Levi, with an introduction and notes by Anthony Levi, Oxford: Oxford University Press, 1995.

REFERENCES

Adams, Robert. "Truth in Landscape." In *Beauty in Photography*. New York: Aperture, 1981.

Alaimo, Stacy. Lecture at Arizona State University. February 6, 2004.

Albers, Josef. *Interaction of Color*. New Haven, CT: Yale University Press, 1975.

Alexander, Christopher. *A New Theory of Urban Design*. New York: Oxford University Press, 1987.

Alexander, Christopher. *A Pattern Language*. New York: Oxford University Press, 1977.

Alexander, Christopher. "A City Is Not a Tree." Architectural Forum, April 1965, 58–62, May 1965, 58–61.

Allen, Stan. "Los Angeles: 4 (Artificial) Ecologies." *Hunch 1 — The Berlag Institute Report 1998/1999*. Rotterdam: Berlage Institute, This is a journal. 1999, URL added to text footnote 18–23.

Allen, Stan. "Logistical Activities Zone: Users' Manual." www.stanallenarchitect.com.

Allen, Stan. *Points and Lines: Diagrams and Projects for the City*. New York: Princeton Architectural Press, 1999.

AlSayyad, Nezar. *Hybrid Urbanism: On the Identity Discourse and the Built Environment*. Westport, CT: Greenwood, 2001.

Angelil, Marc and Anna Klingmann. "Hybrid Morphologies: Infrastructure, Architecture, Landscape." *Daidalos* 73 (1999): 16–25.

Appleyard, Donald, Kevin Lynch, and J. R. Myer. *The View from the Road*. Cambridge, MA: MIT Press, 1964.

Architectural Design March/April 2004. Special Issue on Landscape Urbanism.

Arrien, Angeles. *The Four-Fold Way*. San Francisco: Harper, 1993.

Baird, George. *The Space of Appearance*. Cambridge, MA: MIT Press, 1995.

Banham, Reyner. *Theory and Design in the First Machine Age*. Cambridge, MA: MIT Press, 1980 (1st edition 1960).

Barley, Nick, ed. *Breathing Cities: The Architecture of Movement*. Cambridge, MA: Birkhauser, 2000.

Barbasi, Albert-Lazlo and Reka Albert. "Emergence of Scaling in Random Networks." Science 286, 509–12. 1999.

Barnett, Jonathan. *Redesigning Cities*. Chicago: American Planning Association, 2003.

Barnett, Jonathan. *The Elusive City*. New York: Harper and Row, 1986.

Barth, John. *Tidewater Tales*. New York: Putnam, 1986.

Bateson, Mary Catherine. *Composing a Life*. New York: Grove Press, 1990.

Beatley, Timothy. *From Native to Nowhere: Sustaining Home and Community in a Global Age*. Washington, D.C.: Island Press, 2004.

Beck, Don E. *Spiral Dynamics: Mastering Values, Leadership, and Change*. Malden, MA: Blackwell, 1996.

Beck, Ulrich. *Risk Society: Towards a New Modernity*. Translated (from German) by Mark Ritter. London: Sage Publications, 1992 (1st edition, 1986).

Beck, Ulrich, Wolfgang Bonss, and Christoph Lau. "The Theory of Reflexive Modernization." *Theory Culture & Society* 20 (2) (April 2003): 1–34.

Bell, Jonathan. *Carchitecture*. Cambridge, MA: Birkhauser, 2001.

Benjamin, Walter. "Naples." In *Reflections*. New York: Schocken, 1986.

Benyus, Janine M. *Biomimicry: Innovation Inspired by Nature*. New York: Perennial, 1998.

Benzel, Katherine. 1997. The Room in Context: Design Without Boundaries. New York: McGraw-Hill.

Bergman, Sunny. *Keeping It Real*. Amsterdam, 2000. Documentary, First Run/Icarus Films, Brooklyn.

Berke, Deborah. "Thoughts on the Everyday." In *Architecture of the Everyday*. Edited by Steven Harris and Berke. New York: Princeton Architectural Press, 1997, 222–26.

Berlage Institute. Spring newsletter, 2005.

Berlage Institute. "What Will the Architect Enact Tomorrow?" *Public Events* (Autumn 2002/03).

Berrizbeitia, Anita and Linda Pollak. *Inside Outside: Between Architecture and Landscape*. Gloucester, MA: Rockport, 1999.

Best, Steven and Douglas Kellner. *Postmodern Theory: Critical Interrogations*. New York: Guilford Press, 1991.

Bhaba, Homi. *The Location of Culture*. New York: Routledge, 1994.

Blum, Andrew. "The Peace Maker." *Metropolis* (August/September 2005): 118–23, 155, 157.

Borges, Jorge Luis. Obra poetica. Emece Editions. 1989.

Borgmann, Albert. *Crossing the Postmodern Divide*. Chicago: University of Chicago Press, 1993.

Caan, Shashi. Personal communication. 2004.

Calthorpe, Peter. *The Next American Metropolis*. New York: Princeton Architectural Press, 1993.

Calthorpe, Peter, William Fulton, and Robert Fishman. *The Regional City: Planning for the End of Sprawl*. Washington, D.C.: Island Press, 2001.

Calvino, Italo. *Invisible Cities*. New York: Harvest/Harcourt Brace Jovanovich, 1978.

Calvino, Italo. *Six Memos for the Next Millennium*. New York: Vintage, 1988.

Campbell, Robert. "Why Don't the Rest of Us Like Buildings that Architects Like?" *Bulletin of the American Academy* (Summer 2004): 22–26.

Capra, Fritjof. Center of Ecoliterary, www.ecoliteracy.org/, 2005.

Capra, Fritjof. *The Web of Life*. New York: Anchor, 1997.

Castells, Manuel. *The Network Society*. North Hampton, MA: Edward Elgar Publishing, 2004.

Castells, Manuel. *The Rise of the Network City*. Cambridge, MA: Blackwell, 2000.

Chase, John, Margaret Crawford, and John Kaliski, eds. *Everyday Urbanism*. New York: Monacelli, 1999.

Childress, Herb. "Review of Architecture of Fear." *Environmental and Phenomenology Newsletter* 9 (3) (Fall 1998): 7–8.

Condon, Patrick. Presentation at "Urbanisms: New and Other," University of California at Berkeley, 2001.

Confurius, Gerrit. "Editorial." *Daidalos* 72 (1999): 4–5.

Corner, James, ed. *Recovering Landscape*. New York: Princeton Architectural Press, 1999.

Corner, James. "Field Operations." In *Architecture of the Borderlands, AD 69*. Edited by Teddy Cruz and Anne Boddington. New York: John Wiley & Sons, 1999, 53–55.

Corner, James. "Highline/Fresh Kills and Other Projects." In *Landscape Urbanism*. New York: Institute of Urban Design, 2004.

Crisp, Barbara. *Human Spaces*. Gloucester, MA: Rockport Publishers, 1998.

Cruz, Teddy and Anne Boddington, eds. *Architecture of the Borderlands, AD* 69. New York: John Wiley & Sons, 1999, 7–8.

Csikszentmihalyi, Mihaly. *Flow: The Psychology of Optimal Experience*. New York: HarperPerennial, 1990.

Cullen, Gordon. *The Concise Townscape*. New York: Reinhold, 1961.

Daidalos 73 (1999).

De Sola-Morales, Ignasi. *Differences: Topographies of Contemporary Architecture*. Cambridge, MA: MIT Press, 1997.

De Landa, Manuel. "Extensive Borderlines and Intensive Borderlines." In *BorderLine*. Edited by Lebbeus Woods and Ekkehard Rehfeld. Austria: Springer-Verlag/Wein and RIEAeuropa, 1998.

De Landa, Manuel. *One Thousand Years of Nonlinear History*. New York: Zone Books, 1998.

Deleuze, Gilles and Felix Guattari. *A Thousand Plateaus*. Minneapolis, MN: University of Minnesota Press, 1980.

Deleuze, Gille and Felix Guattari. Anti-Oedipus: Capitalism and Schizophrenia. University of Minnesota. 1983.

Derrida, Jacques. *Margins of Philosophy*. Translated by A. Bass. London: Harvester Press, 1982 (1st edition, 1972).

Derrida, Jacques. *The Truth in Painting*, Chicago: University of Chicago Press, 1987.

Doordan, Dennis. "Simulated Seas: Exhibition Design in Contemporary Aquariums." *Design Issues* 11 (2) (Summer 1995).

Duffy, Francis. "Designing the Knowledge Economy." 11.

Dunham-Jones, Ellen. "Real Radicalism: Duany and Koolhaas," *Harvard Design Magazine* (Winter/Spring 1997): 51.

Dunham-Jones, Ellen. "Seventy-Five Percent." *Harvard Design Magazine* (Fall 2000): 5–12.

Dunn, Alison and Jim Beach. Personal communication.

Ellin, Nan, ed. *Architecture of Fear*. New York: Princeton Architectural Press, 1997.

Ellin, Nan. "In Search of a Usable Past: Urban Design and Society in a French New Town." Ph.D. dissertation. Columbia University, 1994.

Ellin, Nan. *Postmodern Urbanism, Revised Edition*. New York: Princeton Architectural Press, 1999 (1st edition 1996).

Erickson, Arthur. "Shaping." In *The City as Dwelling*. Edited by Arthur Erickson, William H. Whyte, and James Hillman. Dallas: Dallas Institute of Humanities and Culture,1980.

Fishman, Robert, ed. *New Urbanism: Peter Calthorpe vs. Lars Lerup. Michigan Debates on Urbanism II.* Series edited by Douglas Kelbaugh. Ann Arbor, MI: University of Michigan Press, 2005.

Florida, Richard. *The Rise of the Creative Class*. New York: Basic Books, 2002.

Forman, Richard T. T. *Land Mosaics: The Ecology of Landscapes and Regions*. New York: Cambridge University Press, 1995.

Forster, E. M. *Howard's End*. New York: Modern Library, 1999 (1st edition, 1910).

Fournier, Jim. "Meta-Nature," www.metanature.org, 1999.

Fournier, Jim. Presentation at Paradox III conference at Arcosanti, 2001.

Frampton, Kenneth. *Modern Architecture: A Critical History*. London: Thames and Hudson, 1985 (1st edition, 1980).

Frampton, Kenneth. "Seven Points for the Millennium: An Untimely Manifesto," *Architectural Record* (August 1999): 15.

Frampton, Kenneth. "Toward an Urban Landscape." In *Columbia Documents for Architecture and Theory: D4*. New York: Columbia University Press, 1995.

Friedmann, John. *Planning in the Public Domain: From Knowledge to Action*. Princeton, NJ: Princeton University Press, 1987.

Gablik, Suzie. Reenchantment of Art. New York: Thames & Hudson. 1992.

Gamble, Michael. "Reprogramming Midtown Atlanta." Presented at American Collegiate Schools of Architecture Conference, Baltimore, March 2001.

Gehl, Jan. *Life Between Buildings*. Copenhagen: Danish Architectural Press, 1971.

Gibney, Jr., Frank and Belinda Luscombe. "The Redesigning of America." *Time*, March 20, 2000, 66–75.

Gladwell, Malcolm. *The Tipping Point*. Boston: Back Bay Books, 2002.

Gonzales, Robert, ed. *Aula* (Spring 1999).

Graham, Stephen and Simon Marvin. *Splintering Urbanism*. New York: Routledge, 2001.

Gurian, Elaine Heumann. "Function Follows Form: How Mixed-Used Spaces in Museums Build Community." *Curator* 44 (1) (January 2001): 87–113.

Gurian, Elaine Heumann. "Threshold Fear." In *Reshaping Museum Space*. Edited by Suzanne MacLeod. London: Routledge, 2005.

Harries, Karsten. *The Ethical Function of Architecture*. Cambridge, MA: MIT Press, 1998.

Harris, Steven and Deborah Berke, eds. *Architecture of the Everyday*. New York: Princeton Architectural Press, 1997.

Hartman, Carl. "Seeing the Future of Construction through Translucent Concrete." Associated Press, July 8, 2004.

Harvey, David. *The Condition of Postmodernity*. Cambridge, MA: Blackwell, 1989.

Hawken, Paul, Amory Lovins, and L. Hunter Lovins. *Natural Capitalism*. Boston: Back Bay Books, 2000.

Hawthorne, Christopher. "Captain Koolhaas Sails the New Prada Flagship." *New York Times*, July 15, 2004.

Heidegger, Martin. "Building, Dwelling, Thinking." In *Poetry, Language, Thought*. Translated by A. Hofstadter. New York: Harper and Row, 1971.

Hill, Kristina. "A Process Language for Urban Design." *Arcade* 21 (4) (Summer 2003).

Hillier, B. and A. Penn. "Dense Civilizations: The Shape of Cities in the 21st Century." In *Applied Energy* 43. London: Elsevier, 1989, 41–66.

Hinshaw, Mark. "The Case for True Urbanism." *Planning* (September 2005).

Holl, Steven. Web site.

Honoré, Carl. *In Praise of Slowness*. New York: HarperCollins, 2004. (especially "Cities: Blending Old and New," 87–107).

hooks, bell. "Choosing the Margin." In *Yearning*. Toronto: Between-the-Lines, 1990.

Hough, Michael. *Cities and Natural Process*. New York: Routledge, 1995.

Huxtable, Ada Louise. *The Unreal America: Architecture and Illusion*. New York: Penguin, 1997.

Ingersoll, Richard. "Landscapegoat." In *Architecture of Fear*. Edited by Nan Ellin. New York: Princeton Architectural Press, 1997, 253–59.

Iovine, Julie V. "An Avant-Garde Design for a New-Media Center." In *New York Times*, March 21, 2002.

Iovine, Julie V. "Just How Much Convenience Can a Person Stand?" *New York Times*, January 13, 2000.

Iyer, Pico. "Nowhere Man: Confessions of a Perpetual Foreigner." Utne Reader. May–June 1997. 78–9.

Jacobs, Allan and Donald Appleyard. "Toward an Urban Design Manifesto." *Journal of the American Planning Association*, 1987. 53 (1): 112-20.

Jacobs, Jane. *The Death and Life of Great American Cities*. New York: Vantage, 1961.

Jacobs, Jane. *The Nature of Economies*. New York: Modern Library, 2000.

Jencks, Charles. *Heteropolis*. London: Academy Editions, 1993.

Jencks, Charles and Karl Kropf, eds. *Theories and Manifestos of Contemporary Architecture*. New York: Wiley-Academy, 1997.

Jenkins, Henry. *Textual Poachers: Television Fans and Participatory Culture*. New York: Routledge, 1992.

Johnson, George. "First Cells, Then Species, Now the Web." *New York Times*, December 26, 2000.

Johnson, Philip. "How the Architectural Giant Decided that Form Trumps Function." *New York Times Magazine*, December 13, 1998, 77–78.

Johnson, Steven. *Emergence: The Connected Lives of Ants, Brains, Cities and Software*. New York: Penguin, 2001.

Jones, Tom, Willliam Pettus, and Michael Pyatok. *Good Neighbors: Affordable Family Housing*. New York: McGraw-Hill, 1996.

Katz, Peter. "Form First: The New Urbanist Alternative to Conventional Zoning." *Planning* (November 2004).

Kelbaugh, Douglas. *Repairing the American Metropolis*. Seattle: University of Washington, 2002.

Kelbaugh, Douglas, series ed. *Michigan Debates on Urbanism I, II, and III: Everyday Urbanism (Margaret Crawford v. Michael Speaks)*. Edited by Rahul Mehrotra. *New Urbanism (Peter Calthorpe v. Lars Lerup)*. Edited by Robert Fishman. *Post Urbanism & ReUrbanism (Peter Eisenman v. Barbara Littenberg and Steven Peterson)*. Edited by Roy Strickland. Ann Arbor, MI: University of Michigan, 2005.

Kemp, Mark. *New York Times*, August 9, 1999.

Kenda, Barbara. "On the Renaissance Art of Well-Being: Pneuma in Villa Eolia." *Res* 34 (Autumn 1998).

Kent, Fred. "Great Public Spaces by Project for Public Spaces — Instructive Lessons From Here and Abroad." *Project for Pubic Spaces Newsletter* (2005).

Kent, Fred. Interview. *The Planning Report. 2003.*

Kerr, Laurie. "Greening the Mega-Projects: The MTA and the Second Avenue Line." In *Urban Design Case Studies 1/2*. New York: Urban Design Institute, 2004.

Kimmelman, Michael. Interview with Howard Gardner. *New York Times*. February 14, 1999.

Kinzer, Stephen. "Concerto for Orchestra and Hopeful City." *New York Times*. September 4, 2003.

Knipp, Shirley Cox. "Thinking Outside the Box (Cubicle)." *High Profile Arizona* (Winter 2004): 12, 23.

Koh, Jusuck. "Ecological Reasoning and Architectural Imagination." Inaugural Address, Wageningen University, The Netherlands, November 11, 2004.

Koh, Jusuck. "Success Strategies for Architects through Cultural Changes Leading into the Post-Industrial Age." In *Environmental Change/Social Change,* Proceedings of 16th EDRA Conference. Washington, D.C.: EDRA, 1985, 10–21.

Koolhaas, Rem. *Delirious New York: A Retroactive Manifesto for Manhattan*. New York: Monacelli Press, 1994 (1st edition, 1978).

Koolhaas, Rem. "Pearl River Delta, The City of Exacerbated Difference." In *Politics-Poetics Documenta X — The Book*. Edited by Jean-François Chevrier. Kassel, Germany: Verlag, 1997.

Koolhaas, Rem. "Rem Cycle." *Vogue Magazine,* November 1994, 335.

Koolhaas, Rem. *SMLXL*. New York: Monacelli, 1996.

Kostof, Spiro. *The City Assembled*. London: Thames and Hudson, 1992.

Kraft, Sabine. "The City upon the City." Translated (from German) by Irina Mack (personal translation).

Kurokawa, Kisho. *Intercultural Architecture: The Philosophy of Symbiosis*. Washington D.C.: AIA, 1991.

Landry, Charles. *The Creative City*. London: Earthscan, 2000.

"Landscapes." *Praxis 4* (2002).

Lasn, Kalle. *Culture Jam: How to Reverse America's Suicidal Consumer Binge — and Why We Must*. New York: Quill, 1999.

Leach, Neil. *The Anaesthetics of Architecture*. Cambridge, MA: MIT Press, 1999.

Lee, Mark. "The Dutch Savannah: Approaches to Topological Landscape." *Daidalos* 73 (1999): 9–15.

Lefaivre, Liane. "Critical Domesticity in the 1960s: An Interview with Mary Otis Stevens." *Thresholds* 19 (1999): 22–26.

Lefaivre, Liane. "Dirty Realism in European Architecture Today." *Design Book Review* 17 (Winter 1989): 17–20.

Lefaivre, Liane and Alexander Tzonis. *Aldo van Eyck Humanist Rebel: Inbetweening in a Postwar World*. Rotterdam: Uitgeverij 010, 1999.

Lefebvre, Henri with Catherine Regulier-Lefebvre. *Eléments de rythmanalyse: Introduction à la connaissance des rythmes*. Paris: Ed. Syllepse, 1992.

Lennard, Suzanne, H. Crowhurst, and Henry L. Lennard. "Principles of True Urbanism." International Making Cities, www.livablecities.org, 2004.

Lerup, Lars. *After the City*. Cambridge, MA: MIT Press, 2000.

Lewis, Paul, Marc Tsurumaki, and David J. Lewis. *Situation Normal, Pamphlet Architecture* 21. New York: Princeton Architectural Press, 1998.

Lifton, Robert Jay. *The Protean Self: Human Resilience in an Age of Fragmentation.* Chicago: University of Chicago, 1993.

Lindwall, Peter. "Impact of the Strand on the Townsville Community." *Queensland Planner* 44 (2) (June 2004): 18–19.

Logan, John R. and Todd Swanstrom, eds. *Beyond the City Limits.* Philadelphia: Temple University, 1990.

Lootsma, Bart. *SuperDutch.* New York: Princeton Architectural Press, 2000.

Lootsma, Bart. "Synthetic Regionalization." In *Recovering Landscape.* Edited by James Corner. New York: Princeton Architectural Press, 1999, 251–74.

Louv, Richard. *Last Child in the Woods: Saving our Children from Nature-Deficit Disorder.* Chapel Hill, NC: Algonquin Books, 2005.

Lynch, Kevin. *Image of the City.* Cambridge, MA: MIT Press, 1960.

Marcus, George E. *Ethnography Through Thick and Thin.* Princeton, NJ: Princeton University Press, 1998.

Marcuse, Peter. "Not Chaos, But Walls: Postmodernism and the Partitioned City." In *Postmodern Cities and Spaces.* Edited by Sophie Watson and Katherine Gibson. Oxford, U.K.: Blackwell, 1995.

Martini, Kirk. "Beyond Competence: Technical Courses in the Architecture Curriculum." *Architronic* 4 (3) (1995).

Mau, Bruce. "An Incomplete Manifesto for Growth." *I.D.* (March/April 1999).

McAvoy, Peter V., Mary Beth Driscoll, and Benjamin J. Gramling. "Integrating the Environment, the Economy, and Community Health: A Community Health Center's Initiative to Link Health Benefits to Smart Growth." *American Journal of Public Health* 94 (2) (February 2004): 525–27.

McHarg, Ian. *Design with Nature.* Gardern City, NY: Natural History Press. 1969.

Miller , Alice. *The Drama of the Gifted Child: The Search for the True Self.* New York: Basic Books, 1997 (1st edition 1979).

Milun, Kathryn. *Pathologies of Modern Space: Empty Space, Urban Anxiety, and the Recovery of the Public Self.* New York: Routledge, 2006.

Mitgang, Lee and Ernest Boyer. *Building Community: A New Future for Architectural Education and Practice.* Pittsburg, PA: Jossey-Bass, 1996.

Molloy, John Fitzgerald. *The Fraternity.* St. Paul, MN: Paragon House, 2004.

Moore, Charles and Donlyn Lyndon. *Chambers for a Memory Palace.* Cambridge, MA: MIT Press, 1996.

Moore, Thomas. *Care of the Soul.* New York: HarperCollins, 1992.

Morton, Patricia. "Getting the 'Master' Out of the Master Plan." *Los Angeles Forum of Architecture and Urban Design* (October 1994): 2.

Morton, Patricia. *Hybrid Modernities.* Cambridge, MA: MIT Press, 2003.

Mumford, Lewis. *The City in History.* New York: Harcourt Brace Jovanovich, 1961.

Mumford, Lewis. *The Culture of Cities.* New York: Harcourt Brace and Co., 1938.

Muschamp, Herbert. "A Happy, Scary New Day for Design." *New York Times,* October 15, 2000.

Muschamp, Herbert. "Architectural Trendsetter Seduces Historic Soho." *New York Times,* April 11, 2001.

Muschamp, Herbert. "Forget the Shoes, Prada's New Store Stocks Ideas." *New York Times,* December 16, 2001.

Muschamp, Herbert. "Imaginative Leaps into the Real World." *New York Times,* February 25, 2001.

Muschamp, Herbert. "Swiss Architects, Designers of Tate Modern, Win Pritzker Prize." *New York Times,* April 2, 2001.

Muschamp, Herbert. "The Polyglot Metropolis and Its Discontents." *New York Times,* July 3, 1994.

Muschamp, Herbert. "Woman of Steel." *New York Times,* March 28, 2004.

Muschamp, Herbert. "You Say You Want an Evolution? OK, Then Tweak." *New York Times,* April 13, 2004.

Muschamp, Herbert. "Zaha Hadid's Urban Mothership." *New York Times,* June 8, 2003.

Nilsen, Richard. ••• *Arizona Republic,* July 4, 2004.

Nilsen, Richard. "Postscript to Modernism: It's Style Over Substance." *Arizona Republic,* April 25, 1999.

Orr, David. "The Education of Designers." *ACSA Newsletter* (January 2001).

Otero-Pailos, Jorge. "Bigness in Context: Some Regressive Tendencies in Rem Koolhaas's Urban Theory." (MS, presented at ACSA conference, May 2000).

Otto, Frei. "The New Plurality in Architecture." In *On Architecture, the City, and Technology.* Edited by Marc Angelil. London: Butterworth Architecture, 1990.

Ouroussoff, Nicolai. "Making the Brutal F.D.R. Unsentimentally Humane." *New York Times*, June 28, 2005.

Ouroussoff, Nicolai. "Sobering Plans for Jets Stadium." *New York Times*, November 1, 2004.

Overbye, Dennis. "The Cosmos According to Darwin." *New York Times Magazine,* July 13, 1997, 24–27.

Parsons, Richard D. "Connecting Dots." *New York Times*, June 12, 2005.

Pawley, Martin. *The Private Future.* London: Pan Books, 1973.

Pearson, David. *New Organic Architecture.* London: Gaia Books, 2001.

Pecora, Vincent. "Towers of Babel." In *Out of Site.* Edited by Diane Ghirardo. Seattle: Bay Press, 1991, 46–76.

Peirce, Neil. "Megalopolis has Come of Age." *Arizona Republic,* July 29, 2005.

Peirce, Neil. "Neighborhoods Closing Doors." *Washington Post Writers Group*, July 15, 2005.

Peters, Tom. *The Circle of Innovation.* New York: Vintage, 1999.

Pimentel, O. Ricardo. "Clinton Puts Good Advice on the Menu." *Arizona Republic*, May 2, 2002.

Pine, B. Joseph, II, and James H. Gilmore. *The Experience Economy: Work Is Theatre and Every Business a Stage.* Cambridge, MA: Harvard Business School, 1999.

Pollak, Linda. "City-Architecture-Landscape: Strategies for Building City Landscape." *Daidalos* (1999): 48–59.

Polshek, James Stewart. "Built for Substance, Not Flash." *New York Times*, January 22, 2001.

Project for Public Spaces. "Letter to the *New York Times*." July 2004.

Project for Public Spaces. "What If We Built Our Cities Around Places." November 2004. www.pps.org.

Purdy, Jedediah. *For Common Things: Irony, Trust and Commitment in America Today.* New York: Vintage, 1999.

Putnam, Robert. *Bowling Alone.* New York: Simon and Schuster, 2000.

Redfield, Wendy. "Reading and Recording the Elusive City." ACSA Conference, Baltimore, 2000.

Reich, Charles. *The Greening of America.* New York: Random House, 1970.

Ritchie, Ian. *(Well)Connected Architecture.* New York: John Wiley & Sons, 1994.

Roach, Catherine. "Loving Your Mother: On the Woman-Nature Relation." *Ecological Feminist Philosophies.* Karen J. Warren, ed. Bloomington: Indiana University (1996): 52-65.

Roberts, Marion, et al. "Place and Space in the Networked City: Conceptualizing the Integrated Metropolis." *Journal of Urban Design* 4 (1) (February 1999): 51–66.

Rosaldo, Renato. *Culture and Truth.* New York: Beacon, 1989.

Ruby, Andreas. "The Scene of the Scenario." *hunch* 8 (2004): 95–99.

Rugoff, Ralph. "L.A.'s New Car-tography." *LA Weekly,* October 6, 1995, 35.

Sara, Rachel. "The Pink Book" and "A Manifesto for Architectural Education," *EAAE Prize* (2001–02): 122–33.

Sassen, Saskia. *Cities in a World Economy.* Thousand Oaks, CA: Pine Forge Press, 1994.

Sassen, Saskia. *The Global City.* Princeton, NJ: Princeton University Press, 2001.

Schwartz, John. "Internet 'Bad Boy' Takes on a New Challenge." *New York Times*, April 23, 2001.

Scully, Robert. "Systems of Organized Complexity." *Arcade* 21 (4) (Summer 2003).

Sennett, Richard. "The Powers of the Eye." In *Urban Revisions: Current Projects for the Public Realm.* Compiled by Elizabeth A. T. Smith. Cambridge, MA: MIT Press, 1994, 59–69.

Serres, Michel. "China Loam." In *Detachment.* Translated by Genevieve James and Raymond Federman. Athens, OH: Ohio State University Press, 1989 (1st edition 1986).

Serres, Michel. *Genesis*. Translated by Genevieve James and James Nielson. Ann Arbor, MI: University of Michigan Press, 1995.

Serres, Michel. *The Natural Contract*. Translated by E. MacArthur and W. Paulson. Ann Arbor, MI: University of Michigan Press, 1995.

Shane, Graham. "The Emergence of 'Landscape Urbanism.'" *Harvard Design Review* 19 (Fall 2003/Winter 2004): 13–20.

Shulman, Ken. "X-Ray Architecture." *Metropolis* (April 2001).

Simmel, Georg. 1969 "The Metropolis and Mental Life." In *Classic Essays on the Culture of Cities*. Edited by Richard Sennett. New York: Apple Century Crofts, 1969, 19–30. (1st edition 1903).

Smith, Elizabeth A. T. comp. *Urban Revisions: Current Projects for the Public Realm*. Cambridge, MA: MIT Press, 1994.

Smithson, Alison and Paul Smithson. *The Charged Void: Urbanism*. New York: Monacelli, 2005.

Speaks, Michael. "Big Soft Orange." In *Architecture of the Borderlands*. Edited by Teddy Cruz and Anne Boddington. New York: John Wiley & Sons, 1999, 90–92.

Speaks, Michael. "Plausible Space." *hunch* 8 (2004): 90–94.

Spellman, Catherine. ed. *Re-envisioning Landscape/Architecture*. Barcelona: ACTAR, 2003.

Spretnak, Charlene. *States of Grace*. New York: HarperCollins, 1991.

Spretnak, Charlene. *The Resurgence of the Real: Body, Nature and Place in a Hypermodern World*. New York: Addison-Wesley, 1997

Staal, Gert. "Introduction." In *Copy©Proof: A New Method for Design and Education*. Edited by Edith Gruson and Staal. Rotterdam: 010 Publishers, 2000, 16–19.

Steinitz, Carl. "What Can We Do?" Symposium in *Harvard Design Magazine* 18 (Spring/Summer 2003).

Swaback, Vernon. *Designing the Future*. Tempe, AZ: Herberger Center for Design Excellence, 1996.

Szenasy, Susan S. "(Re)defining the Edge." Bruce Goff Lecture, University of Oklahoma. September 8, 2004.

"The Hybrid Spaces of Walter Hood." *Land Online*, May 2, 2005.

Trancik, Roger. *Finding Lost Space*. New York: Van Nostrand Reinhold, 1986.

Traub, James. "This Campus Is Being Simulated." *New York Times*, November 19, 2000.

Tschumi, Bernard. *Architecture and Disjunction*. New York: Princeton Architectural Press, 1994.

Tsing, Anna Lowenhaupt. *In the Realm of the Diamond Queen*. Princeton, NJ: Princeton University Press, 1992.

Tzonis , Alexander. "Pikionis and the Transvisibility." *Thresholds* 19 (1999): 15–21.

Tzonis, Alexander and Liane Lefaivre. "Beyond Monuments, Beyond Zip-a-ton." *Le Carré Bleu* 3–4 (1999): 4–44.

Van Berkel, Ben and Caroline Bos. "Rethinking Urban Organization: The 6th Nota of the Netherlands." *[Hunch 1 — The Berlage Institute Report 1998/1999*. Rotterdam: Berlage Institute 1999, 68–73.

Van der Ryn, Sim and Sterling Bunnell. "Integral Design." In *Theories and Manifestoes of Contemporary Architecture*. Edited by Charles Jencks and Karl Kropf. London: Academy Editions, 1997, 136–38. ["Integral Design" was originally published in The Integral Urban House, Helga Olkowski, Bill Olkowski, Tom Javits and the Farallones Institute Staff, San Francisco: Sierra Club Books, 1979.]

Van der Ryn, Sim and Stuart Cowan. *Ecological Design*. Washington, D.C.: Island Press, 1996.

Venturi, Robert. *Complexity and Contradiction in Architecture*. New York: Museum of Modern Art, 1966.

Wade, Nicolas. "Life's Origins Get Murkier and Messier." *New York Times*, June 13, 2000.

Wall, Alex. "Programming the Urban Surface." In *Recovering Landscape*. Edited by James Corner. New York: Princeton Architectural Press, 1999, 232–49.

Walljasper, Jay "Town Square." Project for Public Spaces Newsletter September 2004. www.pps.org.

Weber, Max. *The Protestant Ethic and the Spirit of Capitalism*. New York: Penguin, 2002 (1st edition 1905).

Wexler, Mark. "Money Does Grow on Trees — And so Does Better Health and Happiness." *National Wildlife* (April–May 1998).

Whyte, David. *Crossing the Unknown Sea: Work as a Pilgrimage of Identity.* New York: Penguin, 2002.

Whyte, William H. *The Social Life of Small Urban Spaces.* New York: Project for Public Spaces, 2001 (1st edition 1980).

Wilbur, Ken. *A Brief History of Everything.* Boston: Shambhala, 2000 (1st edition 1996).

Williams, Margery. *The Velveteen Rabbit.* New York: Doubleday, 1922.

Wiscombe, Tom. "The Haptic Morphology of Tentacles." In *BorderLine.* Edited by Lebbeus Woods and Ekkehard Rehfeld. Austria: Springer-Verlag/Wien and RIEAeuropa, 1998.

Woods, Lebbeus. "Inside the Borderline." In *BorderLine.* Edited by Lebbeaus Woods and Ekkehard Rehfeld. Austria: Springer-Verlag/Wien and RIEAeuropa,1998.

Woods, Lebbeus and Ekkehard Rehfeld. eds. *BorderLine.* Austria: Springer-Verlag/Wien and RIEAeuropa, 1998.

Yamamoto, Akira. *Culture Spaces in Everyday Life: An Anthropology of Common Sense Knowledge.* Lawrence, KS: University Press of Kansas, 1979.

Yeang, Ken. *The Green Skyscraper.* New York: Prestel, 1999.

Zellner, Peter. *Hybrid Space: Generative Form and Digital Architecture.* New York: Rizzoli, 1999.

INDEX